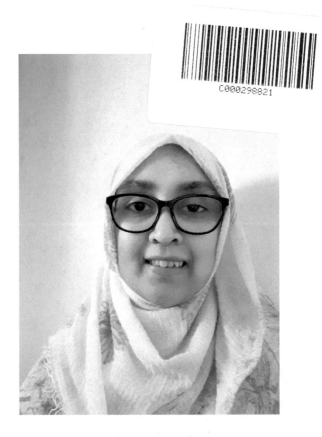

About the Author

Yasmin is a single, disabled mum, to two beautiful daughters. Who have been a driving force, for Yasmin to achieve her long lived dream of becoming a children's author. After publishing two children's books. Yasmin has shared a personal account of her journey of when she was diagnosed with a life long neurological disorder. *Transverse Myelitis, My Journey to Self Discovery*, explores various aspects of Yasmin's experiences whilst she was hospitalised.

Transverse Myelitis, My Journey to Self-Discovery

Yasmin Nahar

Transverse Myelitis, My Journey to Self-Discovery

Olympia Publishers
London

www.olympiapublishers.com
OLYMPIA PAPERBACK EDITION

A CIP catalogue record for this title is
available from the British Library.

ISBN: 978-1-80074-489-9

This is a work of creative nonfiction. The events are portrayed to the
best of the author's memory. While all the stories in this book are
true, some names and identifying details have been changed to
protect the privacy of the people involved.

First Published in 2022

Olympia Publishers
Tallis House
2 Tallis Street
London
EC4Y 0AB

Printed in Great Britain

Dedication

I dedicate this book to all the wonderful members of the healthcare team, who did not give up on me. Thank you.

Acknowledgements

Thank you to my parents and siblings for always being there,
supporting me in every which way possible.

A little bit about me

My name is Yasmin Nahar; I am a thirty-nine-year-old single mum, living with my two daughters. I suffer from a chronic neurological disorder, which affects my day to day living, this condition has been a trigger of my body suffering from Transverse Myelitis. I will explain what this condition is for those of you who might not have heard of it before.

It has been playing on my mind for a while now that I wanted to share some of my experiences with readers out there, in the hope that it may help them or someone that they know that has been through a similar experience to see the light at the end of the tunnel and live a happier and productive life. As I have managed to, during all these years.

It has not been easy, I will admit it's been like a game of snakes and ladders, where I have good days when my body functions quite normally for me to carry out my day-to-day general living tasks. After which comes the downward spiral, suffering from the bad days where the body becomes so stiff, so numb that coming out of bed seems like a chore, eating breakfast seems daunting and everything surrounding me seems to have stopped.

That sense of feeling sorry for myself, for not being able to do something such as cooking and cleaning for myself, without the help from my family members. The overwhelming feeling of ringing the school and explaining to them I am unable to bring the children into school, hence I need assistance for the children to travel to and from school. The constant feeling of being a burden to the ones who care for me.

However, all is not gloom and doom for me in my story, with the help from my family, my beautiful girls, my mum, dad, sisters, brother, and my dear friends who have stayed with me encouraging me at each hurdle, I have achieved a great deal for me to be proud of myself.

How it all started

Today, I decided to sort through a file that has been sitting inside my cupboard, holding so many memories. The file which contains many pieces of papers documenting moments from my life's experiences, handwritten notes, typed up notes and medical examination notes, from various hospitals. Up until now I have always kept this file as a reminder to myself of how well I have done in my life, to achieve a dream I always thought was impossible, which is becoming a children's author.

Ten years ago, I was diagnosed with a neurological disease which changed my life forever, it left me paralysed for a short period of time. These notes tell me how far I have come on the days I feel a little sad or when my body does not want to function the way I hope it would do. These notes were my first point of setting myself free when I felt trapped and helpless sitting on a hospital bed for weeks and weeks, months, and months.

Going through all these notes and scruffy little handwritten diary entries I want to share my story just so I can reveal how my faith in my religion Islam, my family and my positivity made the impossible possible for me. This is my story as to how I have discovered myself and my self-worth over a course of the last ten years.

I was a perfectly healthy person of my age, but at the age of twenty-nine things changed for me with quite a dramatic effect.

It was the 25th of December 2011. I remember coming downstairs at seven a.m. with my two year old daughter Zara, and four months old daughter Jannat. After feeding both girls their breakfast, I sat down to have my own breakfast, it was quite funny as I watched Zara, take out all her toys from the toy box then she happily went inside, pretending it was the bath tub. As she knew that it would be bath time soon because it was something, she had every morning. Meanwhile Jannat was in her bouncer making funny faces at her sister, before looking up towards the TV and giggling to herself as she watched Cbeebies.

I finished cleaning the dishes and joined the girls in the sitting room, it was Christmas day and they had quite a lot of good movies showing on TV. I was excited to watch "The Borrowers" with Zara, as she understood a little, to what was happening.

After the movie finished, around ten a.m. I went into the kitchen to prepare a little mid-morning snack for Zara, she was very excited to see me go into the kitchen and followed me, as she was used to me giving her a snack in the mornings "Pi-e-aaapple, pie-aaaapple," she said, pointing towards the pineapple. I laughed at her cute accent, as I acknowledged that I had understood what she meant and started preparing the pineapple by peeling it before chopping.

This was the moment that had changed my life forever. Who would believe that just a while back I was playing and laughing with my girls. When suddenly, I felt a sharp pain rapidly walk up the middle finger of my left hand, which at the speed of lightening travelled up the whole arm, then across my shoulders before travelling down my right arm then the hand.

I screeched, as the knife fell out of my hand. There was a sudden feeling of pins and needles, burning, prickling all at once. I felt my chest tighten just seconds later. Silent tears rolled down my eyes, but even that seemed to tingle as it came down my cheeks. However, as I did not wish to alarm my two-year-old. With great difficulty I managed to chop the pineapple in completely disproportionate sizes and handed her the plate.

I got rid of the peelings and struggled to walk back into the sitting room after taking two paracetamols for the excruciating pain and constant pins and needles sensation. I sat down on the sofa, "I am having a heart attack, no I must be very tired, no I can't feel my back properly, I am having a stroke," I started saying to myself. I could see Zara looking at me, offering to share her fruit with me, I managed a faint smile back and said, "no I don't want any." Minutes passed like hours, I kept looking at the clock, hoping the pain and pins and needles would go away, but it just did not happen.

After struggling with what was happening to my body, I told Zara to come with me and call her dad, as I knew I needed help.

With the fast changes to my body, I was now unable to take full steps. I crawled up the stairs, at this point I tried taking my mind off what happening to me. My family and friends who are aware of my nature, know that I am amongst those who try to use humour even in the worst of situations, so just for amusement, I told myself I resembled the T1000 robot from the movie *Terminator-Judgement Day*. I laughed and winced in pain at the same time.

Once upstairs I called my husband EH, to wake up and look after the children for a while, as I was convinced, I was having a heart attack. EH reassured me that I should calm down, relax, and sleep for a while, as these sensations could be a result from all the overworking. Since I had been managing two incredibly young children all on my own, after recovering from a traumatic pregnancy and labour, just a few month ago. My body was bound to feel tired.

However, I knew this pain was not due to being sleep deprived or from my workload. Nevertheless, I could not explain what this pain was, knowing that I wouldn't be taken seriously, I decided to listen and sleep for a while to see how it goes.

It was not easy, the pain made it difficult to relax. So, after what seemed like ages, I got up from bed thinking there was no point in lying down as the pins and needles made it difficult to feel comfortable. I looked at the time, it was only twelve noon. Not much time had passed, my body felt tight, heavy and there was a constant tingling, pins and needles sensation running up and down my body.

My hands trembled as I used them to move the blanket aside. I did not feel the slightest bit better, I noticed that my grip had become weak as I tried tying up my hair, I just about manged to loop it around the ribbon twice and went downstairs.

I asked EH to call the paramedics because I was unable to feel my limbs properly. I was beginning to get scared and just wanted to be reassured that I was going to be ok. EH could see my discomfort and knew I was not overreacting, so he called 999.

When the paramedics arrived, I was sitting on the sofa, on one side, as I could not sit up straight anymore at this point. Even when I tried, my body just slid to one side all on its own. The paramedic took out a machine from his bag and monitored my heart, having carried out all the tests, he told me that I was not having a heart attack, which was an instant relief for me, as I was worrying how my children would cope without me if I had to be taken into hospital.

I was advised by the paramedic to take a lot of rest because at that point, this was all he could advise, after speaking to me about my medical history and lifestyle, he thought that my body was sleep deprived and all the stress I was going through mentally may have impacted on how my body was reacting now. He did advise though, that if I felt that my condition was getting worse then I should call for an Ambulance and go into the A&E for further tests, but to prepare to wait as it was Christmas day so the hospital would be remarkably busy.

After the paramedic left, I tried to convince myself to be as normal as possible, so, I decided to get the kids ready, as they were still in the pyjamas, which was beginning to bother them, as they were in the routine of having their bath after snack time, now it was almost lunch time.

I then made my way to the kitchen to prepare lunch, I remember as I turned on the hobs, I had missed clicking on the ignition button a few times, until I finally managed to place my finger on the button, it was almost as if a magnetic force was holding me back from using my hands properly.

Waiting for the food to warm up, I went to lay the dining table, I struggled as I set the table for lunch whilst EH went to take a shower. I could now feel that I was dragging my right leg to walk, as it started to feel numb and tingly.

I felt my hands were burning when I touched the water. What would usually take me fifteen to twenty minutes, that day it took me roughly forty-five minutes to set the lunch table.

The children were getting hungry, but I felt myself incapable to move properly, after sitting down to start feeding Zara, I knew I would be unable to feed her, because when I tried lifting the spoonful of rice from the plate, it started to shake so much that I could not take the spoon near her mouth, without it flopping back onto the plate. So, I asked EH to feed Zara her lunch.

I then told him that I was unable to nurse Jannat as usual because the strength in my arms were beginning to get so weak. It was at this point, that with a heavy heart, I had to make the difficult decision of moving her onto formula milk. It was even more difficult to convince myself that this was the right thing to do because up until now I had not even introduced her to the concept of it. As there had been no need for it till this point. This for me was one of the most difficult decisions that I had to make without even having time to think or contemplate over.

I watched helplessly as EH took the bottle of formula milk near her mouth, she kept turning her face from side to side trying to get the bottle away from herself. I could see that she was unfamiliar with the taste and did not understand why she was being given this. She kept looking at me, reaching out her arms and moving forward, indicating that she needed me to go and pick her up from her bouncer. I winced in pain and went and sat next to her, holding her hands in mine, there were huge tears balancing on the corner of her eyes, as she looked at me, I apologised to her, feeling powerless and defeated. What was happening to me?

I felt helpless and lost. "What is happening to me? When would I get back to feeling better?" These questions kept playing in my mind.

I looked at both my children, seeing confusion in their eyes, as they could feel something was not right about today. Things were happening differently to normal. I felt weak as I looked into their eyes, trying to put up a brave face that I was ok.

It was three p.m., EH started to get ready to go to work, I told him that it was not possible for him to go today because my body was acting too strange. He had to stay behind and look after the children. At which he suggested that maybe I should call my mum to lend me a hand. I told him that this was not an option today, any other day and that would be fine, however, I could not just ask my mum to jump in and babysit the kids for me today, as she was hosting a huge lunch and dinner party (that had been pre planned for some time now) at her house, because in the whole year, Christmas was one day when each and every member of the close and extended family had a day off.

Mum had planned and prepared for everything and I just could not worry her at the last minute. None the less EH thought that if mum came and looked at my condition once, she may be able to help and take me to her house with the kids, as he insisted on going to work. I reluctantly agreed for mum to come and have a look at me.

As soon as she walked in with my brother Mo, I could see how overwhelmed she looked. I could see how tired she was from cooking for about twenty to twenty-five people. I instantly put on a brave face and told her I was fine and just felt very tired, needed resting and could not attend dinner later that evening.

My mum stayed for half an hour she rubbed some oil on my toes, to try and circulate the blood properly, all that time the touch tingled and burned but I did not let my pain show on my face, as I could see how sad and worried my mum was. I persuaded my mum to go back and attend to her guests and that I would be as fit as a fiddle in no time. Obviously, mum left without being convinced, but she also had a house full of guests, that she just could not cancel just like that. Plus, we were unsure at this point what exactly was wrong with me.

As EH prepared to leave for work, I explained that it was not fair to worry my mum, when she was managing a huge family do, that she had already set and prepared for. I finally managed to convince him stay and look after the kids up until eight p.m. just so I can rest a little more and once the dinner rounds were over, I would take the girls to bed that way he can work the whole night (as he was a private hire vehicle driver, so there is that flexibility to start at different times).

Agreeing this being a fair plan I settled down to rest. Praying all that time for a miracle to take place and for me to be back to normal. However, as the time passed, I only felt more feeble. To add to my worries, I realised how bad I actually was, when I needed the bathroom. I realised that I could not get off the sofa. I was left without any feeling from waist below. Shocked at what I was feeling and not feeling, I cried out for help. "I need the bathroom, but I can't get up and go," I told EH. At first, he thought I was overreacting but after watching me struggle and falling backwards on the sofa as I tried to stand with my hands and legs shaking, he understood that I was just not panicking, but really finding it difficult to stand. So, he had to carry me up the stairs and helped me, to sort myself out.

"I need to call for an Ambulance. It has only been around seven hours since my symptoms first started and now, I can barely move, I need help, before I completely become paralysed. What if I am unable to speak soon, how will I explain what's happening to me?"

I blurted out crying, as I was convinced now that I would only get worse. By now my EH could see the changes in my condition himself and we both agreed that we had to be as normal as possible in front of the girls, as Zara was walking around me the whole time wanting to play and sit next to me, but due to the constant tingling and pins and needles I was unable to cope with any sort of touch to my skin.

I called Mo to come over so that he could go to the hospital with me, when the Ambulance came, just so EH could stay behind to be with the children, as the girls had to have one parent next to them so that they would not get upset because the whole day's events had already unsettled my eldest who now knew something was not right.

Upon the Ambulance arriving, I repeated the full scenario of what had happened to me. I was convinced that I was becoming paralysed, but after carrying out checks from their side the Ambulance staff told me that I was not paralysed because my legs were responding to their equipment. It was only when they told me stand up and walk into the Ambulance when they noticed that I could not stand on my feet, and I was sliding sideways to me left side the whole time. They quickly assisted me to the vehicle themselves. My brother followed us to hospital in his own car.

Throughout the journey to the hospital, I could still hear my children's voices, "Mum, mum, why are you going without me?" Zara had been calling from behind me, Jannat was crying when she saw me leave with the strangers, I could just hear these words and sounds repeating themselves.

Just as any mum would feel, I felt the unbearable pain, of being separated from my children in uncertain circumstances, it hurt me so much, there are no words to describe these painful feelings. "I will be home before morning my darlings," I convinced myself half-heartedly as we stopped outside the A&E.

It was an awfully long wait at the A&E. After about two hours of waiting since we arrived at the hospital, I felt I was completely paralysed from down below, when my name was called out, I was stuck in my position. Without knowing what to do and worried my turn will go I raised my hand like a schoolgirl, making the teacher aware that she was present in class. I asked Mo to ask for a wheelchair so I could be taken to my station.

Once I was in the bay, Mo had to lift me up from the chair and place me on the bed for examination. I once again, reiterated the full story of what had happened to me since morning. Up until then I was confident that the doctor will leave me on drip to get my energy levels back up to normal and once the pain and tingling had subsided, I would be able to return to my family.

However, this was not the case, the doctor looked confused, and the nurse looked confused. After close examination I figured out that they could see that certain areas of my body were responding to the equipment and certain areas were just motionless.

As they used this tool which looked like an oversized drawing pin with a large round head and a blunt point at the end. I could see my arms and legs sort of jump/vibrate at the touch. They then used a tiny pin and asked me to close my eyes and to let them know if I felt anything when they gently touched different parts of my body with it. They did this around my head, chin, cheeks, neck area then both my arms, hands, across the tummy, waist, thigh, knee, and toes areas. My results were not clear therefore I was told that I would have to be admitted, to have further tests as it was Christmas day many of the departments were closed. In the meantime, I did have an X-ray done, before being shifted into a ward.

Coming to terms with the new reality

From here starts my real journey of getting to know what the unknown is and how I was going to beat this situation and not let it beat me. The whole time my brother was with me, I could see the worry on his face, but I put on a brave face, not only to be strong for him but more importantly for my own self. After all, I had to get back to my children as they needed me.

As there was nothing more anyone could do until the following morning, I told Mo to update everyone at home with what was happening and just go home to rest, as it had been awfully long since we had arrived at the hospital and there was nothing more to be done for the time being. By now, my arms too had started to give up, I found it difficult to move them. I told Mo that he should not worry about me, as I was in good hands. He left after making sure I was comfortable enough as possible.

That night I looked up towards the sky and prayed to Allah (The God Muslims believe in) for only one thing, to get well as soon as possible and just be next to my girls. I knew in my heart that Allah would look after me and make sure my children were alright, as Allah tests with uncertainties and then makes sure that we overcome the difficult times, as that is what being human is about, to go through many different experiences, and seeing how we manage. I felt better in my mind after making my prayer, I felt a sense of peace inside me, even though my outer body hurt, I could feel my mind at peace as I communicated with Allah.

Throughout the night the dedicated teams of nurses and health and social care staff came and checked me and changed my position from side to side, as I was unable to turn sides by myself now. "Recovery seems to be a long way away, but not impossible," I kept reassuring myself. "Allah will make things easier for me I just have to have faith." I repeated these words to myself through out what seemed like one of the longest nights of my life.

The following morning a lovely lady came and gave everyone breakfast, I remember the golden-brown cup of tea and that fresh smell of a slice of toast, it seemed like the best smelling food I had ever smelt, I realised at this point, that I had not had anything to eat since the morning before. No wonder this food looked and smelt so good to me.

As I was helped to sit up, I stared at the breakfast in front of me. I tried picking up the butter knife, but could not, I then tried to just pick up the toast and put it in my mouth. But failed that attempt too. Helplessly I tried to use my mouth to pick up the toast, but could not manage that either as my mouth could not feel the toast, I was aiming at the tray then the plate etc. It was no use, as my co-ordination had become very muddled.

"Okay, I am unable to do anything, my limbs are not working, I cannot feel anything. I cannot even sit up on my own." I sat on my bed with hot tears rolling down my eyes. Just yesterday morning my routine had been completely normal, I would have never imagined in my wildest dreams that within a timespan of twenty-four hours my life would be turned upside down.

A little while later a nurse came to clear away the breakfast items from all the bays, when she came up to my bedside and looked at the untouched breakfast, she asked me if I was not hungry. I told her I was but could not eat it myself. She listened to my story carefully and smiled at me kindly, then immediately sat down next to me and put the little knob of butter onto my toast and helped me to eat. I felt incredibly grateful, but more emotional, as I was surprised at the nurse's caring attitude.

Soon after breakfast a senior nurse came with an assistant, from what she was reading I knew she had a little idea of why I was admitted to the ward. She too was extremely helpful and told me what I would be expecting that day. I was told that they would change me into a hospital gown and then a doctor would come round to insert a catheter, to help me with my bladder. After hearing this, I could feel the stinging behind my eyes, trying so hard to hold back the tears, I wanted to show that I was completely okay, because I was convinced the sooner I responded to treatment the quicker I will be discharged, but a catheter, it was a scary thought, how bad was my condition? I just could not work out, how I wished someone could just tell me what was happening with me?

Till this point in my life, I had always believed that going through labour and giving birth was the most difficult stage in my life, as there were many people involved in my care, who had seen me in an undignified state. However, now I had to get used to this. One of the most difficult part of being physically impaired was when others had to jump in and look after my every need, which included my personal care needs.

"Remember, you have to beat this and not let this beat you!" I kept telling myself. Many hours went by, but no one knew what my condition was, initially I was told I could be suffering from Guillain-Barre syndrome. Something I had never heard of before, they told me it was neurological disorder, but further tests would determine this.

I went in for a CT Scan, but that did not manage to shed any light on what my body was going through. Later, Doctor Ward, who had inserted my catheter for me, came back to tell me that he had to do a lumbar puncture, in simple words a spinal tap which would involve a needle being inserted in my lower back to take out some fluid, it is the fluid that surrounds the brain and spinal cord to protect one from injury. So much information was being given to me that I really did not understand what some of the things, words or procedures meant. But I was desperate to find out what was going on with me, that I said yes to any treatment that was being suggested to me, even if it did mean having multiple blood tests, being pricked with needles etc.

I was told I would have to wait for an MRI scan as soon as the department was open. All the waiting made me more apprehensive, but I was determined to stay positive. Even when my family came to visit me in hospital and had to see a catheter by my bedside. I reassured everyone that it was only short term and soon I will start to feel things again.

I started receiving intravenous immunoglobulin as a start to treat Guillain Barre Syndrome. By this time, I started feeling that my world was being attached to wires and needles, I felt trapped inside my own body. However, I needed to stay strong and let the doctors do their work.

During the course of the day, I found that I was finding it difficult to breath properly, therefore the doctors decided that I should have peak flow tests to monitor my breathing. After having a few peak flows tests the doctors looked at the chart and decided that I should be moved into the Intensive

Treatment Unit (ITU).

Up until now I was able to put a brave face on everything but moving into ITU made me realise how serious my condition could be. I was now moved from a general ward into the ITU. I was getting a one to one with the nurse. Which I was really grateful about, but it was intense, when my family members, came to see me, they had to wear apron and gloves. The environment was more quiet and serious. I felt more scared than I had ever been before. Was I ever going to get home as quickly as I hoped? It had now been three days since I came to hospital but instead of getting better, my condition seemed to have deteriorated. Things like sliding sheets were placed under me to move me from bed to bed so that fresh clean bedding could be made up for me. I was being given bed baths. I had a cannula permanently attached to me, to make it easy to have repeated blood tests and to have my IV drips.

Finally, I was taken in for a MRI scan, I was worried about going inside this machine, as I did not like the experience of being under the CT scan machine earlier on the week, I felt the space was tight, but this machine was even more different and scary it was more narrow, more noisy, and more compressed.

I was experiencing so many different treatments, in such a short span of time, that I started to run out of steam, it overwhelmed me to feel that there was little hope of me getting any better, because no one really seemed to know what was going on with me.

Just then things took an optimistic turn. Luckily for me, a neurologist from the Royal Free Hospital, Dr Adams was doing the rounds with the doctors in our ward. When she looked at my MRI scan, she told the team that I had suffered from Transverse Myelitis. A rare neurological disorder. I did not know what the condition was as I had never heard of it before, up until now, neither had anyone in my family. But we were all glad that finally we knew what we were dealing with.

On the third day to my admission in hospital I had started to receive a high dosage of steroid following the diagnosis of Transverse Myelitis. This is where google came in very handy, as I wanted to know what exactly Transverse Myelitis was and when I would recover from it to be able to go home.

My husband read from his phone and I listened, *"A rare neurological disorder, its inflammation of both sides of a section of the spinal cord. It damages the insulating material that covers the nerve cell fibre, called the Myelin. It interferes with the messages sent down the spinal cord nerves to the body."* (Information from google search.) None of the information made sense to me, but I was glad that I would be treated for an actual condition now, sooner I got treated sooner I would be discharged.

Following the response of my body to the steroids, I was moved to the Higher Dependency Unit (HDU), where I felt a little more relaxed than being in the ITU. I was here for five days where my treatment continued. I had to have a second lumbar puncture done and be given enema for my dysfunctional bowel. By now I was feeling extremely low with my mindset because all of a sudden, the progress seemed to have slowed down and the fact that my privacy seemed to be invaded all the time made me really upset. I was grateful for the treatment but just wished that I could have more dignity.

This is where my faith came in as my saviour during the nights after the lights were turned down, I would look up to the ceiling and make a prayer to my lord Allah, making wishes for my speedy recovery. As a Muslim I would usually pray five

29

times a day, but since losing my sensations this was not possible, I would speak to Allah and ask him to accept my salah (prayer) that I could only perform with the movement of my eyes. For me, this faith and my prayers worked, the more I prayed the more positive my progress would be, even though awfully slow, but progress was happening.

Once my progress was stable, with no further improvements, I was moved to Ward 10, where patients who had suffered from heart attacks and stroke were being looked after. From here began my waiting journey, I was waiting to be transferred to the Royal Free Hospital, where I would be under the neurologist Dr Adams care.

The day I was being transferred to the Royal Free, I was full of so many different emotions, I knew I had to go because that is where I could be treated properly for my condition. However, the thought of being away from everyone and not knowing for how long, was very daunting. On the afternoon of my move, my dad came with a bag which contained a carton of orange juice and some croissants. He told me to eat and drink as it would build my strength. Having lost my appetite completely because of the news of leaving my family I did not want to eat anything, but at that moment I felt my dad will be happy to see me eating and drinking normally, and I did not want to show him how scared I was feeling inside.

My dad had just finished feeding me when we were joined by EH. I conversed with my family in the most normal way possible, not letting on how I was feeling from within. Not exceedingly long after that, the ambulance arrived to take me to the royal free, I remember the last thing I managed to do was smile at all the family members who stood in front of me as they watched me being pulled away. My mum was unable to come and visit me because she had taken on the full-time responsibility of looking after Jannat for me.

With mixed emotions and nerves, I smiled and told everyone I was fine and not to worry about me, I held my husband's hand and told him to look after the girls and tell them that, "Mummy loves them, and mummy will be home very soon, not long now." The hard lump in my throat would not let me say anymore, my lips trembled but I kept smiling, I did not say anything else, I held back the tears which zinged behind my eyes.

As soon as I was in the ambulance with the doors closed, I wailed like a little baby, crying my heart out. At this point the kind ambulance man told me to be strong and that I had nothing to worry about. I was going to a very reputable hospital which had the correct facilities to treat my condition.

I cannot remember the time of my arrival to the Royal Free, but it was pitch black, I was wheeled into the stroke department and my file was handed at reception before I was placed on a bed right next to the window. I looked around helplessly, everything seemed so unfamiliar, and I just dreaded the thought of remembering the names of my nurses and doctors all over again, I was worried about being poked and prodded again, the thought of the discomfort was overwhelming.

I lay silently for what seemed like hours, because of the heat and lighting. Finally, a health care assistant came over and took my observations, then I was left alone for a little longer before a lady doctor arrived and performed all the physical tests. The pin/hammer like object was used, to gently knock against my thighs, knees, toes and arms. Then with the pointy part of the object the doctor run it across under my toes. Then came out the little pin that was used to gently prick against different parts of my whole face, shoulders. Then I was told to close my eyes whilst she pricked different areas of my body and I had to say when I felt that prick. As this was happening, I felt like saying out loud that, "this had all been done before, just tell me when I would be absolutely fine and when can I go home?". However, things do not work like that at as we all know, with patience and perseverance results are achieved, deep down I knew what the reality was, but I did not want to believe that my condition was as bad as it felt, like at that moment.

Within the course of the next few days at the Royal Free, Dr Adams came back to visit me and told me that I would need a plasma exchange, as she believed I would benefit from this type of treatment.

Getting ready for the plasma exchange was a trial in itself. The whole process was explained to me, but being prepared for it, was very scary, first I had to put on a pair of compression stockings, as I had been immobile for a while now and this would prevent any blood clots. Prior to the procedure of the plasma exchange a central line had to be inserted into a larger vein in my neck, under the local anaesthetic. During the insertion of the central line, I felt no pain, but only some form of pushing and pulling, I watched as a tube, screws and objects that looked like tiny bolts were used to secure the tube in place and this tube would be used with the plasma exchange machine in due course.

After the insertion of the tube, I had an X-ray to check that the tube was positioned correctly. To my dismay this was not the case for me the first-time round, I had to go back into theatre for the second time to have the tube positioned correctly.

Feeling very rough by this point I could not wait to go back into my ward. However, as we were returning to the ward, my bed caught another stand still bed on the side, and as I was being moved my catheter caught one of the sides, the container carrying all the liquid just spilt everywhere, I was mortified as I watched the staff rushing to clear up the mess. It is at times like this I was reminded of how helpless I physically was. If it were in my hands I would have just got up and run because of the humiliation. I kept apologising to the staff that they had to clear up such mess. But the lovely staff reassured me that there was nothing to be embarrassed of, as they were just doing their job. Also, the accident was not due to my doing so I should not feel bad at all. But I just could not stop myself from feeling that level of awkwardness.

When I returned to the ward, feeling very awkward and red, I saw that my dad, EH and one of my cousin brothers had come to visit me. Straight away I forgot about all the drama that had taken place downstairs and I smiled, the smile that I used as makeup to cover up my true feelings.

I explained what I had been through on that day to my family like as if I was telling a story. I did this not only to show my family that I was okay with what was happening, but I believed that this attitude would help me fight my fears, so it was more for me that I pretended that I was so strong. In the hope that I would recover.

After my family left that evening, I lay in bed thinking about what would happen the next day, when I had to take a trip to the renal unit for the start of my plasma exchange treatment.

The nurses came round in the evening, to carry out the

usual observations for all the patients in the room, there were five of us sharing the one room, out of which three remained incredibly quiet all the time, they were also quite a bit more senior to myself and then there was Emma who did talk every now and then, but she was going through her own trials bless her, hence I sometimes felt I was all isolated despite being in a room with four others.

Every morning and every evening before bed, all the patients were changed for a comfortable night's sleep. Our positions were also changed to prevent any bed sores. That night when it was my turn, a truly kind nurse called Nurse Freida came over to my bedside. When she was taking out the wipes and pads from her trolley, she noticed something was bothering me, as she changed me, she talked me through how I needed to stay calm and let the doctors do their job, she also reminded me that god was watching, and he would not let anything bad happen to me. Straight away I felt connected to someone who had the same feeling as me, about religion and how faith makes the impossible possible at times.

Nurse Freida held my hand and told me how brave I had been up until now, even with the painful sores that had developed around the back of my thighs, from constant pressure of lying down with limited mobility I never complained that I was in pain, neither did I create a fuss to change sides etc. She reminded me of how I was always patient and waited for a positive outcome. After speaking to the nurse, I felt a little happier and less scared. Still, I hardly managed much sleep that night just thinking what would happen to me.

After breakfast, the next morning I was told I would be taken into the renal unit as soon as one of the nurses were available to come round and give me enema for me bowels, because by now with the great changes to my diet and all the medications I was taking, my body was very much constipated.

This was the last thing I needed right now, as I remembered my first experience of being given enema at the HDU in Luton and Dunstable, I had to wait for about thirty minutes before managing to pass a bowel movement. During that time, the feeling of humiliation, embarrassment and awkwardness had been quite an emotional experience for me, as I was handled the way a baby would be, and deep down I knew that the condition I was in, I had no choice but to accept the help, and these carers who were playing a crucial part in my treatment were professionally trained individuals. They were doing their job and they were not judging me for my inability to ask for a bed pan at time, as my sensations were so impaired, I had no idea when and where an embarrassing accident might happen. The fear of having these accidents resulted in me always asking for a special lady's pad in the mornings during my wash, for the peace of mind, that I will not be creating more work for someone out there, who had to deal with my soiled laundry.

Coming out of my thoughts, I really did not want to be given the enema not before such an intense session ahead of me, however I was told I had no choice but to be given them as it was not healthy for me to go without a bowel movement. So, as I lay there with the nurse giving me the suppositories, I felt a strange sensation, one I cannot explain, a burning feeling, a sting that brought instant tears into my eyes. The nurse finished dressing me and told me that the discomfort I felt was from the haemorrhoids that had developed in my back passage due to the lack of bowel movement and constipation. In addition to this, the long duration of hours I spent sitting in my wheelchair until someone put me back in bed again played a part in these uncomfortable sores developing.

I explained that I liked being in the wheelchair as it gave me some mobility, but I was advised laying on my sides would take the pressure off my back and the haemorrhoids would heal faster. I was put to the side registering all this information and waiting to pass a bowel movement before I went in for my first session of plasma exchange, so that I did not need assistance whilst I was upstairs, just then a porter came down with a file in his hand asking for me to be taken to the renal department. I didn't even have the thirty minutes I thought I would have; I couldn't believe the speed at which things were happening that morning.

How I wished the doctor who was doing her rounds that morning, had not advised that I be given enema, "why today?" I asked myself. "How will I know if I need to go, would I be able to ask for a bed pan?" The questions had fully occupied my mind, that I had not realised that I was already in the renal department and a doctor was looking through my notes. Before I knew it, I was attached to a machine, which somewhat resembled an olden day's double panel cassette player with wires coming in and out and turning around, winding exactly like a cassette player.

The mixed feeling inside me had completely taken control over my mind I did not know how to react but helplessly lay there staring at the machine, I watched, as it worked, until finally the session was over. However, as soon as the session finished, I felt sick, nauseas, I thought I was going to be sick, but at the same time I had passed a bowel movement, I did not know what kind of help I was supposed to ask for? Someone to change me, or to give me a sick bowl? It did not take long, for me to admit to myself that I was not in any sort of control of my body at all, so I had no choice but to ask for help so that my needs were attended to.

There are times, where it was best admitting to oneself that you may be temporarily in no control of your body, but to get that control back, remaining positive and co-operating with the doctors, nurses and healthcare team are vital to get better as soon as possible. Though this did mean giving up on my independence and dignity for a while.

This was one of those hardest experiences for me to come to terms with, as I have been an independent individual, since the age of sixteen but suddenly to be depending on everyone for the most little tasks such as brushing my hair and eating my food was very painful for me. None the less, I knew I had to get through this for the sake of my children.

For the next four days the same routine continued until my plasma exchange sessions were over. After which I felt a little positive change. There were some sensations back in my hands, which enabled me to start feeding myself again. Although I was told there was still time before I would be able to do other things, so I should not get my hopes up too high, too soon but should remain positive. This was difficult, because I could not get my hopes up just in case things did not happen at the speed that I wanted them to, but I had to remain positive.

I too knew that remaining positive and optimistic was vital, but it was quite a challenge now as the compression socks had seemed to have become my permanent companion, I was told I had to wear them because of the lack of movement in my legs. I was also being given a dose of Fragmin injection every evening until further advice, in my stomach to help prevent blood clots.

With all these things, I found it hard to even think that "would it ever be possible for me to do anything by myself again?" I seemed to need something, for reducing the level of inflammation in my spine, then I needed something to help me with my bowel movements, I needed help with preventing blood clots. I then needed the hoist to be lifted in and out of bed or to sit on my wheelchair. With so many things, it was hard for me to imagine that I can get home as soon as I had hoped.

It had almost been a month of me being admitted to hospital and so far, I found that I was only able to feed myself. I was unable to sit myself up on my own, I still could not wash and dress, I could not use the rotate turntable aid for my transfers. I was beginning to feel trapped in my own body. During all this time at the hospital I was only able to start feeding myself. I had begun to feel frustrated and upset, especially when I wanted to just sit up by myself without the need for someone else to help me to do it.

Every night when the lights went out, I would do a little count in my head of what I had and had not been able to do that day. This was a way of me setting myself my own goals of what I needed to achieve. If I had not been able to do something, then I made it my personal goal to try and at least give that activity a go the next day. For example, when I used to be taken into the gym for my physiotherapy I tried and tried to stand for at least ten seconds holding my therapist's hands. I did the same thing during my wash and dress sessions; I had started to insist that I be taken to the shower room and using the help of a bath board I started to have some sessions of giving myself a shower with my therapist standing right next to me whilst I did this. This way I started to feel a little bit more normal, and it was a huge confidence boost for me. I realised that if I did not push for independence, it may not just be offered to me. Plus, we did not have physiotherapy every day, so I wanted to make the most of it when I did have it.

With time I started to use a mini exercise bike, my therapist would assist me with this, my feet had to go into these saddle type pedals then once my ankles were securely strapped onto the machine, she would press the switch and the machine would automatically start pedalling. This was a great feeling as I felt I was riding the bike myself. I would watch with fascination, as my toes moved, it was great watching them pedal.

During one of these physiotherapy sessions, on the 23rd of January 2012, I was noticed by a consultant from the Regional Rehab Unit (RRU) at the Northwick park Hospital.

Dr Lee had been reading my notes. After speaking to my current doctor, Dr Lee came over to me and asked me how I was and if I would want to be transferred to the Regional Rehab Unit as soon as a place became available.

"Rehab? Why would I need to go to a rehab unit," I asked, as I couldn't fully understand how that was going to help me at this moment. I looked into Dr Lee's eyes with a lot of confusion, hoping he can answer my questions with what I wanted to hear, that is to make me recover.

"It's not the sort of rehab unit, you may have heard of in the past, it is not somewhere you go because you need to get rid of a habit that may not be good for you. But it is a unit to get rid of some of, if not all your symptoms. So that you can carry on living your life as normally as possible. You will be receiving therapy timetabled to fit in with your own medical needs. But you must understand that to get the best possible results, you will have to show determination from your side too. It may not seem easy, but as long as you work together with your keyworkers and therapist, I am sure you will make significant improvements." Dr Lee responded to my questions.

I could not believe that I would be able to get back to normal after receiving the treatment that was aimed more specifically towards my needs. Of course, I was prepared to take any chances that would make me recover, I happily agreed and started to countdown to the day I would be able move again.

The feeling was exciting and gave me a lot of hope, which is what I needed the most, if hope is lost then for me all is lost. After Dr Lee left, I was so excited to tell the nurses and health care assistants that I may be leaving the ward soon and thanked them for all that they had done for me during my stay at the Royal Free.

Just as things seemed to look up, I received the news that I would be moving back to the Luton and Dunstable hospital before I can move to the Regional Rehab Unit at Northwick Park. The Royal Free had done all that they could do, treatment wise, so there was nothing else that they could do for me that Luton could not do, the ward was waiting for patients on waiting lists to come through, hence that meant I had to leave.

This was like the spanner in the works for me because I had started getting used to the staff members, and the little physio I received was beginning to have an effect, if I moved now that means I would have to wait again for a physio therapist to be appointed for me, during which time I feared my body might become used to the no movement routine. However, I knew in my heart that I had to leave so someone in more need of my space at the Royal Free could receive the help that they needed.

The move had happened so abruptly though, I was in the middle of my sponge bath when nurse Jones came and told me that I was going to be taken by ambulance to Luton that evening. It was a very emotional farewell, I remember saying my goodbyes to all my friends, and the lovely hospital staff, but one thing that I will always be sad about till date, is not being able to say my final goodbye in person to nurse Freida, who had been so supportive and caring throughout my stay at the Royal Free.

Once I was back at the Luton and Dunstable, I was initially taken into Ward 10, and in the morning, I was moved to the St Mary's Wing, which was in a more isolated part of the hospital. It was a waiting game for about four days, I could not concentrate or think about anything else, apart from what it would be like at the regional rehab unit and most importantly how long would I have to stay?

Already I had moved between two hospitals and it had been over a month. I just prayed that a miracle would happen, and I would recover completely after my first week's stay at the rehab unit. Even though I knew that this was wishful thinking and that I had to remain patient.

When members of my family visited me, I knew that they were expecting to hear good news, but sadly at that point I was only able to move my left hand with which I tried to do my personal tasks, there was not much movement in the right leg at all and I did not like using my right hand because it hurt and tingled at the same time. So, the only area that I could show that was almost fully functional was my left leg, but that too got tired, after lifting it up and down a couple of times.

To my husband who used to visit me every couple of days at the Royal Free, there was not much of a change, but the rest of the family who had not seen me since I left Luton, were delighted that I was not paralysed anymore more.

Although, most of the times when they visited I did not like to show them how weak I actually was feeling, before they came I would get the nurses to help me sit up straight with the support of pillows, and throughout the visiting hours I would sit up for as long as my body allowed me to do so, just so I can prove to my family that I was improving and would be home only after a few more days. I would ask my mum and sisters about the girls and how they were getting on, and they would reassure me that the girls were doing simply fine, and that I should not worry about them and concentrate on getting myself better.

Finally, after what seemed like a lifetime of waiting on the 30th of January 2012, after breakfast I was told that the ambulance would be coming to pick me up and transfer me to the Regional Rehab Unit. I was so relived and happy that I would receive the final instalment of treatment that I needed before becoming the person I was before this disease attacked me.

When I was getting ready that morning, I looked at my reflection in the mirror and could not really recognise who I was looking at. My entire face was moon shaped; I was looking at someone completely different due the effects of the steroids.

I looked at my hands as feet as I tried my best to moisturise them, I noticed that nails had started turning a sort of brownish colour and they had become hard, I did not like this change, I wanted to return to the way I looked before.

Thank goodness that only the shape of my face had changed and not my entire body, I was worried that I would be putting on tonnes of weight because of the steroid treatment but luckily for me this had not happened, one of the reasons could have been that I had completely lost the taste in my mouth everything had a metallic taste and food smelt funny to me. I was told these could be the side effects of all the different types of medication I was on. Hence most of my diet was made up of Weetabix, toast, and juice.

After I finished assessing my looks, I called my mum and my husband to inform them that I was moving the Rehab Unit later that afternoon, so they did not have to come and visit me today.

When I arrived at the Regional Rehab Unit (RRU) I was greeted by a lady called Sue who was the ward manager, she showed me into my room, a single side room, I was told that this would be a temporary room as patients were not allowed to be isolated in a single room for too long, she showed me where the washroom was and where to put all my clothes. After registering this information in my mind and before I could say anything, she left me in the room closing the door behind her.

As I stared at the ceiling lying flat on my back, I asked myself, "How am I supposed to go the washroom and how am I supposed to sort out my clothes? Is this going to be like a boarding school?" I was confused at this welcome. "Do they even know that I am not able to move around by myself?" I was asking myself all these questions when my trail of thoughts was interrupted by a nurse called Charlie.

She explained to me that there were two coloured teams in the ward, one was red, and the other one was blue. She told me that she was the nurse who will be my main nurse and she was part of the red team. If I needed something I should try and ask a member of my team.

The way in which I would be able to tell which member of staff belonged to which team was by their t-shirts. All the staff in the red team would always wear a red t-shirt and all the staff in the blue team would always wear a blue t-shirt. "Ok I need to make a mental note of this information," I started telling myself. But that was not all, Charlie continued, all except for the ward manager, the doctors the physio therapists and the occupational therapist. The physio therapists would always be in a white coloured t -shirt with navy blue trousers or joggers and the occupational therapists would be in white tops with bottle green coloured trousers.

After giving me all this information Charlie asked me if I as okay with all this, I did not know how to respond, I felt like I was sitting in the hall, of high school on the first day, where the head teacher lays out ground rules, of what is expected from their students and how the school together with all students will make big achievements.

Even though, I was left speechless, I smiled and faintly nodded. I thought I would get into trouble if I asked for all that information to be repeated to me again, because I did not have a clue. I was so nervous and scared, this environment was very alien to me, I was in severe pain from not being able to move the way I wanted to.

My thoughts were interrupted once more as Charlie took out some paperwork that needed completing, we started doing this when my physiotherapist Kate arrived, she was joined by

Amy (a student occupational therapist) and Alaina (an occupational therapist). I knew as soon as I saw the equipment in their hands that it was that time again to do the little tests to show what I am and am not capable of doing.

I was made to sit at the edge of the bed, followed by quick assessment of my limbs. I was feeling even more nervous now, just as I was trying to make sense of the red and blue team issue in my mind I was being looked at by even more new faces, so many names to remember, "how was I going to manage?"

Once the assessments were over with, Kate told me that Alaina had come to help her out today, but my OT would be Nikki, who I would get to meet the following day as she was away on training today. Once all the assessments and paperwork were completed, I was left staring at the ceiling once more.

I had to leave the Luton & Dunstable just as they had started to serve lunch, therefore I did not get a chance to eat anything. As a result, I was starving by the time I came into the RRU but was too scared to ask for anything. This is because I could sense that this hospital was quite different in comparison to the other hospitals I had been admitted to, there was something about it that had a boarding school feel about it. My transfer could not have happened at a more worse time, it was just as lunch was being served at the Luton and Dunstable, by the time I came to Northwick Park it was shortly after three p.m. So, the meal cards for the patients for that day had already been completed. I did not have my mobile with me because it was still in Luton and as I could not use the dial pad properly there really was no point in having it with me.

However, I was starving, and I was scared of this new

environment, I thought maybe EH could come over just for a couple of hours to keep me company whilst I registered this new habitat of mine. I also wanted to eat something, as I had not eaten anything since breakfast that morning. Just as I was about to press the button for assistant, a nurse walked into the room. I took my chance and asked if she can take me to the reception so I could make a call, because the bedsides here did not seem to have a phone, like they did at the previous hospitals. She told me that this was because patients could have their own phone, tablets, and laptops, to make the atmosphere feel as homely as possible. However, seeming that I did not have my phone with me she was willing to take me to reception, but for that I needed a transfer from the bed to a wheelchair and reading my notes, she confirmed that my transfers required two people and as she was unable to get hold of anyone I might have to wait till later.

Feeling sad and disheartened I decided that I should just maybe try and fall asleep maybe the next morning will come quicker.

As I settled down to fall asleep, Dr Bheroze came in. "Oh dear", I told myself, "get ready for further poking and prodding." By now I was feeling grumpy and upset with all these changes. They were a little overwhelming for me and I really did not want another assessment right now. But me being me, I smiled at the doctor and went through the whole process again for the third time since arriving that day. "How sure did they have to be?" I asked myself.

After a quick assessment by Dr Bheroze, I raised my concerns about how soon I can be discharged from hospital as I really had to get back to looking after my children. Dr Bheroze went through what I had heard from the doctors at the

Royal Free. It was all up to how my body reacted to the physiotherapy and most importantly how I dealt with my condition, as I might have to accept the terms that I would probably never be the same prior to this condition. I was told that I had to stay in high spirits and to help me along the way a counsellor was going to come round every week to see how I was progressing.

After doctor Bheroze left, I was unsure of the timescale I was going to get better within. One thing was for sure though I would have to accept that the tingling and pins and needles sensations would probably be a permanent side effect and I would have to manage that with the treatment plan the doctors had in mind for me. It had been an exceptionally long day and I fell asleep going into a whirlpool of mixed emotions, there were echoes all around me going around the room at a speed of around fifty miles per hour, soon enough the echoes faded away, tomorrow was going to be another day. "I am fighter, I will never give up," I told myself.

31st of January 2012

I woke up being greeted by a friendly lady called Anette, she was going to be the person making sure that each patient received their breakfast, lunch, and dinner on time, along with the tea and coffee throughout the day. However, I was informed that there were set times for every meal and I had to complete my order form, which would be left at my desk every morning that I would have to complete and return it to the reception desk before ten a.m. each day to ensure my orders went through.

After breakfast I waited in anticipation for someone to come and give me my shower, before being taken down for physio. As the minutes ticked on the clock, I found out that everyone's keyworkers would be going around to check their patients and discuss their timetable for that day. "Timetable" I repeated to myself. "Why do we need a timetable? Doesn't someone just come out to take us to the gym where we practice standing and sitting?" I was in conversation with myself when Nikki my occupational therapist arrived, with a clipboard in her arms. I was quite excited to see her, finally I was going to do some exercise again. The last few days had been completely physio free, and I was worried that all the progress I had made might stop.

I was ready as ready I could be, we started with the bed transfers. This was moving out of the bed using a tool called a Banana board, which looked like half the size of a surfboard.

The board was placed just under my left thigh, once positioned I had to use all my strength to slide down the Banana board onto a wheelchair. To do this, transfer I needed the assistance of my occupational therapist (OT) Nikki, who was holding the other end of the board which was on the edge of the wheelchair as a safety measure just in case I slipped. Amy, who had come to assist Nikki, positioned me onto the board so that I was fully sitting down onto the board and Kate my physio was behind me as a guide, this was so that when I was sliding from the bed onto the chair if I wobbled over or slipped from position, then she could quickly grab hold of me.

At first, I thought it was a simple manoeuvre and I would be able to do this with no problems at all. However, it was quite different in reality. I sort of froze in position, even though my mind was telling my body to move down the board, I just could not manage this on my own. Kate had to lift me up a little and guide me down the board with her hands holding onto my waist from both sides. It was a real struggle, and I felt the horrible sensations of the pins and needles and the tingling multiply beyond all levels of discomfort.

However, I did not want the keyworkers noticing this, otherwise they would take each step slowly, from what I had learned from my past experiences at the Royal free. I did not want slow progress, I just wanted to fix myself, just like when you would go with a car to a garage to get back on the road. In my case I just wanted to go back to my girls Zara and Jannat. I smiled through my transfer and tried to vocalise my experience in the most positive way.

However, luck was not on my side and the three keyworkers had decided that the Banana board transfer was just too difficult for me at this stage, and it required too many people, this was not very practical for a daily basis. So, Nikki told me that they had decided that my transfers shall be from the bed and it would be done using a hoist. I felt upset at first coming to terms with the fact that I would need a lot of assistance for my every move. However, if I wanted to get better, I knew I had to follow the advice and the timetable.

After my transfer session Nikki provided me with two Wheelchairs, one was manual, and the other was electronic. So, I had a choice which one I wanted to use, depending on the strength of my arms. I then had to go through more paperwork, this time a questionnaire about myself.

Finally, before Nikki went, I asked if I could have some paper so that I could start keeping a diary for myself. To remind me of how I started my journey till the point I was going to leave the hospital. Nikki thought it was a great idea it would give me something to do and keep me motivated.

My fingers hurt as I picked up the pen and started to write. The pen would fall out as I tried to grip it. It is strange how picking up a pen was something I did everyday but now it seemed like a mission itself to just hold the pen firmly and write.

Kate came into the room to put up something called a Bed Statement. A sheet of paper that was placed above my headboard. This was an information sheet about myself, to make the health care team aware of who I am? why I am here for? and it also contains data about how my transfers were to be done, what my goals are? and the date by which I was expected to achieve these goals? The main reason for having this statement is so that any member of staff regardless of what team they belonged to, if they were on that particular shift, would know how to do my transfers and what sort of activities

I needed to do for me to achieve my goal. Even though Nikki and Kate were my physio and OT they would not always be on each shift.

The physiotherapy team had a timetable which contained the names of the patient and the times they needed to be doing an activity. In some ways it is like being at school. There were timetables, rules, guidance, and advice that had to be followed. The team were very thorough in their approach.

"It was my first proper day at the Regional Rehab Unit (RRU). I have started to make myself comfortable, this is going to be home for at least the next few weeks." The sooner I settle in, the sooner my body will start responding to the treatment. It is all about patience and perseverance. Even though the environment felt very alien yesterday, today has been much more positive in terms of me understanding how things work around here and what sort of support would be available to me throughout my stay.

Later on, the day, I spent a lot of time thinking how I was going to get better, making a list of things that would help me achieve my goals, when once again I was taken out my thoughts by Nikki. This time she came to help me unpack my hand luggage and transfer all my belongings into the wardrobe to the side of the room. I had not been able to do it myself because I thought I was going to be moved to a room shared with other patients. However, after my assessment the team had decided I should use the single room for a few days to see how I progress. It felt strange putting things on hangers and placing them in a room which was neither a room in a house or a hotel but a hospital.

I was advised that I did not need just pyjamas in my wardrobe, but to have someone bring in actual day wear clothes, as this too was part of making one feel as normal as possible, rather than a vulnerable patient. It is a great idea, because I too believe that looking good and well, helps to heal the body and soul. I have a good feeling about this place, even though I am physically not strong right now, to have some form of normality in the routine is quite nice, much better than just lying down in bed all the time.

1st February 2012

Charlene – one of the nurses – came in after breakfast to assist me with washing and dressing. She told me that from now on they will be doing a bowel routine every day, this was to ensure that my body knew how to react every day. I was relieved to hear this in one sense but somewhat embarrassed at the same time, because this meant someone would have to come in early, every day and make sure that I had passed a bowel movement. Before I was even allowed to have my shower and go for physiotherapy. I told myself that this was a bitter truth that I had to come to terms with, if I wanted to get better and it would also mean that I would not have to take suppositories every day, to assist me. In the long run this is all for my own benefit but trying to convince myself that I have to go through the whole same process every day is very daunting.

I was also told that they would change my catheter to a more practical one to do my exercises in. The new one would not only be discreet as it would go inside one of the legs of my trouser, but I would also be able empty it out every day by myself, by going into the washroom. Instead of the Health Care Assistant (HCA) doing it for me during the course of the day, like it has been done up until now. This would again give me independence and control. However, to start off with someone will assist me every day until I get most/all of the strength back in my hands.

I am beginning to understand now why this department in

the hospital is called the regional rehab unit. It is like being in a boarding school, having to follow rules and instructions. But I kept telling myself, "This is not going to be for ever, Allah is testing me, and I just have to remain patient and rise above all difficulties." I made a silent prayer, seeking help from my lord to give strength to endure the embarrassment I would have to face in the coming days.

After all the adventure I had in the morning, I was allowed to go to the library, one of my favourite places to be when I needed to relax. I love reading, I love reading children's fiction the most. Where there are fun, adventurous characters that can face any difficulties and always coming up with solutions to save the day.

This was my first independent trip outside of the corridors of the regional rehab unit. I was given a code so that I could punch it into the box outside of the ward when I needed to come back in. This was a safety measure for all the patients, to ensure that only the patients and the patient's next of kin were allowed in the ward. Visitors would have to wait outside until someone came to receive them from inside the ward. It was also to give patients freedom to independently go in and out of the ward, for reasons such as going to the cafeteria or to sit outside in the hospital garden.

I happily took in all the information and instruction and rode on my electronic wheelchair for the very first time. At first it felt like being in a car and trying to control the vehicle trying not to bang or bash into anything. There were controls on the arm of the chair and trying to get used to using them was quite a task. The chair would pick up speed immediately and trying to make sure that it just run smoothly took me a few banging into the lifts and walls before I got the hang of using it. "I definitely failed that driving test." I laughed to myself.

Finally, I arrived at my destination following the signs. I opened the door excitedly and went into a room, which I was expecting to be colourful and full of aisles with many different genres of book. The reality was somewhat different, the library was as big as the room I was staying in. I found myself wheeling through the narrow aisles in which the room had been organised. I looked around and discovered that there were just a few shelves, with a small range of books to choose from. Not the sort of library I was expecting, but it took a minute or two, to register that I was in a hospital so to have a room with just a few shelves was good enough. Luckily, the genre I was interested is reachable from my chair, so I will not need assistant there. Only if I want some of the travel or cookbooks then I would need someone to get them down for me from the top shelve, which I am not allowed to reach until I can start walking again.

The library has a little front desk with a register, so that in the absence of a staff member patients can enter their details along with the books they are going to borrow. There is a returns bin outside the library, so if for any reasons the library is closed, we could still return the books.

After my quick observation of the environment, I was in, I went past some of the shelves, I came across the No 1 Ladies Detective Agency books by Alexandra McCall Smith. "Perfect," I said to myself. I had first heard about these books from one of my best friends from work, who I call Aunty Lily. She would tell me how funny and charming these books were, during our lunch breaks when I was working at the college. I remembered how we used to laugh over the characters and discuss how great the writing was. I picked up the first book in the series and excitedly took it back to my ward. "I need to try and laugh as much as possible; this will be the perfect medicine for my recovery," I kept telling myself.

However, no matter how hard I tried, the thought of being away from little girls, always ached my heart.

I returned to my room to have a drink of water and put the book on my bedside desk. As I lifted the jug to pour water into my cup, I must have moved in an awkward way, because I felt a funny sensation run down my back, which run though my legs. I looked down at my legs, which were a little shaky from the movement. I tried to apply pressure on them, to get rid of the spasm. I even tried moving them a little to straighten them out as both legs were brushing into each other, forming a triangular shape from the thigh area to where both the knees were, this was an uncomfortable position to be in, so I decided to move them a little.

I feel helpless and defenceless every time I try moving my legs. They are still very heavy, and I have to use my hands to lift them up and down. After getting rid of the spasm, I finished drinking water and went near the mirror to make sure I was looking presentable.

I looked at the clock on the wall, "Time to get ready for my gym session," I reminded myself as I looked at the timetable. I started to make my way out of the room to the gym, this time making sure I did not crash into anything.

I entered the gym in hope that we would practice a lot of sit to stands. But to my dismay it was more assessments of the legs, it seemed like I was not progressing onto anything major that will speed up the process of me walking again.

Kate told me just to hang in there, soon enough I would be able to walk, but every little milestone had to be met. I knew what she was telling me was the most effective way towards recovering, but as humans we have the tendency to be impatient at times and I think I was just having one of those moments. Soon enough I realised that I could not let the cloud of worries overshadow my dreams of positivity.

I sat in my chair watching as tape measures, rulers and lots of other equipment that looks like a shoe sizer came out of Kate's magic box, I wonder how she managed to fit in all that stuff into a bag that resembled a doctors home visit bag. I was full of curiosity as to how this was going to help me. None the less I did promise myself that I would let the professionals do all that they had to do to help me recover. Yet, my heart kept telling me that I just wanted to go home to my children and sit by their side watching Cbeebies. I closed my eyes and prayed for the best.

2nd February 2012

Today's OT session consisted of Nikki and Amy helping me to wash and dress. I was wheeled into the bathroom from which point I was able to have an unassisted wash. Once finished, I pulled the red cord by the shower to inform the staff that I had finished taking my shower.

I do still have to have help with dressing, I cannot reach certain areas, and my legs are still out of action right now. Amy helped dry and brush my hair, which had been tangled into a huge bushy mess. Since being admitted to hospital I have not had a chance to condition my hair, therefore it has become damaged to quite some extent. Amy managed to untangle the stringy mess and tied up my hair into a neat plait. It felt so good to have all the hair brushed out thoroughly, it has been almost a month and half since I had my hair combed properly. I looked at myself in the mirror and thanked Amy for making me look so good. I turned around from the mirror to see that Nikki had made up my bed with clean sheets. It was so good of them to do this for me, I like having my things organised first thing in the morning. I happily got myself ready to go into the gym, I thanked both my care workers and made my way out of the room.

Throughout my physiotherapy session this morning, Kate and Ruby helped me to stand on my feet using a crest. This is a piece of equipment that has an area for standing and then there are sections where belt attachments come out, for holding onto the different weak areas of the body, such as the ankles, knees, thighs, and waist. From the region in front of my chest I was able to see a table type attachment where I placed and rested both of my arms.

I was securely attached to this piece of equipment so that there were no risks of me falling accidently and it meant I was standing on my own without a staff member helping me. However, Ruby was standing behind me to keep an eye on my posture. I tried hard to stand up as straight as I could. But my body ached, there were many different sensations running across my entire body, I felt tingling, pins and needles, shooting pains and even muscle spasm.

It was an unpleasant feeling to try and stand for more than a few minutes, it took a lot of my energy and strength both physically and mentally as I tried to hold myself up without slanting sideways. Though I knew that as soon as I mention discomfort and pain to the staff, they would take me off and let me rest for the session. I could not do that because this would have meant taking things even more slowly. Slow progress in therapy means slower recovery time.

I stood straight and smiled. Whilst Kate started the next part of the session, which was to play a game of catch and throw, at first, I thought this would be simple, I have played catch and throw many times in my life, so this should have been easy. Little did I know that my reaction times had been affected by my condition, every time the ball came towards me my hands would either go up to slowly or I would just push the ball away, I was unable grab hold of the ball. It is quite scary realising the extent of the injury the nerve damage has caused.

After a very tiring game of catch and throw, Kate took me

back to my room and completed, my goals sheet. I was then encouraged not to eat lunch on my own in my room, but instead go into the day room and have lunch with other patients.

I was not comfortable at first, but I knew that socialising was also a part of the healing process. After a lot of eerming and uumming, I thought I would be brave and face one of my biggest fears, which was making new friends and being surrounded by strangers.

3rd of February 2012

It was a quiet sort a day, I did not have any physiotherapy timetabled, so I had to find things to do on my own. I went and sat in the garden for a while. Later, today, Joe from benefits came to see me. he went though some forms and informed me of what sort of help there may be out there, to help my family's financial situation. As I have been in hospital for about six weeks, EH has been unable to go to work because of childcare purposes. Even with my mum taking full responsibility for Jannat, Zara prefers to always be with her dad. She has a lot of confusion in her mind and is in shock that I have not returned home yet, so for her peace of mind and to make her feel at ease her dad is always there with her.

I discussed with Joe my worries, about how I was not sure in what way we would manage financially, as it has been over a month and a half, and no income has been coming in. Joe reassured me to not worry and to concentrate on getting better, once the necessary forms are completed and assessed then things will start to fall into place.

I have so much to think about, even though I am in hospital, working on recovering, my mind is at home, I have Zara and Jannat to worry about, but I also have our financial circumstances to worry about. How are we going to make ends meet? I am so unsure of when I will be able to get back home and take over, looking after the children again, for a start my children will feel much more happier and secure that their mum is back. But also, EH can return to work and there will be a flow in our income again. I feel so responsible for everything that is happening around me and how it is affecting my family.

Please Allah, make this journey easy for me, please do not let me be a burden on anyone, I am scared and worried. I am not sure how I can make things normal again, you are the most merciful and kind, please accept my prayers and show me the light at the end of the tunnel.

4th February 2012

It Is hard for me to see patients, who are now almost ready to be discharged from the hospital and start living their lives as normally as possible, go home for the weekend. This is a trial period for them to see how they will manage with life outside of the RRU. I watched as family members came and picked up their loved ones.

I looked at my bed statement above my headboard. It is going to be some time before I would be able to go home to spend time with my family. Though I rather not go until I can manage things on my own. There is no point going home only to become a burden on my family members, it is not very practical for me to rush and leave hospital only to depend on my family to look after not only my children but to look after me too.

Putting all my anxiety and worries aside, I must look at how I will fight against this condition, it is not end of the world, if I put my mind to it, I know I can manage. Till now I have always faced many difficult situations in life, and I have coped. So, it is nothing different now, I just have to remain optimistic that I will recover as best as possible for me to manage independently with my day to day living. I am a strong person; "I have never let anything drag me down to stop me from handling things in my life. It is no different now, I am only facing a speed bump, this is to test my endurance, I can beat this, I will beat this," I kept telling myself. But no matter how much I reassure myself, why do these tears keep bothering me?

Once I had finished, with the feeling sorry myself session, I quickly reminded myself of the plan to get better. First of all, I needed to try hard with my transfers, so that I need minimal help to get in and out of bed. I made up my mind that I would put all my effort into my transfers over the coming day, so that I too would be able to join the patients who are packing excitedly, to go home for the weekend.

After more than quarter of the patients left from the ward, I just browsed through the corridor, it was incredibly quiet, and it felt strange.

To keep my mind from feeling sad I sat down and did my prayers asking Allah for his guidance and help to get through this as happily as I could. I was always thinking about Zara and Jannat. "Have they eaten? Have they had their showers? Are they thinking of me?" so many questions just went round and round in my head. Although, I knew in my heart that Allah will guide me through this difficult time.

After finishing my prayers, I asked to be put into bed, as the pain and tingling was just too much for me to bear.

"Mma Ramostwe is going to keep me busy today," I thought, as I picked up the No 1 ladies detective agency and opened it to read.

5th February 2012

I started the day telling myself something really important, "I need to make friends if I am going to call this place home for a while now." I got ready and decided to introduce myself properly to some of the other patients in the ward.

I could feel a hard lump in my throat, as I nervously wheeled myself into the day room during lunch. I scanned the room to find a table where I could easily park my wheelchair. I saw a big enough space near one of the tables in the middle of the room. I made my way there, where I met Carol, Dina, Richard, Matt and Anu.

After a quick introduction with the others, I did not feel so nauseous anymore and the hard lump in my throat disappeared. We, each in turn, discussed how we had ended up moving to the regional rehab unit (RRU). It was amazing to find out that all of us had a neurological disorder, but every condition was so different from the other. Yet our symptoms started off with some form of similarity.

I am so relieved that now I can talk about my tingling, pins and needles and the people that I talk to know exactly how it feels and how it affects mobility. I can confidently say that I feel like someone is giving me electric shocks every time I touch water, that it is okay to say I cannot touch things for long because my hand hurts, or it feels like it is on fire. These people understand how I feel.

After a long chat over lunch, I was worn out, my whole

body was aching and feeling heavy from all the talking. "I am tired of talking, I feel like I have put out three loads of washing in the garden. Is this how tired I am going to get from now on, every time I have long conversations?" I thought to myself. "I cannot be like this forever, getting so tired cannot be good, how am I going to cope when I go back home and start my life as a full-time mum?" I told myself, as I wheeled my way back to my room.

Once I was back in my room, I asked to be put into bed, with a lot of questions still playing on my mind. I knew that if I wanted to see change in myself then I had to do something about it. "I need to be much more determined and focused." I reminded myself, I looked at my bed statement again, "I need that statement changed, I want to be able to transfer using the rotator turn table." I repeated to myself over and over again, my eyelids started feeling heavy, and soon enough I was fast asleep.

After my little afternoon nap, I sat up straight wiggling from side to side, grabbing the bed rails to assist me, I did not want the HCA to come and help me to sit up, so I tried and tried until I was finally able to pull myself up. My breathing became heavy, and my arms ached from all the pulling. I did not realise until now how lucky we are every day to able to just sit up straight from lying position when we want. However, when the body is so heavy and not willing to cooperate with the mind then it's a completely different story. "I need to change this; my body must listen to my mind," I told myself.

I picked up the sheet with the list of bed exercises from my table and started to practice them. In my mind I was moving my toes in circular motion, but I could not really feel anything, but I was looking at my toes and I could see that it was twitching a little. This is a relief because it means the message is getting across, but the strength is not quite here yet.

Next, I started the exercises with my hands, I worked on picking things up from the desk. It is easy picking things up that are large and have a body and height to them such as my water bottle. However, flat things are more difficult to pick up my hands were unable to grip them properly, so I have to slide little and flat objects to the edge of the desk then place one hand under it and pick it up with the other. This went on until dinner time with little breaks here and there. But I was determined to make a change.

I am so pleased, that all that determination this afternoon paid off, because towards the end of the night, I was able to pick up my comb and brush through my hair. This is a big step I have managed to comb through my hair without any assistance. "Yes! This is the first step to getting those hands to be much stronger." I told myself almost grinning as I did. I am so happy with the fact that if I try hard and tell myself over and over again that I can do something then soon enough my body will play along with my mind.

6th February 2012

I happily went into my OT session today, I wanted to show Nikki what I could do with my hands. Nikki was impressed and told me that as part of the session today, I would be moving smaller objects because that's where the difficulty lies, so we had to slowly work on improving that. I was so pleased that the night before I had seen an improvement that even though I hated moving smaller objects and putting them down because the sensations in my hands just felt so uncomfortable. I did not mind today, because I knew this would be my road to recovery. I happily moved little objects. I tried to pick up the cards from the table without sliding them to the edge of the table to help me.

I am constantly being reminded, that I have to do things properly so that different parts of my body know how to do things in the correct way instead of just trying to take the easy option. This definitely was like being back at school. But I enjoyed myself.

Physio session was not so fun. Kate had to take the measurements to make the back slabs for my legs which were essential for supporting me when we go to the gym and practice walking. I also needed a splint for my right leg so that I had full support from thigh to toes as we did not want it give way all of a sudden between our sessions.

However, the whole process of creating these slabs and splint was absolutely painful and uncomfortable. Kate made me lie down on the bench with my stomach and chest resting on the flat surface of the bench. She then placed white clay like substance all over both my legs, she did this one at a time so that she could mould the clay into the shape of my legs.

This process was long and painful because it required precision and time to shape the clay to cover the full area of the thigh down to the calf. The other thing this process required was water to help with the moulding, but the touch of water that was all over my clothes felt really uncomfortable, it was like having hundreds of electric currents running down my spine, unlike the shower where the water just runs down the skin, this process had the water sitting on my skin through my clothes for what seemed like a never-ending process.

Finally, after the shaping of the clay out, came the white bandage. This was the top layer to ensure that the mould does not crack or break, because fabric does not crack. I felt like I was going to end up like a mummy at this point. Both my legs were fully wrapped around in white bandage. The right leg was completely covered up to the toes.

Once the whole process was over Kate carefully cut a long slit in what now looked like a cast from the middle so that it created an opening to take the leg in and out of the cast when I would go for my physio.

The splint on the other hand, would now be with me permanently so that I can practise my sit to stands more safely with support. Kate told me my supports would take whole the night, to fully dry up and be strong.

After that traumatic session in the gym, I was glad to be back in my room and change into some dry clothes.

Today I miss being at home, it is difficult to go through so many different procedures and not be able to discuss it with anyone, it is heart breaking. Some might say, "why not use the mobile phone and quickly catchup with your dear ones."

My answer to that would be, "I have never been a big fan of phones, too much maintenance and especially now with most phones being touch screen, I find it difficult to use them." I prefer the face-to-face contact when I feel down.

However, when I think about it logically, I feel it is best if I do not worry my family members, by telling them how upset I am feeling. I need them to continue believing in me, when I keep reassuring them that I am okay with everything that is happening, every time that I do speak to them. We will go through this difficult phase in our lives as a family. For now, I cannot let my emotions come in the way of my recovery.

Ok I must put down the pen now, as I am struggling to write any sort of letters now.

I glanced through the scrap pieces of papers on my desk, thinking when I look back these diary accounts one day, I can tell myself how well I have done to beat this disease.

I then closed my eyes and prayed to Allah. Only my lord will help me keep strong. I need to stay calm, happy and patient. I finished my motivational speech to myself and got ready to fall asleep. Tomorrow is going to be another new challenge.

7th February 2012

I made slight progress, during occupational therapy this morning. I managed to wash independently and required minimal support to dress. It is such a relief that I can now put on my incontinence pad by myself. Even if it means sitting on the commode to help me do this. Up until now, it has been quite an embarrassing experience, to go through every day, where I have needed an HCA to help me do this.

"Now I am at the first step of getting my dignity back, it is only a matter of time, before I get better at most of these tasks, soon I will not need any help with this routine." I promised myself.

Later this morning, I felt reluctant to go into physio session, I knew I would have to use the leg slab and splint, as Kate had mentioned yesterday. This meant that my legs would be in so much discomfort, already any sort of touch makes the pins and needles sensations extremely strong.

I do not know what it is like, to be poked by a porcupine, but all I had in mind throughout that point was, that I was being prepared to be pricked by a bunch of porcupines? Just by going on the appearance of the leg supports it was difficult to prepare myself to put them on, this is how I can best describe my fear for the level of pain and discomfort I was about to go through.

I then told myself, "Right Yasmin, you have to face this once you put these support on. You will be able to walk, you want to walk, you want to go home to your children." I repeated these points to myself all the way into the gym.

Kate put on my aids for me once I met her at the gym, like I had guessed, it was a very painful process, first of all, by placing the support securely on the legs, then wrapping it up in a bandage so it would not come off during the session.

This was the first time I felt something so uncomfortably close my skin. I could feel the muscle spasms, these were immensely powerful, many electric shock sensations went down my legs, but I did not want to express this. Otherwise, I worried that they would stop the session and wait, till I got used to putting these supports on first. This meant losing out on starting the walking process early. Which will lead to delays in going home. "I can do this, just keep recalling Allah's name, he will guide me through this." I confidently told myself.

Finally, with all the supports in place, I sat on my chair with my eyes closed tightly to avoid feeling the different tingling sensations running up and down my legs, I then opened them to see my goal in front of me.

At first, I struggled to stand up straight from my chair, holding Kate's hand, I slowly tried to lift my toes and started to make my way up to the parallel bars in front of me, balancing was extremely hard, I felt there was a strong magnetic kind of a pull restraining me from moving forward. I wobbled and shook all the way to the bars. I felt tingling and burning sensations going down my back as I tried to walk.

Once I reached the parallel bars, with Kate's assistance, I placed my hands on the bars and had a look at the distance I would need to try and take steps towards on my own.

It felt awkward, when Kate was holding my hand, I was somehow able to lift my legs and take at least four to five steps to where the parallel bars were. However, holding onto a bar with each hand and just trying to move but not being able to, hurt my entire body. I became tired of just standing, I took deep breaths to help me, but the pain was too strong. I was unable to lift my legs at all by myself. My hands became sweaty as I continued to hold on, fearing I would fall.

I tried but nothing happened something was stopping me from moving forward, I battled with tears of pain as I tried a few more times to move forward. Kate stopped the session when she saw how much pain and discomfort, I was in, which was clearly evident on my face by then. She reassured me that my body was just getting used to all the new things it was being introduced to. So, it would take just a little time to adjust to.

I was assisted back to my room after all the support was taken off me, I was relieved that the pins and needles had calmed down instantly. I was put in bed and advised to rest, as the session had been an intense one. I was reminded to practise my bed exercises once I had a little rest.

I had stopped writing my daily accounts for a few days, as I had become a little too poorly from all the different exercises I was trying to get used to. As a result of trying so hard, my hands became very weak and after my physio sessions I was unable to write my diary accounts for the 8th of February 2012 till the 13th of February 2012.

14th February 2012

During my morning physiotherapy I went to the gym and practised what seemed like a never-ending session of just transferring from wheelchair to bed and bed to wheelchair. Kate explained the importance of why we had to do this. "It is not just about sliding from the chair to bed and bed to chair. Your posture has to be strong, as in the long run your body will use the correct postures to help you balance and walk," I was told.

Even after being told the importance of doing things properly, it was very tempting to use my hands to push myself up from the bed, in order to correctly move from the bed. I had to take out my hands in front of me, just as one would do when doing squat exercises. This was another uncomfortable and difficult task, but I could not avoid it.

One reason being that I want to recover as soon as possible, and the other I do not want my keyworkers to feel that I am not motivated enough. They will slow down the process of how they introduce different exercises to me if I complain of pain and discomfort.

I cannot let them notice that I am struggling. I want that bed statement changed, I wanted my transfers from bed to chair to require the assistant of one HCA instead of two, just as the hoist transfer requires at the moment.

With all these thoughts pushing me harder, I was able to transfer a few times. Although Kate stopped the session when she noticed me slanting towards my left side, which is my stronger side for support. I guess you cannot hide how tired your body gets from a therapist who has been doing the job for a good few years.

In the afternoon Martine, one of the regular physiotherapists, came in to support Kate with me using a new aid I had not seen before. It looked like a big standing trolley that you see in places like BnQ (DIY stores) for loading big items such as wooden panes, big bags with compost etc. The only difference was there was a part to stand inside and arms coming out from the top with straps and belts. When I asked what it was Kate told me it was an Advanced Reciprocating Gait Orthosis (ARGO) stand, to help me with my posture when I walked.

There are two things I am getting used to, number one everything used in the patient's treatment has a name I have never heard of before and number two I have to start using the term *orthosis*, for anything that comes in direct contact with my legs and arms to help me correct my posture of how I do things. I am very used to the term AFO which stood for Ankle Foot Orthosis but initially it sounded like some kind of UFO. *(This is how I humour myself amidst all the sad feelings inside me, naming things or describing things in a way which would make everyone around me laugh.)*

Anyways, that is me drifting onto another topic. Martine and Kate helped me with putting on my AFO and then strapped my wrist and ankle to the ARGO stand. One reason for using this stand was to separate both my legs from one another. Since I had the Transverse Myelitis, my right leg has turned in towards my left leg and it was almost impossible to stand, sit and lie down without both my legs touching one another.

This is not good because it causes friction which in effect has caused for the skin on my left leg to become sore. Kate also told me that if we did not practice walking in what I described to myself the Terminator pose, then my leg will become used to standing with both legs touching each other and this would in turn, cause a lot of problems for me later on. When I do start to walk on my own, the right leg will turn inwards which can then cause falls and problems with balancing.

I can now understand why since the beginning of my treatment, a pillow is placed in the middle of both my legs when I am lying down and sitting on my wheelchair. It is a constant effort to use the correct posture.

After understanding the importance of standing up correctly, I managed to use the help of the ARGO stand to walk up to the nurse's station and back to my room, it is a small distance for now, but it is a start. Kate and Martine did not touch the stand but stood remarkably close on either side, just so that I would not run into anything or anyone.

These were my first steps without the assistance, from any of the therapist. The ARGO stand acted like huge rollator frame the only difference was I would not accidently fall as I was strapped onto the stand.

Just when I thought that I had done extremely well with my posture and transfers today, my therapist suggested and made sure I finished my day with some more bed to chair and chair to bed transfers.

I was so relieved when I was put back in bed after my sessions today. My entire body ached and, on this occasion, I felt strong muscle spasms. I was in so much pain. Today I was glad for all the medication rounds that the nurses did for the set times, I needed the painkillers to help me feel more comfortable.

15th February 2012

I woke up feeling very tired from the physiotherapy yesterday. My hands are trembling as I am trying to write this point down on paper. The Paper keeps moving sideways, I am unable to have a firm grip on it. I will not write anymore during the day today; my fingers are tired and numb from trying to grip onto the parallel bars yesterday.

After an awfully slow start to the day, I half-heartedly went into the gym with Kate and Martine. They helped me put on the orthosis for the back of my legs, my entire body felt someone was pricking me from every angle. The pins and needles sensations were so strong.

My agony did not end here. After putting on the back slabs, which covered the thigh to calf area (a bit like a cricket leg pad but instead of covering the front of the leg it holds the back of the legs straight) of both legs, out came the turn for the AFO for my right leg only, holding together the knee to ankle area. It was very strange to lie on a bench whilst my therapist securely put on all my orthosis.

Kate helped me to stand after that routine. Now I felt even more uncomfortable, I felt stiff, and I could not think how I was going to move when I felt like a mummy *(metaphorically speaking)*. I was assisted to the parallel bars. At that moment, the feeling inside, me was something I cannot explain. When I was asked to hold on to either side, by placing a hand each on the bar, one on the right side of me and the other on the left side. I stood in that position for a few seconds. When asked to try and take a step forward, at first, I was unable to move at all. In my mind I was telling my leg to move forward, and I could feel a strange kind on a tremor going down my legs. However, I had not moved forward even an inch.

Hence at first Martine bent down and sat where my legs were, and she assisted me to lift my toes and placing her hands one on my calf and the other on the ankle and she started to do the actions of what one would do when they must walk. It is only at times like this that we realise that how lucky we are that when we want to move ourselves from one location to another, we would normally start with standing and walk forward without even thinking how lucky we are to be able to do so.

It takes a tragic circumstance to genuinely appreciate the way our bodies function. I just wanted the session to end because I felt the back slabs were somehow stopping me from moving at all. But I was told it was for my safety. I had to do some hip extensions, again I needed Martine to do the actions whilst I tried hard in my mind to move my legs. Finally, towards the last quarter of the session I was able to walk a little without the back slabs, but I had to use the AFO (Splint). I was told the splint might be a permanent aid for me to walk from now on because of the amount of movement and strength in my right leg.

16th February 2012

I am in a lot of discomfort from wearing the back slab, as my skin has become quite thin from all the medication, plus during the early days I was more bed bound, hence some of my muscles look as if they have shrunk, both my legs look very bony. So, from now on it is a task in hand to do a lot of muscle building exercises, and all the right kind of physiotherapy has the biggest role to play.

I was put on the ARGO stand for the first half of the morning session, to walk up and down from the nurse's stations. My posture is improving with every trial, but at the time, I felt I just could not stop myself from feeling exhausted. These strenuous exercises are having a big impact on how quickly I feel tired, even though I try to stay calm with the different breathing activities, I cannot stop feeling tired.

For the latter half of the morning, I was given a rollator frame (Zimmer frame) to aid me to walk the width of the gym for about four times in total, twice going one way and twice the opposite direction. Thankfully, I did not have to wear my back slabs, but I had the splint on the entire time. In fact, I have the splint on pretty much the whole duration of the day except for when going into bed for rests, or when doing floor exercises in the gym.

During the afternoon I was put in the intermediate group, which meant being in a group with patients who had the similar levels of strength in their limbs as myself. We were also restricted to using only some of the less advanced equipment. I was put on the motor med which is a machine that assists one's leg to pedal automatically whilst sitting on the seat which resembles an exercise bike. I was on this machine for about twenty minutes.

Then to finish off I was put on the crest to play a game of catch and throw whilst standing straight. I was able to play for the first ten minutes, then my arms were far too exhausted from all the movement, even when I tried, I was unable to lift my arms. So, I just stood and watched the other patients play for the final ten minutes of the session.

17th February 2012

I did not want to do anything too intense today. My body felt it was being pulled down by some strong force. I wanted to take it easy and see how I feel. Even though I want fast results, today I realised that sometimes we must listen to the signs that our body is giving us. If a session is too intense or difficult then it is best to speak up. Otherwise, you will have to spend more time in resting and taking it easy until your body is able to function in the way in which you would like it to. A big lesson learnt; I am not speeding up the process of recovering quickly to be discharged from hospital. In fact, by forcing myself to go through every session it is having a knock-on effect. From now on I will tell Kate when something is too hard for me to do.

Later on, I waited for Nikki, who had told me that I could use the computer room to give myself a break. I am so relieved to have my login details. I could now type my diary entries rather than writing them down every night. My hands will get some relief from this method, holding a pen can be quite tricky at times.

I do not want to give up writing my daily accounts because this is what helps me take some pressure off myself. I feel by writing things down I am actually sharing the burden with someone, without actually sharing it with anyone, causing worries that could be avoided.

I also want to be able to one day, when I feel ready, share

my story with other people out there, who may have or are going through some kind of health problem, restricting them from living their life as they would have liked to.

I hope I can be of inspiration to others, after leaving my job at the college, I did start to feel a void in my life. I miss being part on an environment where a dedicated group of people work to help students achieve their goals in life.

In the afternoon I decided to use my electric wheelchair to go downstairs and try and manoeuvre, inside the cafeteria and the shop.

I was okay at first enjoying myself driving in and out of aisles, but then all of a sudden, for no reason at all, I felt my chest tighten and my forehead started to sweat. I knew at that point that I needed to get back into the ward before I pass out or something. I immediately made my way upstairs and immediately asked the nurse to be put I bed.

I could not understand why I felt like that, it was completely unexpected. I had become claustrophobic all of a sudden and it felt really bad, my chest tightened, my arms felt heavy, and my palms became extremely sweaty, as I was making my way back up to the ward. I could not press the buttons on the lift and the keypad to enter the ward. My fingers kept slipping because my arms felt extremely heavy.

I may need to mention this to Bianca, who is the patient psychologist in the ward, she might be able to shed a little light on why I felt like that today. I hope she can help, up until now I thought I would be okay and would not need to speak to Bianca, as I am a positive person and I know that I have to listen to my carers and follow the plan they have in mind for me to recover the best I can. However, after my little experience today which I have no explanation to, I need someone who is more skilled in those areas to be able to advise me.

Why am I feeling like this suddenly? I do not remember anything new upsetting me.

18th February 2012

After the events of yesterday I woke up feeling very stiff. I could not stop wondering why I felt so scared being the middle of so many people. Is this something that is going to stay with me from now on?

My thoughts were interrupted by Nikki, who had come into my room to speak to me, checking that I was okay, she had heard from the team about yesterday's episode. We spoke about the events from the day before and she too told of me what I already had thought of, which is, that it would be best to raise these worries with Bianca who might be able to suggest some exercises to help with the worrying feeling. I started to feel a little better after speaking to Nikki, because she did not think I was overreacting or being a drama queen.

What Nikki did next was really kind, to distract me from my worries she asked me whether I wanted to try having my shower unaided as well as dressing on my own. This was a challenge and I like challenges. It meant Nikki had faith in me, that I am capable of managing this on my own from now on.

I agreed immediately, I was assisted to sit on the commode, just in case any embarrassing accidents took place during the session. I did have a few embarrassing accidents during the early days, but I was incredibly lucky that Nikki was always very discreet, and she would just clean up after me without embarrassing me at all. She has always been very considerate about my self-respect, when she has helped me through those embarrassing times.

I am receiving regular bowel training sessions from Charlene, who is the main nurse in my team. Therefore, I do not have embarrassing accidents every day but every other fourth or fifth day. I have been made aware that there is a chance that this problem may fully resolve itself or there may be some obstacles that I may still have to face but they would show me how I can manage with this issue, with life outside the Regional Rehab Unit.

Coming back to my wash and dress session, I was able to meet one my goals. I showered and dressed myself fully. One of the areas I have always required assistance with, up until now was putting on my pad and trousers. But today I was shown how I could do this on my own. I shifted from side to side on the commode and with only some difficulties, I managed to put on my pad and trousers by myself. It took me a little while, because my hands and legs were shaking like a leaf as I bent forward. I had to hold onto the left-hand bar of the commode so that I did not fall as I bent forward.

The entire time, my whole body felt like that there was a constant burning and tingling sensation running through it, as I moved back and forth, with all my concentration.

Again, this task is one of the things that most of us healthy people might take for granted at times. We do not think twice as we wash and dress, we just do it. But when your limbs become so weak, this whole process feels like half a day's work.

I feel even more grateful now, that I can live my life with dignity and independence. I thank Allah with all of my heart, that he is guiding me through these challenges, making me think about how lucky I am to be receiving such great care. I am incredibly happy with my progress today; it has really given me a new lease of life.

Later, today I requested to go into the computer room. I spent the afternoon watching a video on self-catheterisation. As I want to be discreet when I go back home if I leave with unresolved issues with my bladder. Even though, this process seems scary and uncomfortable, I must overcome my fears and prepare myself to undertake this task as it is something I have to face sooner or later.

After my little session on researching on this topic, I spoke to Nikki afterwards about this matter, asking whether this is something I would have to do when I leave the hospital. Nikki reassured me that the decision would be mine entirely.

Another reason that this would depend on, is how effectively my bladder would be trained. If and when my catheter is taken out and if I do not have any problems with passing water then I wouldn't need to do this, but if there are some minor problems then there were clinics I could go to where they may suggest using incontinence pads to stay discreet. However, these were all things Nikki told me not to worry about yet as my treatment was going on right now, and thankfully I was responding well to it and improving, so I just had to remain optimistic and see what happens.

19th February 2012

I did not have a lot of physiotherapy and OT timetabled for today. Hence, I decided to go back downstairs to the shopping area and see how I felt. I told myself I would not go into the shops but just go around the outside and see how I feel because I was not ready to go into a crowd just yet.

So, I wheeled down to the lift and went downstairs on my own. I roamed around outside Adams fruits and then wheeled up to WHSmith and just looked on from outside.

I did need two rest breaks during this time. This is because today I did not take my power chair, but I had decided to take my manual wheelchair, only to see what my endurance levels were like. It was not a surprise to me that my hands continuously shook, during the whole time. I used them to drive the chair and it also got quite sweaty because I was extremely nervous.

Nevertheless, I was quite lucky today as I had not experienced the same problems as I previously had, with claustrophobia. Feeling quite pleased that my chest had not started to tighten today I came back up to the ward.

Once I got back to my room, I decided to sit down and read my book for a little while, just to relax my muscles, plus I did not want to fall asleep before lunch today. I am trying to see how much I can do during the mornings before I need a nap to help me build up my strength.

After lunch I decided to search for some simple cooking

recipes. This is because soon, I will be spending some of my time in the kitchen for my occupational therapy sessions. As this is one of my personal goals, which I would have to meet before leaving the hospital, because I am going to be a full-time housewife/mum after I leave, so I need the training.

I had spoken to Nikki right at the beginning of my treatment, of areas that concern me the most, the areas that I need to be strong at because my lifestyle depends on it. Nikki had a plan in mind for me and she told me that we would take things one step at a time, in order to make sure my body was coping properly with all the changes it was being introduced to.

20th February 2012

Today during occupational therapy, I got the chance to work on one of my other personal goals. Being a fulltime housewife and mum, I would need to train myself to be able to do ironing. So, Nikki took me to the OT kitchen, where she laid a tabletop ironing board and plugged in an iron for me. All I had to do was sit in my wheelchair and iron a square piece of cloth.

It is exceedingly difficult to sit on a wheelchair whilst ironing, but I was told that for my own safety it is good practice to do so, within the regional rehab unit and life outside the unit.

This is because the iron will be hot and the steam, could cause burns or light headedness. Standing up and ironing may cause a risk of suddenly falling if my head got dizzy but sitting on my wheelchair or an ordinary chair if I preferred, would ensure I do not go crashing on the ground.

The information all made sense to me as it was all logical and with Zara and Jannat being so young, it is best that I do things which are risk free not only for me but for them too. However, to follow this rule proved to be more difficult. As this whole process required adjusting everything so that reaching all the things was easy.

I sat in my wheelchair in front of a table with the desk ironing board placed on top of the table for easy to reach purposes. I was talked through of how I can make these simple adjustments at home too, when I do the ironing so that everything is within my reach without any difficulties. But most importantly I would have to ensure that before I switched on the iron, I would assess the safety of the environment. Initially I encountered some teething problems when I tried ironing from sitting, as my body kept slanting towards the left. It took me a while to sit with a good balance. My body ached and I felt a lot of tingling as my hands moved across the board. Something else I have to practice conscientiously to improve on.

After an eventful morning with lots of positivity, I was a little bit thrown back by some unexpected news. In the afternoon, I became a little upset because I was informed that my physiotherapist was moving upstairs to the renal unit, therefore someone new would replace her.

I have become so used to receiving instructions from Kate every day and now I will have to receive these instructions from someone who I do not know. As soon as I am comfortable with a certain way of doing things, circumstance seem to always change, it has been happening since my treatment started. I have moved from one department to another, meeting many different people supporting me. sometimes it is quite difficult to embrace all the changes, so many questions arise in my mind.

Nevertheless, I must remain positive and give the new physiotherapist a chance, so far everyone has been brilliant, so I am sure the new therapist will be really good too, in how she handles my treatment.

As I waited to be collected for physiotherapy Kate arrived with Miranda who was introduced to me as my new physiotherapist. I felt a little silly for worrying myself over who the new physiotherapist will be. Miranda seemed really nice, and she looked really understanding. All the time Kate spoke to her regarding my condition, Miranda would smile at me, like as if it were a signal to let me know that I should stop worrying, she had everything under control. The other great thing was she had read my notes before coming to see me, so I did not have to repeat my story. Saying that she still wanted to see for herself what I can and cannot manage.

Therefore, we made our way to the gym, where I joined my fellow patients, in the intermediate group. I started off the session by going onto the motor med machine whilst Miranda assessed my progress.

I then had to demonstrate my transfers from wheelchair to plinth and vice versa with support from Martine, who had joined us.

Miranda wanted to see how I managed on the crest, so I stood on there for fifteen minutes playing catch and throw with her. I was glad to do this because this helped to break the ice. I realised that Miranda was just as fun as Kate and I would not have a problem communicating with her. I was quite exhausted though because I had demonstrated quite a few things.

Hoping that the crest activity would be the last one for that session, I asked Miranda if I would finish for the morning.

Miranda told me that it be a good idea to do some hip extensions, as I still needed some assistance with that and so, she just wanted to see how I get on. At first, I was reluctant to do my hip extensions. This was one of the exercises that I dreaded the most because I was not particularly good at it and I always needed some help to lift my legs so that a stretch went down my legs.

Later on, I did not mind so much because I could see that Miranda was pleased with what she saw, even though I hardy managed to lift my legs, once Martine helped me, I managed to stay in the position for about ten seconds without complaining that I wanted to put my leg down, like I had done previously due to the pain factor.

I met Nikki in the afternoon and told her how pleased I was with Kate's replacement, even though I would miss her a lot because of all the time and effort she has put into my treatment. Having said that Miranda seemed very thorough in her approach and I felt that she would support me in the same way Kate has done.

Nikki was pleased to hear that I had stopped worrying, but that did not stop her for taking me into the OT kitchen to practice my ironing. One thing I have learnt from being here at the RRU is that the exercises we try to avoid are the ones that we have to practice the most until we get to a good level with it. Though I do understand the reason behind it, obviously it's preparation to do things as normally as possible when we are discharged. If we do not practice, then we will not be able to cope, here at the RRU, we have carers looking after our every need, but when we go home, it is going to be different. It would be up to us to be as independent as we can.

Today has been an exceptionally long and tiring day. The ironing has made me very tired and doing all that physiotherapy on top has caused a lot of pain. Therefore, I asked to go into bed straight after dinner and for the first time I had to be woken up to take my night medication. Usually, I would be reading my book for a while and only go to sleep after the night nurse had left my room after giving me my medication. Today however, I was too tired to stay awake for the night-time medication rounds.

21st February 2012

After waking up this morning, I felt the aftermath from the ironing yesterday. To start off with, I found it difficult to lift my breakfast spoon and place it properly towards my lips. Every time I tried, I ended up putting a little bit of Weetabix on my chin or the spoon went past my mouth. This did alarm me at first because I thought my hands were losing strength in them again.

So, I decided to do the hand exercises that I had been practicing from my occupational therapy session. I continued to do this for about thirty minutes. Then I tried combing and plaiting my hair to see how well I managed to do this. Throughout the whole process I felt my arms required extra attention than usual to complete the task.

When I raised this with Nikki, she completed her checks and told me it is normal for the body to have good and bad performing days. This was like a side effect from the Transverse Myelitis. I did mention that I started feeling the change after the ironing task. Nikki told me that it was possible that the ironing too, may have been a reason to feel like this.

Feeling relieved that I was not going to go back the way I had been since my Transverse Myelitis attack, I prepared to go to the gym. Once my session started, I went on the moto med machine for fifteen minutes and then I had a standing session using the rollator frame.

After lunch I wanted to take a quick nap, because I was

not feeling too strong, worrying about my hands had made me feel heavy from inside. I felt like there were weights inside of me which were refraining me, from moving freely. I thought that if I relaxed properly then that would release the muscles that had tightened with worry. I was right, after my nap I felt bright and fresh.

I had been booked in to be in the OT kitchen this afternoon. I was going to be cooking for the first time in almost two months. I had the choice to use some of the ingredients available in the cupboards and given the option to cook anything of my choice.

The kitchen looked quite different from my kitchen at home. All the worktop heights were adjustable, there was a handle that could be turned to bring the height up or take it down for each individual patient using the kitchen.

I was told all patients had to start off using the kitchen by remaining seated in their wheelchair throughout the whole session for their own safety, only after reviewing the progress of each patient, standing up and cooking in the session would be allowed. Again, this task was a preparation for life outside the regional rehab unit. The utensils were in cabinets that were easily accessible.

Every day I was learning something new, I listened to all the safety advise and then started cooking. There was plenty of space to manoeuvre with my chair around but not being able to stand to cook was quite frustrating. I had to go to the sink numerous amounts of times to carry back the washed ingredients with a bowl placed on my lap. I had to be careful to wheel myself back to the worktop without dropping anything. This process lasted pretty much the whole session. I had to go back to wash utensils, pots, and pans. It took a lot of time to go back and forth in a chair. Walking would have saved double the time used. However, finally after all the preparation I successfully managed to cook a spinach, tomato, and chickpea curry.

Cooking is usually quite easy for me; it is what I do regularly on a daily basis. But now that my limbs were weak, this whole process seemed difficult and tiring, it really tested my endurance levels. Nikki encouraged me throughout the session, making sure I was safe all the time. Especially when I was working by the cooker.

After a very strenuous session, I was happy with the end result. I had actually managed to cook a dish, which looked and tasted really good, on my own, with supervision. Although, the thought of how long it had taken me to cook a simple dish, was a little upsetting at first. But Nikki told me that with time it would become easier as I would get used to cooking with such adaptations.

22nd February 2012

At half past eight this morning I had to go into the orthotics clinic. I was told that a mould had to be taken of my leg, for a plastic splint to be made for my right leg. I was informed that the plastic splint would be a more secure AFO compared to the soft fabric one I was currently using. The plastic is rigid and would not bend like the soft AFO, plus it would be easier to wear as it did not require a bandage piece to be wrapped around the top to secure the AFO in place like my soft one.

Coming back from the clinic I had to prepare myself to face the toughest part of every morning, that is going through with the bowel training session. Today I was allowed sit on the commode without any suppositories. Unfortunately, even after having a bowel movement I was told I was not fully empty, so in the end, I still had to have the suppositories. I was told that this would become a regular part in the training method now to ensure that bowel was responding properly.

Each day there is just so much information I have to start taking in and accepting them in the hope that my body will react appropriately and recover quickly. Today has been one of those days, where my legs were being examined more than usual.

After coming into the regional rehab unit, I have developed a large painful boil just on the tip of my right knee. Before the boil had formed, the skin on my leg had been rubbed a little hard just as the nurses were securing the belts into place for my hoist transfer.

At first the skin looked red in an area of a five pence size. I did not feel any pain or irritation because of the limited sensation I have. Within a few days the skin started cracking a little and then the boil stated forming, because the skin was being rubbed repeatedly because my AFO met the boil on my knee. Gradually It burst and there was a little bit of infection. Hence, I had to be put on antibiotics. I was told that I would have daily dressing to prevent further spread of infection.

I was informed not to get that area wet when I was taking showers, because that would prevent the healing process. When I asked, "How I can keep that area dry?" Diane, the nurse who was looking after me today suggested covering most of the leg from thigh down to the calf with some plastic and taping it onto place then removing it after the shower. I am not happy about doing this every day, because it means moving and touching the skin on the right leg directly a lot more than usual. The tingling and pins and needles feeling will get worse.

"I need to try though, the sooner the antibiotics start taking affect, and if I follow all the precautionary steps, the sooner this boil will completely go away," I told myself. "It makes sense, but why do I feel so reluctant just at the thought of it?"

It has been a long day today, especially with having the orthotics clinic first thing in the morning. In my physiotherapy session I used the rollator frame to walk in and outside of the gym. I then had to practise my sit to stands from the chair.

I asked Miranda if she could possibly look at changing my transfer method from the bed to wheelchair now. As I was using the rollator frame to practise walking almost daily now. My standing posture is also beginning to get stronger.

Currently two members of staff are coming in at least twice on a daily basis, to help me with transfers. However, if I did not need the hoist any more then only one nurse or one HCA will need to help me each day, this would take off some pressure from the staff." I explained to Miranda, in the hope she would listen to my request.

I personally felt bad I told her, that two staff members always had to come into my aid, the unit is always so busy, and the staff hardly get a free minute. Miranda listened carefully to my views and said that she would have to assess how I transfer using the rotator stand, which is the second safest way to do my transfers. I needed to practise using the rotator stand before it becomes my permanent transfer method.

Safety is going to be the key factor always. Miranda reassured me that the staff members were not feeling the pressure any more than usual, because they had to do my hoist transfers twice a day. Nevertheless, she was prepared to look into the matter and would change the transfer method if she felt that it was safe to do so after assessing me.

I was excited to talk about what I had discussed with Miranda to Nikki, as I exercised my arms during OT.

I managed to exercise my arms and shoulders only for a short duration of time because today had been an exceptionally long day with all the different activities I had completed.

Therefore, I was happy to come back to my room later on. I excitedly called EH, updating him on the progress I had made today and what changes could possibly take place in the next few days. I then talked with Zara for a little bit, she told me she is building a house with her Legos. It was so lovely listening to her; how I wished I was home right now sitting next to her; I miss playing with the children. I put the phone down and then rang my mum to see how she was coping with looking after Jannat full time for me.

Jannat has started taking her solids now, my mum is doing so brilliantly, cooking new meals for my little girl every day. I am incredibly lucky that my mum has the energy to become a full-time nanny to my daughter, without really knowing the timeframe of how long this arrangement will be for.

Mum told me that Jannat was doing simply fine, and she is beginning to babble a lot more, she has become playful and sometimes she is even a little mischievous. Listening to mum, made me feel relaxed, as I knew that Jannat was happy staying with my mum. My mum told me not to worry about the children or for the rest of the family and concentrate on getting better, everyone was ok, and they were looking forward to hearing about how I was managing at the RRU.

It has been an exceedingly long day today because I have talked about so many different things throughout the course of the day. Therefore, I must have built up my anxiety levels.

As I was having dinner in the day room with my friends, I had the most horrible panic attack, whilst I was eating, out of nowhere. I was shell shocked and completely unable to move. One minute I was sitting and chatting with the others and then the next I felt my throat starting to swell, blocking my airways. My chest tightened and I was unable to breath properly. The spoon I was holding fell out of my hand and I started to flutter my arms for help. Carol and Dina thought I must be choking and immediately called for help. A couple of nurses (Dolly and Shaila) walked into the day room and took me back to my room.

Once in my room, I was helped to go onto the bed and they immediately carried out all the necessary observations and called for Doctor Bheroze to come and check what was going on. I winced in pain and faintly asked if I was having a relapse.

Dr Bheroze came in and completed a full check-up, assessing the strength in all my limbs. He then reassured me that I was not having a relapse, as I had feared at first because I suspected that since my body had become stiff, I was having a relapse, due to the limitation in my movements.

I was told that stress and anxiety could be a reason for the body to behave in the way it did. After listening to me about if anything had upset me today, or was I worrying about anything, Doctor Bheroze suggested that I take it easy for few days. Also, to try not to rush through my treatment, things will happen in due course. I was not to worry about being a nuisance on the healthcare team, that they were there to help all the patients, which included me.

Annette who had seen what had happened, whilst she was delivering the evening cup of tea to the patients, brought me my hot cup of tea with a biscuit and looked at me with a kind glance. She told me I looked good smiling and that soon I would be smiling again like usual, but today I just needed rest.

After having my tea, I felt relaxed, the tightening feelings had gone away, I could feel my body again, so that was a relief. I decided to read a little and then fall asleep, straight after the night medications were given. Just then, Carol and Dina walked in after everyone else had left, to make sure I was okay, they had gotten worried, seeing me like that earlier on. I told them I was feeling better than before and thanked them for calling out for help. We chatted for about ten minutes, before they left me alone so that I could get some rest.

I am tired I want to sleep, but I cannot for some reason.

That is why I am still up, writing down what I had experienced today. I wish I can stop worrying so much, why do I always end up worrying to the extent where I feel so poorly. I do not really think about worrying thoughts, it's almost as if they creep up on me. Even talking too much about condition, and looking at ways forward with the treatment, triggers something. I feel quite helpless at times, with how my body reacts to things.

23rd February 2012

I was unable to sleep peacefully after the fright last night, so when I got up this morning, I did not feel very energetic. I had my morning physiotherapy session before breakfast. I thought it would be difficult to concentrate because I was so tired. To my surprise the exercise helped me feel refreshed. It was a good feeling to shower straight after the workout.

I was able to dress myself fully, all except for putting on the splint. The soft material of the splint is a little wobbly so trying to put my leg through the slit, which starts from the calf all the way down to the tip of the toes (I can only describe it like a jacket for the leg) is a challenge, then wrapping the bandage around the whole thing and tying it into place is the more tricky part, as I was unable to bend down and hold the splint in place without it sliding off. Therefore, Nina came down to assist me, then I was helped to sit on my wheelchair.

I was extremely excited about the remaining physiotherapy sessions today. Prior to the panic attack episode yesterday, Miranda had taken on board my determination for changing my transfers to the rota turner stand transfer.

As I started the session, I was happy to practise the whole routine a few times, but I did feel at a point that it was getting very repetitive, due to the initial difficulty I had with standing up straight. I had to place both my toes on the base of the frame, like you do, when you need your shoe size checked. Placing each toe on either side. I then used all the strength I had in my arms to grab onto the middle of the frame, wrapping my arms around the wider section, still in sitting position. Then I tried hard to lift myself from the bed. This part was tricky because my sensations below my waist are still very weak, so I did not know how to push myself up.

So, I had some help from Martine who placed her hands around my hips and helped me lift whilst Miranda held onto the stand so that it did not move. Then once I was standing up straight, hugging onto the stand, Miriam rotated the stand to where the wheelchair was and slowly, I had to sit down. I felt discomfort and a lot of pins and needles. But I did not want the session to stop so I tried the bed to chair and vice versa using the rota stand a couple of times.

After which, even with Martine assisting the lower half of my body to push up and stand straight, I was unable to do so. As my legs wobbled like jelly and the strength to stand up straight, just was not there. Miranda and Martine reassured me that I was making good progress and naturally my body will feel weaker because it is a big change for it to adapt to, but with consistent practise it will get better.

For the remaining of the session, I walked only around my room using the rollator frame. At this point I would have happily just sat back down in my wheelchair and practise my leg extensions. However, I did not want to feel like someone who gives up so easily, so I walked around the room once (just for self-reassurance) and then asked to be sat down because realistically that was all the strength I had at the time, to do so.

At two p.m. two members, one from the nursing team and one from the HCA team Sham and Niyah joined me in my physio session to see how I was walking around the room and how I managed to do my rota stand transfers. They advised

Miranda that they were pleased with what the saw, but it was still too early to change the transfer method just yet.

As a result, Miranda told me that as long I was wearing the correct footwear, not my slippers, but my trainers or shoes, something that would not slip off and my AFO, then it would be possible to change my transfer method.

Wow! That is it, those were the words I had been so eager to hear, of course I will take all the necessary safety steps. I am so happy today this is great news if I can build up my endurance levels and keep focused, soon I will be on the next step to my recovery. I cannot wait to share this with my family.

I told myself, as I happily went into the gym with Miranda to practise sitting on the floor and balancing exercises.

24th February 2012

In the morning when Dolly (a nurse) and Lianna (a HCA) came in to assist me with my transfer, I told them that soon I would not need the hoist anymore. They checked the notes from Miranda and decided that they would try the rota stand transfer to see how I do. With both the members still present in the room for safety reasons just in case my legs gave in, Dolly did my bed to commode transfer using the rota stand, so that I could go in and have my shower. Whilst I was in the shower Dolly and Lianna made my bed and when I had finished my shower in the presence of both members of staff Lianna helped me with transferring from commode to wheelchair using the rota stand once again. Only when I was safely on the wheelchair Dolly left the room, leaving me with Lianna to get dressed fully.

Finally, I can tick a lot of boxes, for what I have achieved after coming into the regional rehab unit. I can shower myself and get dried and moisturised inside the bathroom without anyone being inside the shower room with me, which is a big relief, as it has given me back some of my dignity. I can clothe the top half of my body and put on my incontinence pad inside the bathroom before I am assisted out into my room. I am only left getting dressed in the presence of a member of staff for the lower half of my body.

Now I need to really focus on using the rota stand as a permanent method of transfer. This will enable me to pull up my trousers whilst I am standing holding onto the frame, because I can put my legs though the trousers up to my knees in my sitting down position. Rather than wiggling into my trousers whilst I am lying down in bed. Moving from hoist to the rota stand will give me back my full privacy. I echoed this piece of information to myself repeatedly.

From now on, I want to focus on permanently getting my transfer method changed, therefore, Miranda decided to centre the physio session this morning, completely on practising this transfer method. I have to admit, it became quite repetitive after a while, but I was determined to make this work I want to go home, and I want to go home feeling strong, I kept telling myself.

Please Allah help me keep calm, strong and positive and make this possible for me. I made this prayer believing that I will not be left disappointed because so far, I have been going uphill with my progress all I need to do is to stay motivated.

I was left with Martine for the remaining of the session, where we practised sit to stands on the plinth. Once I came back into my room, I was advised to rest in bed for a bit, just to give my body some respite because I had been working extremely hard. I happily took on board this advice, since my body was getting a little tired and I could tell it was because just sometimes, I struggled to make my body do the simplest of exercises such as putting out my hands in front of me, like one does when practising to do the squats. This was all the aftermath of practicing hard on my transfer method.

I went into bed and practised my bed exercise, even though I could not feel my toes, to do it I closed my eyes and with all my concentration started rotating my toes in making the number 6 and then the opposite direction making the number 9. I am doing much better with my left toe as there is more movement in that leg, in regards to the right leg at least I can feel it vibrate a little.

25th February 2012

This morning, I was extremely excited, as one of my good friend's was coming to visit. As a result of me feeling so energetic and great, I wanted to try making my bed by myself today. I was so full of energy, at the thought of having a friend coming over. I had so much I wanted to just share, to someone who can listen to me without taking any worries back home with them.

I have not been able to tell any members of my family exactly what I have been feeling or going through since I have been admitted to hospital. This is because I did not want them to worry. Finally, today I can take off the mask of being super brave and chill out for a few hours.

After taking my morning medicine, I decided I should tidy my room, it was a little bit tricky with placing every item on my lap to move it from one side of the room to the other, then organising things into their places. I have not been given authorisation to use my rollator frame to move around alone in my room without supervision just in case I have a fall. Therefore, I must move around only in my wheelchair. It had been an okay task, I just had a little bit difficulty, due to the restriction of moving around freely.

Making the bed was extremely hard, using the remote to lift the bed's top and lower ends to get the sheets under it, then wheeling my way round from one end to the other to straighten out the sheet. Using my arms to flatten the sheets required almost all my strength. After making my bed I had to rest for thirty minutes, because my heartbeat was racing much more faster than usual, and I could feel my balance on the chair was not great either. I kept sliding towards my left side, which is the stronger side of my body.

Now I understand the importance, of why we are told that we must put on our belts, when we sit on our wheelchairs, in a situation like this, it would prevent us from falling out of the chair.

Despite the little problem of feeling exhausted throughout the time I was making the bed; the end result was very satisfying to look at. I had made my bed, all by myself and I managed to make it look good.

Feeling pleased with myself for trying to take new challenges on board, I went to have lunch in the day room. I am not sure what the others thought of me today, as I could not stop talking, I do not think I gave anyone else a chance to talk, I was just so chatty and full of life.

Carol and Richard picked up on my more than usual positive behaviour and asked me what the reason was for being so happy. I told them my friend Deena was coming to visit me. I then went onto telling them the whole back story of how myself and Deena met, and the fact that before becoming such good friends Deena was my manager at my first proper job after graduating. I then went onto telling them how much fun I had working in the college and how I had transformed from being a shy mouse to a loud chatty confident individual.

Today I felt good, I talked to my friends, in the hospital about my friends outside of my hospital world. It feels good and refreshing to talk about something that moves you away temporarily from your worrying surrounding.

Deena arrived shortly after lunch and we went down to the cafeteria. It was so good to see her, yet emotional at the same time, as I just poured out my heart to her. And for once I did not have to be careful about what information to hide and what not to hide.

I told Deena exactly how anxious I feel all the time worrying if I ever will manage to live my life normally outside the hospital. She was such a good listener and made me feel good about sharing my worries, she has, always been a good listener, right from the start when I met her.

We then moved onto talking about life at the college and how things have changed since we both moved on in our lives.

I resigned after my maternity period was complete after the birth of my eldest daughter as EH did not want Zara being looked after by anyone else. So, I gave up my job to dedicate my time to my girl to make sure she gets the best possible care in growing up.

Deena had moved on from working at the college because she met this wonderful man, and they got married shortly after I went onto my maternity leave.

As we talked about everything we were laughing so much, there are so many fond memories of having been part of a great team. We were like a huge family of thirty people, making early morning teas and coffees for one another having tea, lunch's etc. We were a lively team I suppose we lived up to our name. We were the Health and Social Care team after all.

Deena left, leaving me to feel further motivated and full of bursting positivity, I felt like I was moving around, inside a happy cloud, I was smiling all the way back to my room. In my journey, for the first time today I was making conversations with people I met in the shop and lift. I was feeling excited to such an extent, that I did not mind conversing with new people around me. I did not even realise that I was talking to complete strangers, until I calmed down from all the excitement.

I came back to my room and took out my therapy putty that Nikki had given to me during my OT sessions and told me to practise using it to strengthen my hand movements. Up until now I have been very reluctant to use it because there are different coloured putties for different resistant levels, and I will be given the green coloured putty as soon as I demonstrate that I can handle the yellow one.

It feels strange using the putty, my hands tingle and I do not like the sensation it leaves behind. But today I did not need reminding to use it. I stretched the putty then rolled it onto the desk. Smiling because I felt happy, I had been able to talk to someone close to me, who is not my family member but a really good friend. I felt as if I had let go of two big, heavy bags, off from my shoulder, that freed up my arms.

Renita, the blue team's nurse in charge came in, to give me my evening meds, I excitedly told her about my day. However, soon after, my happiness somehow seemed to be short lived because Renita thought that because I was so full of positivity and energy today, it was a good time to remind me that I had to start thinking about self-catheterisation, a process of emptying out my catheter on my own when required.

It was a very daunting thought, one that I do not feel extremely comfortable with, how can I safely do that without causing a spill, or even worse what if I accidently pull it out of place? After listening to my worries, Renita smiled and reassured me that since I was making so much good progress with my personal care and with all the practice walking, then this would be something else that would give me that extra bit of independence and privacy, that is when the penny dropped, all of a sudden, my smile returned.

Yes! it means I do not have to disturb a member of staff when I feel uncomfortable because the bag is too full. No one would have to see my catheter except for the staff who help me first thing in the morning with my wash and dress routine. I am ready for this; I need to do this, I told Renita.

Renita was pleased that I did not want to avoid this topic any further, since she first mentioned it to me, I had been avoiding the whole thing. I kept coming up with so many excuses to delay the process that little bit longer. All that time knowing that one day I would have to face it and do something about it. Finally, today she managed to put her point across to me. I suppose partly because of the fact that I felt that extra bit more positive after Deena's visit. I am ready for my next challenge, Renita told me she would assist me through the whole process, on Monday morning, as it's always best to start something like that first thing in the morning, so that the body starts to follow a certain process. Just like my bowel treatment, things have to be done properly to maintain a discipline.

26th February 2012

Niyah stayed behind this morning to make sure I was not getting too tired when making the bed, because last time I was sleeping for a while after making the bed on my own. She told me I have to gradually build up the strength because I was using my arms to move my wheelchair and to straighten the sheets, which my arms were finding a little tiring all at the same time.

After my shower I went into the computer room, today I picked out some card designs. I am going to make a card for Zara and Jannat using wool to thread onto the design. This is because my brother Mo had bought me some wool, the last time he came to visit, so I can do some knitting when I get bored. I can only manage to do the knit stitch properly, and just getting used to doing a few purl stitches.

Usually, I love creating embroidery patterns using various thread colours and old pieces of fabric lying around the house. Since the birth of my children, I have not managed to make a lot of time for myself to do things I enjoy. This is because throughout the whole day I am spending time attending to their needs, then when they are having naps, I get to catch up with all my household chores, such as the cooking, cleaning, laundry, and ironing. After completing all the tasks, I used to get so tired that I did not manage to pay attention to any of my hobbies.

I love reading books, especially children's books, I love

all the Roald Dahl, Enid Blyton stories, recently I finished reading the Harry Potter series for the second time. However, after finishing with that I did not manage to get to the library to pick up any new books. As a result, I did not have anything do in the little, my own time I had.

At first, I was finding that my life had started to revolve just around the children and the house, which I was okay with to start off with. Then I found myself getting upset and bored because I was not doing anything for myself. So that is when I turned to embroidery and knitting, it is something I was quite good at and it was different to just household chores. I started creating patterns in the children's dresses, which looked quite impressive.

Coming back to present times, at this point knitting or fine embroidery is a little bit out of my league because it is extremely fiddly and requires a lot of consistent hand movements, which is something I do not have right now because of my pins and needle feelings. That is why I have decided to use the wool Mo brought with him, to colour in the pattern for the card instead of paint or felt tips, as it feels more personal, and it reminds me of still having that creative touch. It is really important to me, to remind myself that when I put my mind to something, I can create something good. It gives me some confidence in myself, which is something I am really beginning to lack at the moment. Hence, doing this for my girls make me feel proud of myself. I know they will be happy to see this card from me.

In the afternoon, I had been scheduled to go the kitchen to use the iron for my laundry session but due to short staffing the session had been cancelled. Which I did not mind because I wanted to carry on reading more of the No 1 Ladies Detective Agency.

27th February 2012

After my usual morning routine, which is to have my shower and make my bed, I practised using my Theraband. This is the resistance band that I place under my toes and pull it up with both hands making a U shape. The reason for using this band is help with the movement in the legs as well as building up the strength in my arms. It is quite hard using this band, but like the putty, If I can use the colour that has less resistance then I can move onto a colour that has more resistance later on. Saying this to myself I started practicing all the exercises that were demonstrated on the sheets of paper, Nikki had printed off for me. So that I could carry on doing the strength building exercise on my own time too, twenty minutes after playing around with the band I put it away, feeling the struggle to hold it in position properly.

During physiotherapy Miranda assisted me to walk the length from my room, past the nurses' station to the day room and back to my room. I used the rollator frame to take each step with Miranda right next to me, who had my wheelchair with her as we walked. This was so I could take rest breaks as soon as I felt my legs beginning to wobble.

It is strange how tiring it can be to walk the length of six rooms, that is my room, which is a single room, then another single room. Then there is a room that is shared by a group of four male patients after which comes a room shared by a group of four female patients. We arrived at the nurses' station next.

After which there is one more single room, and then a room shared by only two female patients. Finally, we come to the day room, which completes a list of all the rooms, that I had passed on my right-hand side. Opposite to the day room are two more rooms, each with a group of four male patients. So, I walked past approximately eight rooms, that is if I include the nurses' station. For which I had to take two rest breaks in between because my legs started wobbling and I could feel myself losing balance.

I asked Miranda if this is how I will be walking in the future, because I felt a little upset that I needed to sit down twice for what seemed like a short distance. She told me stop worrying and my body will soon build up on strength and I would be able to walk much more without breaks if I kept practising. I felt as though Miranda was being kind to me and did not want to hurt my feelings. The truth is I may never be able to walk properly, and when I do start walking on my own, I will be wobbling and struggling to lift my leges properly as I take my steps. This is because I have always felt a strange kind of a pull, preventing me from walking properly since we started the standing and walking exercises. All that time the pain and pulling feeling have stopped me from performing my tasks properly.

I am scared, how will I manage walking around the house? whilst making sure that I do not come in Zara and Jannat's way, as my walking aids are quite bulky, and I do not want the children getting hurt if I suddenly lose balance.

During the intermediate session today, I did some push ups, but not really the full push up I was sitting down on a mat and just used my hand to do a half push up, because my legs are not strong enough yet to place them in a plank position.

And I do not know if I will ever be able to go into a plank position because my right leg might permanently stay this way. Something I have had to come to terms with. However, even doing the half push ups was quite a challenge, after completing a few, my arms started shaking as I positioned them on the floor. The shaking was so strong that my therapist noticed and immediately made me stop to get some rest.

I then did my sit to stands on the plinth. I had to hold my position for about twenty seconds between each sit and stand position, I have been told, doing this will maintain a good posture and build up the strength in my core muscles.

28th February 2012

It has been an intense day; my timetable is getting fuller now. I feel like I am back at school, going from one class to another. The only difference is that my teachers remain the same for most of the sessions.

I started the day doing floor exercises, which are quite hard to do even though I am mostly in sitting position. It is the balancing on both my knees which is uncomfortable. Sitting on my knees with my back and shoulders straight is extremely hard because to maintain a balance is difficult because I cannot really feel if I am sitting up straight with all the tingling and pins and needles running through my body.

I had to sit on my bottom then raise up to my knees, with my hands straight out in front of me. Best I can describe this position is like a sitting down squat. I repeated this five times and towards the last two I was bending over like the leaning tower of Pisa; hence I was made to stop to take a rest break, something that I seem to do more frequently these days.

For my next session I was put on the exercise bike that actually required for me to cycle with both my legs, unlike the moto med, where the power of the machine had pedalled my legs for me.

I was put on the machine for ten minutes to see how well I managed, there were straps to hold my legs so I would not fall off.

This was a difficult task, because pedalling with an AFO

on my leg made it tricky to try and tell my leg to move. It took time but I managed to pedal a little.

This afternoon did not get any less tougher. I was practising sit to stands, then transfers. All of which required my hundred and ten per cent of energy. But I laughed and giggled my way through it, even though I felt discomfort and pain down my legs and excruciating pins and needles around the core, which in turn affected my balance. However, I could not let Miranda see how much discomfort I was in otherwise she would have started to ease some of the exercises which in turn means, my recovery will be slower, and I can't go home soon.

One of the things I wanted to raise with Miranda today, was the self-catheterization issue. I did not want someone to accompany me to the toilet every time I needed to empty my fluid bag, or worse having to empty it out into a kidney dish. I would feel much more comfortable if I can just empty it out into the toilet discreetly. This would make me feel more dignified. Miranda took on board what I said and agreed to support me in that area next.

Later this afternoon, as a precautionary step for my next new exercise, we agreed and had decided to check, how well I can walk to the bathroom from my bed side, which is like three metres walking distance. We practised this a few times using my rollator frame, at this point I am only allowed to use my rollator frame within my room, preferably in the presence of a nurse or an HCA member of staff.

After completing the exercise, I was told that from now on I can walk a little to go and take my shower in the mornings. Having said this, I was reminded to use my wheelchair to go up to the door of the bathroom, making sure beforehand, that my rollator frame was already placed next to the door, so when I wheel myself to the bathroom, I am able to just stand up and use the rollator frame to go into the bathroom. Once inside the bathroom I have to sit on the commode, which will allow me to shower on my own. Obviously the commode would be placed and locked by a member of staff, next to the shower ready for me to use when I need to.

I have been told that I am not allowed to do this exercise on my own, just yet. However, once I am able to demonstrate that I am confident with the rota stand transfers from bed to wheelchair, then this would be the next step, standing up from siting position using the rollator frame.

I need to concentrate on these exercises now, once Miranda is satisfied that I can stand up safely from sitting using my frame then I can have a lot more independence. I will not require a transfer anymore because I could stand and walk a little using my frame. From now on I am really going to try with my sit to stands. Even though I do not like it, I will make sure I stand with my legs apart from one another and I am going to put all my strength into this. I reiterated this to myself for a few minutes. This was my little pep talk to myself.

I was extremely excited to share my day with Nikki in the afternoon, telling her about the bike then the possibility of walking in and out of the bathroom. Nikki was very encouraging and told me that it was all a matter of time and I will make further progress. She tied some weights on my arms as we spoke, and I had to lift my arms from the table then straight up ahead of me then repeating that pattern for fifteen minutes with as many rest breaks that I needed to complete the session.

29th February 2012

Today has been a great day I have tried so many new different exercises. It was life changing moment when Miranda asked me if I wanted to try walking up and down the stairs. "Yes, major progress," I said to myself. "If I can do this then I am almost fit to go home." I cried out in joy not being able to contain my delight. Miranda laughed at my excitement but at the same time told me it was particularly good to be optimistic.

I only managed to go up and down the three steps just by the day room but for me it was a big step. I was holding onto the grab rail with one hand and a quad stick with the other. It was a little tricky to understand how Miranda wanted me to go up and down safely. Before I was allowed to lift my legs to take a step I had to place my quad stick onto the first step, making sure that it was not wobbly or diagonal. Only then I was able to take a step forward with my strong leg first which was my left leg, so my left toe was on the step which in turn lifted my body a little automatically so the right leg knew what to do, which was to follow what the left leg had done. So then once both toes were on the first step, I was able to repeat this pattern. It took a while to get my body, brain, and aids all to coordinate together, but I always had Miranda and Ivan next to me so that they could catch me if I wobbled or lost balance.

After my little adventure with the steps, I was able to play a little game of catch and throw behind the parallel bar without holding onto anything just standing on my legs alone. But the bar was in front of me just in case I lost balance, so all I had to do was hold onto the bar quickly to prevent me from falling and having an accident. Throughout the whole exercise, Martine was behind me, as a guide to make sure that she could grab hold of me in case I fell sideways or went back.

It is very reassuring to know, that my therapist will always watch out for me and they want the best for me. They want me to improve just as much I want to improve. But my safety is their main concern. They plan everything around my needs but ensuring that I will be safe and not get hurt in any way.

Before lunch I was given a little go to use a single headed stick, straight away I felt the difference from using a quad stick. With the quad stick there are four little bases at the bottom of the stick that resemble a claw. This design helps to have a steady grip on the ground without causing a wobble. With the single end stick, the stick just slides down if your body cannot hold up straight by itself, so I realised the single headed stick was just not for me to try out now. I am happy with the rollator frame and the quad stick as well as my crutches. As time progresses, hopefully I will be strong enough to use the single ended stick.

After lunch I had my key working session with Nikki, today we discussed what my goals were. Fortunately for me I have managed to reach all of my targets so far. Therefore, I have been given my next set of challenges, another thing for me to look at every night before bed and to repeat these goals to myself before falling asleep.

Straight after key working, I was due in the kitchen for my cooking session, where I made blueberry pancakes. The recipe of which I had printed off from the BBC Good Food website. I realised that measuring the ingredients was a little bit tedious and I found that making pancakes was a little bit advanced for me as the batter had to be perfect to make the ideal pancakes. After struggling to pour in the batter for the first few pancakes, I managed to get the hang of it later on. Once I made the first two pancakes and was pleased that they had turned out right, I carried on, till all the batter was finished.

Satisfied with the outcome of my cooking today, I told the staff members that I had cooked some pancakes and that they could help themselves in the kitchen. The staff, who were able to go and eat the pancakes gave some really positive compliments, which gave me a real confidence boost.

It has been another successful outcome in the kitchen. I am getting used to cooking and manoeuvring in a wheelchair at the same time. The only thing I worry about now, is how will I be able to fit the chair into my own kitchen when I go home?

My final physiotherapy session of the day comprised of me walking from my room to the day room with my rollator frame and back with only two rest breaks on the chair. Finally, I finished off by demonstrating how well I was doing with the bed exercises.

Today has been good, I have practised many different things, I know I feel very exhausted, but this is the taster of how it is going to be like in the real world when I go back home. So, I must just side-line the pins and needles and tingling sensation to concentrate on what really matters to me.

Saying this to myself, I started to get ready to fall asleep. The packed timetables are definitely having an impact on how drained I feel by the end of the day.

1st March 2012

I had been wondering why all this time, I was still in a single room by myself, I was told at the beginning of my stay that I would have to move into a sharing room very quickly after arrival. Now I can understand why? I am still a little bit behind in my progress from the three other ladies who are already sharing a room. They can all independently get washed, dressed, and ready for their day without any nursing team support, except for when they need to take their medication, plus all those ladies can go on their weekend visit to see their families. I suppose the healthcare professionals are trying to get me ready similar to the other patients' level so I would not feel left out or demotivated in anyway sharing the same room as them.

Which brings me onto the topic I have been so upset to talk about. For the past few days Renita has been coming in to see me to talk about my bladder needs and how best we can manage it to make me feel more independent. At first, we were looking at the option of independently going into the bathroom every time I felt uncomfortable to empty out the bag myself. However, as I was not too comfortable with the whole idea especially because I thought I could make a mess and not be able to clean it up if an accident were to happen. We have been discussing another option, which is to have the catheter taken out completely and it if it does not work out then have it put back in again.

The latter is a better option, but I keep telling myself, "Am I ready for this step, what if it does not work out, what if I am not able to control myself during physiotherapy, worse still if I am not able to cope and what if the line has to go back in again?" These questions were eating away at me, I could not help worrying. But I knew if I did not prepare myself, I would never know.

Hence, Miranda has been working so hard to prepare me to independently go into the bathroom by myself, we have been using all the safety measures and I can take a few steps inside the bathroom by myself holding onto my quad stick and the grab rails on the sides of the bathroom till I reach the commode. Even though I would be using the toilet I was told that initially until my core gets stronger and I am able to lift myself up from the seat and sit down without jumping on, I cannot sit on the toilet seat on its own because it is too low down. That could be one of those things that takes a long time to get used to because even when I go home, for my safety so I do not hurt myself, they will be providing me with an additional toilet seat so I can easily get on and off. But for now, the commode is the more comfortable option.

Finally, the day arrived, which I have been so apprehensive about, even though I have been preparing myself. At six a.m. today my catheter had been taken out but at this stage, my independence must wait a little while longer, till I am passing enough water. For which a health care assistant must be called in every time after I have been to the toilet, so that they can measure the amount of fluid coming out. I thought it would be as simple as the line coming out and I can tick off one more thing from my list of what I had achieved. Looks like I will need to wait a little longer before I can fully get my independence and privacy back in that area.

I understand why all these measures are in place, it's so that my body has fully trained itself to behave as normally as it would have before I became ill. Especially with the reduced levels of sensations and not knowing when I needed to go to the bathroom because the body acts faster than the brain sending a message to say, "I need to go". I kept saying these things to myself just to keep myself positive and motivated.

Today, every time I went to the toilet, I needed to have a scan straight after to see if my bladder was fully empty. I was going after every three and a half hours, partly because I was so scared that I will embarrass myself. This is going to be the same story for the next forty-eight hours, after which if there are any problems or if I am not emptying fully then I would have to self-catharise.

During my OT session I was rather quiet because I did not know when I would be able to return to my room and be next to the toilet just in case I had to go. I was using the weights but as I was lifting them at the back of my mind, I kept thinking "What if I embarrass myself what if I need to go now?"

It had been the similar story during intermediate session in physiotherapy. I was told to go on the bike and cycle for ten minutes. However, I was so scared that I might embarrass myself that I asked to come off after eight minutes just so I can be back at my room and be ready.

All in all, today has been very scary. When I had the catheter, I was so eager for it to be taken out because I wanted privacy, but now that it is not there anymore, I am scared I will wet myself in any situation whether it's when I am sitting in my wheelchair, or when I practise walking or maybe even in bed.

What am I going to do? How can I get over this fear? No, I can do this, I will just time myself, I will try to reasonably increase the hours in between of how often I go, so I won't go after every three hours, Renita told me, good practice would be to go no more than four to six times in twenty four hours, so I will try to go after every five hours, that way even if I can't feel anything at least I would go, but not too often that I am not passing enough to empty fully. I repeated these lines to myself repeatedly throughout the whole day today. It was quite good, because as I gave myself this little talk, my mind was diverted from going into the bathroom just because I thought I would need to go.

2nd March 2012

"Yahoo!" Last night I was so exhausted from all the pep talk I was giving myself that I slept for most of it. I woke up at 5.30 a.m. and managed to empty my bladder fully. Then at 9 a.m. I passed 500ml of fluid. It was an exciting moment when the doctors had decided that I did not need any further scans or measuring the amount of water I was passing.

If I was not feeling any pain or discomfort and my progress was as good as yesterday's, then that is it. I can attend to my bladders needs by myself. "Yes, yes, yes finally I have achieved this goal. Now I need to focus on trying to get my bowels to behave in the normal fashion. I have been told that patients usually manage to resolve their bowel needs first and they have more difficulty with the bladder, but my case was different I had managed to resolve my bladder needs but still need assistance with my bowel. "Well one out of two is not bad at all, well done me, now just keep focused and disciplined. You can do this," I reminded myself.

During my physio I was much more relaxed, I looked out for where the toilets were based outside of my room, so that if I felt I had to go then I can go. I managed to walk one hundred and eighty metres with three rest breaks. But I was chattering my way through the whole session. I was telling Miranda all about yesterday almost as if it was the best adventure story ever and even though Miranda had been part of some of my sessions yesterday. I had been so preoccupied with nerves that

I was just not myself, so today I came back with extra pizzazz.

I used crutches for the first time today, I happily practiced my stair exercises, went up and down three steps and repeated it three times. I even played tennis with Mick standing next to me the whole time, whilst Miranda threw the ball to my side. It was a completely different experience of playing tennis, the ball came to me and I had to get to it in the safest way possible, which meant missing it. But just the feeling of doing something new was extremely rewarding. I finally feel a big progress is taking place with me. It will only be a matter of time before I can go home. I cannot believe it has been over two months since I was home. But I am grateful that I have come this far. "Thank you, Allah, for answering all my calls, it would not have at all possible without your guidance and keeping my spirits so full of positivity." I made my prayer and smiled with gratitude.

3rd March 2012

The last few days have been incredibly challenging in their own way. I have been trying to get to terms with so many different changes and I am happy that these changes are happening but for some reason I feel overwhelmed today.

After making my bed and carrying out the usual morning routines, I went to see Bianca for a chat. I just needed to find out if I was being childish that I just wanted to cry for no apparent reason. Bianca was kind and explained that I am taking big steps now to recover and sometimes our minds and bodies do not always keep up with one another that is why these feelings may sometimes creep up upon us, but it was normal to feel a little anxious at times. Bianca told me I can make an appointment with her on a fortnightly basis just to see how I am, otherwise, we can leave it to when I feel comfortable to talk about things.

I was glad I went to see Bianca; after my conversation with her I felt a little bit more confident with myself that I was not going crazy with all these unexplainable feelings. So, I went to look through some websites that have support communities in place for people like myself, who have or are suffering from a brain and spinal injury. It helps when you can be part of a community that knows what you are feeling and how changes can affect the mind and soul.

Later, I went downstairs with Carol, using both my crutches instead of my wheelchair. I wanted to see how much

I can endure without feeling too worn out. we manged to get to the cafeteria area and then after that, I sort of struggled up to WHSmith. Then I had to have a sit down because my legs felt all wobbly and I could not balance properly, I was going from one side to the other. At times, my crutches would just slide forward a bit because my balance was quite poor. So, I rested for twenty minutes before walking up to my room again.

Whilst waiting for my legs to regain their strength, Carol told me about her plans, for when she would be returning home, her children had seen to the necessary adaptations being completed, so that when she went back home, she had all the safety elements taken care of. It was lovely to hear how happy Carol was with her discharge date almost nearing now. We carried on chatting until I felt I was able to stand firmly on my legs again, so we started to make our way back to the ward.

Finally, after coming back up to the ward, Carol went back to her bay to rest and I came back to my room. Once I came inside, I closed the door behind me, which is something I rarely do, apart from when I am getting washed and dressed. For some reason I just wanted to be on my own today, the anxious feeling or anxiety, I do not know exactly what it is, bothered me a lot. I felt it in my performance. I stayed in my room for the rest of the day except for dinner time. I joined the others in the day room but came back straight after my cup of tea. It was almost nine p.m. before I finished for the night. I wrote in my journal and updated it with the days event, before getting ready for bed. As I put my journal on my desk I told myself that tomorrow will hopefully be a different day.

4th March 2012

It has been another challenging day, the anxiety has not been particularly good for me, there seemed to be a magnetic pull that kept me from moving. It was so difficult to shift it off. Even during physio my therapist noticed something was on my mind. I was not talking away, like a moto mouth, as usual, I listened to all the instructions without asking any questions, which was very unlike me, because I laugh and talk through every session.

The most difficult part of today has been going down to see EH who had come with Zara to surprise me. I had to keep fighting back the tears that were trying to force their way out. I smiled and talked to Zara in her baby language and just pretended that nothing was on my mind. I knew there was no point in talking about how I was feeling because that would bring no good to anyone. How I wished I could go home with my family. It was painful when I had to see them off at the end of the visit. I felt Zara's touch next to my skin even after she went home with her dad. She kept looking back as she was leaving, I think she was confused as to why I did not go home with her and EH. I want to see my family as much as possible, but I hate saying goodbye to them, it makes me feel uncertain as to how long I would be away from them.

I am glad that I am back upstairs now, it is almost eight p.m. and I am happy to just sit by the window and write all this down. It is easy when I can let these feelings just come out without worrying about anyone else around me.

I was in my thought process when something just occurred to me, I am a big chocoholic, but I have not had any chocolate in almost two months now. Tomorrow I must buy one bar, I think that will really help me feel a little more light-hearted. In the past two days, I have felt like my heart is being weighed down by something.

But it is enough now Yasmin, you have had two days where you have felt sorry for yourself, you are improving, you are managing to do a lot more independently. You just cannot expect to be fully normal like the way you were before you got admitted to hospital. You know that. Come on all that reading you did on your condition and how it can leave you long term. All the possibilities of what can be expected have also been discussed with you.

Do not make comparisons about how you are managing here, with how you will manage outside the RRU. When you get home you can manage also, you may need some help from others along the way. But that is where family come in. Hop along now go and brush up then get ready for bed. Tomorrow you will bounce back, you cannot be soppy forever, it doesn't suit you.

Phew! that felt good, all of a sudden, I was starting to feel better, writing everything down makes so much more sense, rather than, just speaking the words, and the best part is, these are all my secret thoughts, no one needs to know how weak I am because I will not and can't let them think that.

5th March 2012

Today was brilliant, I started the day making my bed all on my own without any supervision. My morning physiotherapy involved doing my bed exercise, I am improving but the clam exercise will really take some time and effort to master. I just cannot stand the sensations I feel when I am trying to lift my knee apart from one another whilst lying down sideways, it is horrible, but hopefully I will get there soon. I did a lot more of sit to stands with arm stretches. The exercises were on a repeat for most of the session, which was getting a little tedious.

I was so glad to be out of the gym, Miranda has put me on clam and sit to stand exercises for most of the week, just because I said those were the ones I really did not like because they really challenged me. For some reason Miranda thinks I need to do more of the exercises that I find difficult, because that is where the focus is needed. It is no point in frequently doing the exercises that I find easy, because my body is used to them. I can understand her point, but I still do not like clams or sit to stand.

In the afternoon I walked in the corridor with Aiden, whilst Ivan did my assessment after that. I felt a lot more chirpy today, I think I am getting back to my normal self. I did feel at one point today that the weight that was pulling me down was releasing itself.

Hmm, I wonder whether the chocolate had something to do with my mood changes. whatever it is I am simply happy that the smile on my face at that point was real and not one that I had to plaster on for the sake of the situation.

6th of March 2012

Another brilliant start to the day. I showered and got dressed, made my bed, and hummed my way through to the gym. I felt I was ready to face anything today just maybe not the clam and sit to stands. Too bad I still had to do them, but I did get over and done with them first thing. So that was lucky.

I managed to walk four lengths of the corridor today, without having to sit on my wheelchair for breaks. Although, I did hold onto my physio therapist for a few seconds when I almost stumbled.

During occupational therapy I had one hundred questions I wanted to run past poor Nikki who was trying to answer me and making sure I was using my hands properly for my exercises. She did have to remind me a few times that I had to pick up the beads and the pens from the table using my fingers. Instead of just sliding them to the edge of the table and letting them fall into my other hand. It was really tempting to do that, but I did use my fingers to hold the small objects and place them in their required areas in the end.

I am so happy to be feeling full of energy again from within me.

7th March 2012

Today I had to go into Moorfields eye hospital for my eye check-up. It was necessary to rule out the possibility of developing Neuro Myelitis Optica that is a central nervous system disorder affecting the eyes, which is likely to happen to someone with my condition. I have been quite nervous about this appointment regarding what they will find. But fortunately for me after the check-up I was told my eyes were fine and everything looked healthy. The hospital was just next to the Northwick Park Hospital. Hence, Carla had very kindly taken me there first thing in the morning and she also brought me back to the Regional Rehab Unit.

It was still early when we came back, so, Carla watched me brush my teeth and brush my hair in standing position. I managed quite well, there were only a few times that I had to hold on to the desk but most of it was, without using any aids, apart from having my AFO on but that is something I cannot take off except for at bedtime.

After finishing with getting ready, I made my bed, using my rollator frame for walking and balancing with. Later I made the bed in standing position, instead of being sat down in my wheelchair. This was a fresh lease of life for me. Standing and making the bed felt so much more comfortable and I did not have to keep going back and forth I was able to use my hands to sweep away the creases.

In the afternoon I made some delicious potato and onion

pakoras which were loved by the staff, which I had left in the kitchen, after I had finished. I received so many compliments. Best part of making these pakoras was that I could use my rollator frame to walk around instead of sitting down in my wheelchair. Walking gave me a lot more freedom, now I knew that I could stand and cook, on my own at home, because my worry all this time has been that wheelchair will not fit in my small kitchen.

However, for my safety Nikki did say, that I would have to use a perching stool, which is a chair that looks a little bit like a rollator frame but with a seat on top and a back rest and arm supports on either side. After looking at a image on the internet, to find out what Niki was referring to, I was satisfied and happy to use the perching stool because I can sit and rest whilst focusing on my posture and do a little bit walking, it will be a combination of both things.

I have made my own record today. I stood for about thirty minutes in the whole day without any aids except for using my AFO. This is great progress, I just need ensure, that I stay focused and disciplined at all times from here on. Just like I have today, the more I practise, the better I will get and the better I can handle my pain issues.

8th March 2012

"Wow!" What a day it has been today, I have walked so much for the first time, since being admitted to hospital. I started my day with walking up and down the three steps in the gym. Then finished my morning physio session with practising my walk to and from the day room returning to my room. I have only used the two crutches during the morning today.

At first, I thought I can just place the stick in whatever way I felt comfortable. But like the sit to stand exercise there always is a proper way of doing the exercise. I was reminded throughout the whole day that I had to place my left crutch and left foot in front of me first followed by my right crutch the right foot. I was not allowed to just walk in any fashion, I had to follow this specific pattern.

Miranda explained to me that maintaining that discipline was good practise because it strengthens the muscles. Plus keeping a good posture throughout the whole process was particularly important. It took me lot of time to get this correct because the brain almost sent the message a little late because my body just reacted, as I thought I just had to move. After a lot of practise, I got used to the pattern that Miranda had explained to me.

Past lunch, Miranda and Mick took me to the larger set of stairs before entering the corridor. There must have been at least ten steps and I managed to walk up and down with a little assistance from Mick. I mostly held onto the rail with my weaker hand to support me but with my left hand, which is my stronger hand, I held onto one of the crutch to aid me to take the steps. It was very nerve racking because the larger set of stairs itself looked so much more challenging than the three practise steps in the gym.

After a rocky start I managed to walk up and down once on my own, but throughout that whole time my hand just held onto the crutch for dear life and I was almost glued to the rail. I was reminded, to not lean against the rail because that would not help with my balance. It took a little getting used to, but I understood the message my therapists were trying to get across to me. Another area for me to focus my energy on, I told myself.

Occupational therapy was a lot of fun today. Nikki took me out, in my wheelchair, it was so nice to be outside, I mean I am incredibly grateful that I am in a hospital unit that is completely different from a normal hospital ward where we are restricted to staying in our rooms. This hospital is different in the sense that we have the freedom to go down by ourselves to the shops and cafeteria and there is even a hospital garden where we can sit and walk for as long as we like. And I must admit it is a lovely garden it reminds me of the Secret Garden, there is a large pathway, with grass on either side and right in the middle are large trees that are like umbrellas protecting the benches beneath them. There are flowers and plants with the paving. It is a lovely garden.

However, to be out today I felt like I was in the real world. I could see houses, cars, people's driveways. Even the bus stops fascinated me. I was excited to go inside a bus and stop by the supermarket to pick up ingredients for my next cooking session.

This process was particularly important for me, Nikki told me the way we travelled today could be a possible way for me to travel, just locally to the shops etc, with someone with me all the time, when I return home.

I must admit I did enjoy the walking part more because mostly I was in my chair whilst Nikki pushed me to my destination. However, when we were in the supermarket, I felt claustrophobic. I was not used to crowds anymore and waiting at the tills was extremely hard, I did not know how to pack my shopping or how to take out the money to pay for my goods. I was frozen for a while, completely in a state of confusion. Nikki helped me through the whole thing and reassured me that it was very normal to feel this way, practise will help me adjust.

When I came back from my experience of being outside the hospital today, I went onto the bike in the gym. I managed to cycle fifteen minutes and was incredibly pleased with myself. I finished my session by walking on the parallel bars.

Thank you, Allah, I can feel myself getting stronger, none of this would have been possible without your guidance, I am scared though, I just feel what if I stop improving. But you know how I feel, please help me overcome my worries and keep improving my progress, I can only turn to you for help. You have made it possible for me to come this far. Please just make it possible for me to return home very soon. Ameen. I completed this prayer with full faith, before retiring myself for bed, I reminded myself, of tomorrow being another day, hopefully as positive as today.

9th March 2012

After breakfast I started my morning physiotherapy by walking back and forth from the day room. Making sure my balance and the way I move my crutches were in the correct order that I was taught in.

I moved onto the OT session where I used my thera putty to help strengthen my hands. By now I was feeling incredibly nervous and quite anxious because today I was preparing myself to go into an especially important meeting. Everyone that has worked closely with me is going to be there except for Nikki who has to be somewhere else at the same time. But Miranda will be there, Dr Bheroze and Shaila (who had taken over from Charlene at becoming my key nurse) would be present too. My husband, EH has also invited for this meeting to discuss all my progress and how I would be expected to live my life soon after being discharged from the RRU.

After finishing the OT session, I had my shower and got ready, to prepare myself to step into the meeting which was called 'Living with change'. I opened the door of my room and turned right, to walk into the meeting room. Precisely at that moment I felt the floors were all slanting and sloping in different directions. I found it difficult to walk properly, my world seemed to be turning upside down.

Ok take deep breaths and calm yourself down Yasmin, you know you must do this, it is yet again another step towards reaching home to your girls. You can face this, it is going to be ok, focus on what is key, do not let your worries overtake you.

I had stopped for a few seconds to sort out my balance and give myself a calming down talk to, after which I finally made it to the meeting room, where everyone was already waiting for me.

The meeting itself was very intense. I had to relive the whole experience of leading to and ending up in the Regional Rehab Unit. Much discussion took place, there were many do's and don'ts that I must follow, to take care of.

When I look back at how I was when I came to the RRU and how I am now, after a lot of intense treatment, I feel very grateful that I am not bedridden anymore, but the fear that any careless action from my part after I leave the RRU, could mean that I may end up with how I was at the start of my hospital journey.

"How can I always be careful? How will I at all times, manage to consider all the training I am going through right now? What if I miss something?" I kept questioning myself as I sat in my chair, looking blanky at my doctor.

There is just so much that I have to be mindful of. I know I can do this, but I am scared, something in my mind keeps telling me that I may become bed ridden again, I want to just shove this feeling off, but I am struggling to. By the end of the meeting, I felt the base of my palms were all cold and sweaty. I reached into my pocket for a tissue to wipe away all the sweat from my hands and forehead. I then made my way back to my room, so that I could take in all the information that had just been presented to me.

After the meeting I needed time on my own to accept what is now my reality, the reality, that this is now the new normal for me, I must work around my condition. I cannot let this take over my life. "Then what am I so afraid of? What am I worried about? Why am I letting my fears confuse me?" The questions would not go away, in fact the questions seemed to multiply.

I looked through the window and watched the birds fly, they looked so happy, chirping away, the sound of their little conversation amongst themselves soon cheered me up. *At least I have my family beside me, some of these poor creatures do not even have that,* I said to myself as I watched the birds fly. I wondered if they were still with their families? Or have they been separated somewhere in the process? We never can tell the pain that they must feel in their lives.

Surely, we as humans have such a great advantage over animal, insect, and birds, who must face so many challenges since their birth. Yet here they are chirping away, cheering me up with their soothing sounds. I told myself, as I wiped away at my puffy eyes, which were sore from all the crying, that I did not want anyone else to see.

After lunch I walked into the lift by myself and went down to WHSmith. I decided I wanted to try walking up the stairs to return to the ward but gave up on the idea when I saw other people using the stairs, I was scared I would be too slow and hold them up. All these thoughts worried me, so I went up using the lift instead.

During physiotherapy I went on a new machine, the treadmill. It was different, my legs started moving on their own, but I had to keep up with the pace. Miranda set the machine up so that it was not too fast I was just taking large steps left and right, holding onto the bars with all the strength that I thought I had, I was nervous that I would fall flat on my face, but I did not want my therapists to notice this worry otherwise they may not let me go in this machine until I felt comfortable and that to me is slowing down my progress. Right now, I need to work extremely hard and give worrying the back seat.

I moved onto the bike after finishing on the treadmill. I am happy that I went on two different machines today because they worked on different areas of my body.

Later, this evening, some students along with Dr Bheroze were in the ward before dinner they were going round into rooms, asking permission if they can do check-ups on the patients to find out more about how the patient ended up being admitted to the Regional Rehab Unit. I did not mind taking part in their research, as I want to make more people aware of this condition, maybe it will help them with identifying problems with such condition and manage things in a better way.

It was strange though, being checked over from top to bottom all over again being watched by eight to ten students. But I also felt it was important that I share my condition because I have been told it's rare so I would like others to know what this condition is and how it affects a person and their life.

10th March 2012

It has been slightly relaxing today compared to the past few days. I was mostly doing independent activities such as having my shower, getting dressed on my own. I made my bed on my own mostly standing throughout the process. I had to sit only a couple of times to give my arms a rest because my arms hurt. Trying to take out the creases from the sheets using my hands in brushing motion was something, I used to do every day in my life sometimes without even looking properly with my daughter crawling past my legs, talking on the phone etc. it was such an easy task. I cannot believe it now takes me about twenty-five to forty minutes just to make sure my bed looks tidy and clean.

After exhausting my arms from making my bed I decided to walk along the corridor using my crutches without any supervision. It is quite a different feeling when I am walking by myself without Miranda and team watching out for me. I had to make sure to use all my senses to keep myself balanced. I was looking ahead, holding onto my aids, I was listening out for sounds, just in case someone bumped into me, it was very, very daunting but I am glad I have given it a go.

Returning from my walk, I felt my heart beating fast, I was sweating and could feel a sharp pain across my chest. Today I did not get scared as I knew what this feeling was. I became aware that I was going to have a panic attack if I did not get control of my breathing. I immediately sat down in my wheelchair and wheeled across to the window, I put the fan on to cool myself down. I then started to take deep breaths in and out and tried not to breath too fast, so I started to breath in, hold for a few seconds and exhale. Doing this helped calm my nerves. Soon enough I started feeling better. But then a thought crossed my mind, "What if I cannot stand anymore, what if all my strength is gone? because it's this sharp pain and tingling that took away my ability to move in the first place." I questioned myself grabbing onto the sides of my chair.

But this time I did not want to give into my nerves, I wheeled across the room to where my rollator frame was parked. Hands shaking and legs feeling extremely jelly like with a sick feeling in my tummy. I slid a little to the edge of my chair and hands stills shaking I held onto either side of the rollator frame then pushed myself up and stood still for a good few seconds before taking wobbly steps forward. To my relief I was able to stand and even take steps. I immediately sat down again just to make sure that my body got some rest, and I did not overdo it. I do not want to lose my ability again.

I did not want to overexert myself today, therefore I decided to read my books and watch some telly in the day room so that I could relax my body properly for the rest of the day. This helped me too as I was socialising with my friends and it took my mind off the walk I had on my own.

Finally, to end the evening, I went onto the PC room, again just to look through recipes and home and lifestyle websites.

11th March 2012

I woke up and started my day with bed exercises I wanted to feel strong and fresh. I had my shower before breakfast, whilst waiting for breakfast to arrive I made my bed.

Today my family came to visit again. I was pleased that I was be able to spend some time with Zara. We had a great game of playing peeka boo. As I sat in my chair with my hands in front of my eyes, Zara then came up to me and pulled my hands away from my face and before I could say peeka boo, she would say it for me and then giggle away as she felt clever in doing so. Later on, she went around the garden and picked up little pebbles and dropped them onto my lap, she then asked me to make soup out of them. It was so funny as she came up with different game ideas, she too knew that I would give her a surprised expression at her suggestions. But that is what she wanted, and it made her so happy. I loved every minute I spent with Zara, I felt like a kid just being around her.

However, the pain of not being able to see Jannat is something that I just cannot come to terms with. Just sometimes I feel it is so unfair that this condition is preventing me from being with my children. I feel stuck and helpless, if only I could just stand and run around like normal, if only I could just wake up and find myself at home, with my children. Nevertheless, having said this I must be grateful for the fact, that I am in a place where everyone in my care is trying to do their best to prepare me to live a life as normally as possible.

At least today I was in a much positive mood. I did not have to fake my feelings; I was enjoying myself sitting in the garden watching Zara run around. I even enjoyed having a cup of tea with my husband in the canteen.

My mum had sent me cooked food from home, and I enjoyed every grain of rice. It has been exceptionally long since I had a proper Bengali mum's home cooked food. My mum makes the best potato curry. All the potatoes are cut in julienne and stir fried with a few green chillies and lots of coriander. Even the smell is divine.

It is always extremely hard when the time comes to say goodbye, Zara always calls out to me as I wheel myself away from the entrance door. She looks back with her big eyes and stretches out both her hands towards me, calling out to me asking me why I am not going with her.

I watched helplessly, as EH carried her out into the car park area. Hot stinging tears fell down my cheeks, but I was smiling and waving at my little girl, telling her that I will be home soon. "How soon though?" I have been telling her this ever since I saw her first in February. "Am I actually going to go home? Am I actually telling her the truth?" Asking myself questions after questions I returned to my room and shut myself away, from the rest of the world.

I went across to my bed and put a pillow next to my mouth I placed it firmly on my mouth and then just screamed as hard as I could. I wanted to let these feelings out, after a few seconds realising I could not breath properly I moved the pillow away from my mouth and made a promise to myself that I would do everything possible to meet all my goals and prepare myself to be discharged on the day, that was just an expected date.

12th March 2012

From today I was told my bowel management is going to be earlier than usual, this is to maintain a discipline and teach my body when it needs to empty itself. This was a lot of information to take in, because now I am almost in full control of my bladder, I rarely have any accidents. However, my bowels are a completely different story. I just cannot get the hang of going and emptying at the correct time.

The suppository treatment is getting a little overwhelming now. I just do not like to wait every morning, to be given the go head that I can go and have my shower and prepare myself for my day. All my friends are usually at the gym before me, I have to wait till the suppositories do their job. I really appreciate what everyone is doing for me, but just having my personal space invaded makes me terribly upset and I just have no control in my hands to do anything about it. But just like the bladder I must keep telling myself that things will improve. I cannot fall weak now, not that I have come this far.

Whilst I waited, I did most of my bed exercises, apart from the clam exercise, catching me out as usual, I managed quite well with the rest. I must say the bridge exercise is getting easier than before, but Miranda has told me she will make that more challenging for me from now on. Instead of placing my hands on either of my sides and lifting my bottom off the bed creating a bridge shape between my back and thighs, I will now have to cross my arms and place them of my chest and then try to lift myself. This is supposed to strengthen my core.

After my shower I joined the circuit group in the gym, this is a more advanced group from the intermediate group. In this group the patients do not require constant one to one supervision. Which is quite pleasing for me. I feel more independent. I went on the bike for fifteen minutes, my endurance levels are getting better, I used to only manage between eight and twelve minutes, I have almost doubled my time.

My timetable consists of a lot more of exercises now, I had to move onto the parallel bars and worked on my knee and hip extensions. These were exceedingly difficult to do because the AFO on my right leg restricts at least seventy percent of my movement, because my leg just feels more heavy with the AFO on. Already without the AFO I just about manage to take my leg off the floor, with the AFO on, the leg just jumps a little but does not lift up. But I have been told that at any point when I am doing my exercises or standing, I must not take off the AFO otherwise I may have a fall and cause further damage.

I gladly finished the work on the parallel bars, but to my dismay I had sit to stands next on the list. Like the bridge exercise I now had to cross my arms place them on my chest and then lift myself up from the chair. This is difficult to do because I feel tempted throughout the whole session just to use my hands on the side of my chair to lift myself up, holding onto the chair. But I was not left off the hook that easily. Martine made sure I at least did three sits to stands properly. It was exhausting and my heart could not stop racing from all the concentration.

After lunch I took a twenty minute nap before starting afternoon physio. First, I had to practise walking in and out of the bathroom with just one crutch. I had to demonstrate how I can safely have a shower on my own. Because during shower I must take my AFO off. So, I had to show that I keep my AFO just next to the door and after my shower I ensure that I will thoroughly dry myself. Then very slowly get up from the commode, hold onto the grab rail on the wall, using my crutch walk up to my AFO and take it back to the commode where I need to put it on before I can come out of the bathroom.

This experience was so funny I could not stop giggling because Miranda and Nikki stood there like schoolteachers and they were writing or ticking something off on a clipboard. They made me go back and make sure I understood where I had to do certain things to make sure I was safe. I forgot things like drying the underneath of my toes and maintaining a good posture to balance properly. I was rushing certain things, but I was told I had to slow down and make sure I do not miss any steps. If I did not maintain a good posture and balance, then I will need a little supervision again to ensure I was safe.

I reassured Nikki that I have taken everything into account and from tomorrow I will follow all the steps. I have no choice but to make sure I follow the orders as I am being reassessed on this tomorrow morning.

After my shower demo, I was allowed do a little walking, so we walked up to the day room. Then as I walked back towards my room I was told to stop and go into the bay shared by Carol, Kathleen and two other ladies whose names I have not memorised yet.

Later, I had to practise my floor exercises. Throughout the whole session I felt I was reliving what my six-month-old

Jannat must be going through right now. She is holding onto furniture to crawl and stand up; I am doing the same I am crawling on the floor reaching the plinth and then lifting myself up maintaining the rules of how to lift in the correct way.

I was not allowed to just use my hand to support me up, after reaching the plinth I had go on my right knee, place my hands on the plinth then using the strength from my left leg start to lift up supported by my hands which were already on the plinth. I had to do this from my side I am told I should not feel tempted to using my chin and my full arm strength to lift myself up. Which is what I was doing before because I felt this was the only way up. But I was reminded yet again the importance of strengthening the core muscles.

I wish right now that I had paid more attention in my PE classes to understand why all this was necessary. In our busy daily lives, we hardly pay attention to posture and balance but being in the regional rehab unit we are constantly reminded of this.

My Jannat has started taking her first few steps with the support from holding onto the furniture and she is now using the walker as I have been told. I am here in hospital who has learnt to take my first few steps after the disease attacked my body. I too am using a walker in the form of a rollator frame to help me walk. Only difference is my little girl is exploring her surroundings for the first time in her life without any fears, giggling and babbling as she goes along so I am told by my mum.

I am a twenty-nine-year-old learning to explore my surroundings for the second time in my life, but with constant fear in my head, the fear of failing myself.

I am not there to see the first steps my little girl is taking; she is beginning to make conversation in her baby language, and I am not there to see this. I feel frustrated and upset, but I cannot let these feelings overwhelm me. Instead, I must use these feelings to motivate me so that I can recover more easily. It is so easy when I think these thoughts and work them out in my head but applying them to reality is much harder than imagined.

To finish my day Nikki came to see me to talk about housing, I have briefed her on the details of how my house is sized and shaped. We talked about adaptations and how easily they can be installed before my return to home. I did raise concern of the actual size of the property, it is only a one-bedroom house with four of us. I needed a property with two bedrooms so having adaptions done to the one bedroom might not be ideal realistically I need adaptations to a two-bedroom property. We talked about the possibility of having a transfer and talking with Luton Borough Council. But like with most councils I knew there would be a long wait before anything comes through.

As reality hits me I am scared about our future, "How will my condition affect my life ahead?"

13th March 2012

Today was a big day for me, more assessments were on the list. After the usual morning routine, I was assessed at having my shower safely, by walking in and out of the bathroom by myself.

I joined the circuit group in the gym where I went on the treadmill, on which I am getting more confident now.

I then had a ten-metre walking test, Miranda and Nikki used a stopwatch to time me. I did everything in my ability to demonstrate that I can walk outside then indoors without taking too many rest breaks. I manged almost perfectly, the only thing that spoilt it was when I came back indoors, I wobbled a little from not resting enough and lost my balance and ended up leaning against the wall to hold on to, to stop myself from falling over. Precisely at that moment, my eyes felt as though a black cloud had come on its way, blocking my vision. I felt lightheaded and nauseous, I realised straight away my mistake of not pointing out how tired I had actually become. I struggled to straighten myself up right again, therefore Nikki and Miranda gave me a hand, they held onto me, whilst I stood upright again.

I knew what was going to come next, as my therapists were not pleased that I had not taken breaks, even though they had been asking me at regular intervals if I needed to. I was so wrapped up in thinking that I could impress them with demonstrating how well I could cope, that I had disregarded the key point, which was safety comes first.

I was reminded that I must take rest brakes as soon as I feel my legs becoming jelly like. This was a moment like receiving a detention in school. Being a geek in my school years, I hardly ever got myself into detention, only time I ever faced detention was when the whole class used to receive a detention as a lesson to all for someone else's doings.

Today I received a big talking to from both Nikki and Miranda, I know they mean well and are watching out for my safety as their number one concern. But I am a grown up and I feel I know how much I can push myself, but I suppose my body does not want to always listen to me. I apologised as soon as I realised that I could be causing more delays in my recovery than speeding up the process. Because if at any point I have a fall then we do not know how much damage it can cause, what if something is broken during action. I promised to say when I felt tired or feel that the pain is too much to cope with.

I must behave myself, I felt sorry for putting my recovery in threat, just because I wanted to speed things up and show I am okay with everything that comes my way. Today I have learned that it is particularly good to carry on with positivity and determination in what I do. However, I need to always keep in mind the realities of the situations.

I finished my day with carrying out my sit to stand transfers in the best way as I could. I kept in mind posture, balance, and safety though out the whole session. Earlier on the day I had disappointed Miranda with my over enthusiasm but now I needed to get back into her good books. Miranda reassured me that she was not disappointed in me, but she wanted to make sure I did things that would not come in the way of my safety. I felt relieved that she was not upset with me, being a good student all my life I could not bear the thought of any of my tutors being sad with me.

14th March 2012

Martine was on tight ship, with the routine today, she assessed me on many of the floor exercises. We started by watching me crawl across two mats, after which I had to balance on my knees, with my back straight. I then had to throw a ball onto the wall and back. Just when I thought things could not get any worse because balancing on the knees is extremely uncomfortable and I can feel myself wanting to lean on my left side for support, but my therapists make sure I maintain a good posture throughout the exercises.

After a quick break I had to do mini squats again, this required balancing on the knees. Finally, I completed my morning session with doing what I can describe as the Superman pose. I had to raise my arms and legs in the air, but not the same arm and leg at one time, I had to raise my left arm with my right leg, which was impossible because I could not raise my right leg at all. But the balancing was good because I was using my left knee to stabilize myself. The alternate side was also a problem because I can raise my right arm a little and I can raise my left leg for a few seconds, but the balance is extremely poor because I wobble a lot trying to balance on my right knee alone. Looks like in the next few days, this is one exercise Miranda will put on my timetable a lot more, just like the clam exercise.

I just wish I can get good at those. I really do not like the feeling I get across my body when I do these exercises, but I do understand that it is especially important for me because it will only strengthen my core and lots of other muscles.

After lunch Faith from the social services team came into my room. We discussed how I felt returning home and the level of support I will receive from my family. I explained that the one-bedroom house I am living in with my family will not be suitable. Plus, the fact that my husband's plans were to move to Milton Keynes, was very daunting for me. Apart from receiving some support from his sister I will not really have a safety net; in Luton I have my parents and my siblings who can take care of things for me.

I held back onto the other worries I had because at this point in my life I am very uncertain with how well I am going to do when I return home. I need the kids to be comfortable with how life will change with my return. As a transfer with the housing association does not look like a straight away possibility, I must remain optimistic with how I will manage. Right now, mum and my siblings are only a call away, mum can cook for me and my siblings can help with the house chores. I will share the responsibilities of the kids along with my husband.

In my mind, I feel as though I have a well set out plan, but one thing I have learnt from being at the hospital is that with a neurological condition, things are quite unpredictable. We may think we can plan out a day in a certain way, but it is not actually until we wake up to start our day, when we realise if it is going to be a day where we feel strong or weak.

We discussed all this, as Faith wrote down the details on a plan. I also told her that I had discussed with my husband that maybe he could take a further month off work after my return to home, just so I can get used to everything again. But the only problem was, we would have to face financial difficulties. One big issue is, he has to pay monthly on taxi insurance (which is much greater than regular car insurance) even though he is not at work, but we don't really have the disposable income to pay for that. Faith reassured me that she would investigate ways to get support for me and that there are benefits I may look at to apply for.

I am very worried, about how we will manage financially when I get back. I do want my husband to go back to work, because he has been off for so long already having to take care of Zara, as she gets very unsettled with anyone else because I am in hospital. However, if he does go to work how will I manage with Zara and Jannat on my own? I cannot have my mum with me all the time she has her own family responsibility just like my siblings do. Mum is already doing more than enough for me looking after Jannat 24/7 just to take the pressure of my husband. What am I going to do?

The conversation with myself continued inside my mind, all that time Faith was writing everything down. The feeling of possibly becoming a burden on my family is horrible. I must really work really hard on getting better at my exercises so that I am a lot stronger, because my family have to get on with their lives, without having to worry about me all the time.

After Faith left reality had hit me even more than before. It is all good that I want to return home to my family as soon as possible, *But what is the point if I am going to be a burden on them? I know they will not say anything to me, but I know how hard it is to juggle between so many responsibilities.*

I kept asking myself these questions repeatedly, and I could feel myself feeling sick. There was a horrible feeling inside my tummy, and I felt a sharp pain across my temples.

Realising I could make myself feel far worse, just by worrying so much, I decided to have a little nap before going in for my kitchen session.

Waking up after a little power nap helped me get onto my wheelchair, I freshened up and made my way into the kitchen. It was a very therapeutic session, I enjoyed making jam biscuits, the smell it produced was divine. I particularly enjoyed filling the centre of the biscuits with jam and then watching them melt in the oven. Whilst I waited for the biscuits to finish baking, I washed up all the dishes and utensils in standing.

I finished my day doing the usual workout in my circuit group. It is nice being part of the circuit group, everyone is full of enthusiasm and we all help encourage each other with our exercises. However, the big topic on everyone's mind right now was returning home.

Many of the patients in circuit group have already been discharged to go home and some are almost on their way of returning in the next few weeks. Most of these patients have already had adaptions done to their homes, for their safe return.

Everyone was talking excitedly amongst themselves, when I felt as though I had been left there isolated. Although I was sitting on a bike surrounded by three or four other patients, I felt very alone. The voices started to become distant, and I felt as if I was on the bike on my own with no one around me.

Suddenly I was hit by those horrible, pesky little questions again, "What will happen to me? when it is my turn to be discharged. My home is too small for a start. But then there is that bigger problem, of the possibility of maybe moving to Milton Keynes. I can't have any adaptations done to my current home due to the size and space, but the future looks like a blur, full of uncertainty and really scary." All of a sudden, I felt that awful feeling crawling around inside my tummy again.

My best friend right now are these diary accounts I am trying to write as best as I can. Once I reread what I have written, I feel content at how far I have come. But what I will need to do is type all this up next time I visit the computer room, my handwriting is so bad I can just barely make sense of what I am writing. But it is the best way now to offload all my feelings without burdening anyone else.

15th March 2012

In circuit I did all the usual stuff, using the bike, going up and down the mini steps, sit to stands, bed exercises using the plinth and walking on the parallel bars.

In OT session, I had to practice exercises that worked out my upper limbs, my good friend the elastic band had to come out whilst Nikki assessed my finger movements.

I had a fun lunch in the day room, where everyone was excited about the coming days. It was nice sharing positivity with one another.

During my physio session we did the walking length of the corridor and back only using the crutches, today I used only one rest break. I put away one of my crutches back in my room, then walked from bay A to the gym.

To my joy (*not being sarcastic here*) we had to do the floor exercises followed by the mini steps and then onto the treadmill, which was not too bad.

Today was quite an eventful day, along with all my therapy, it was the day I had been looking forward to, the day of my case conference. Dr Behroze, Nikki, Catlin and Shaila were present with me and we were joined by my husband.

Dr Behroze lead the conference, starting off by going through the whole history of my journey, from being diagnosed with a neurological disorder and being hospitalised. Then coming to the Regional Rehab Unit, to how my condition has changed with all the therapy that I had received.

It was very intense, listening to how extremely poorly I had been, when I came first here, to being able to stand again. I had goosebumps throughout, listening to how I had started off to where I am now. Towards the end of the meeting, we had a quick question and answer session.

The good news is that I have been given a date that I may be able to return home if my progress continues, or at least to get to a stage where it is stable, and I am safely able to function, in my day-to-day life being a mum. There was a lot of information to take in, but it is very exciting, if they have decided on an expected return date, then surely, I have improved a lot.

I now have the date, 2nd of May, that I really want to work towards. I need to make sure that I am strong in every area so that I can prove I am well enough to return home. However, I need to bear in mind that if I do not meet all my goals, then the stay may have to be extended. But I am going to stay incredibly positive and focused so that I meet this deadline. If Allah wills, it will be onwards and upwards from here on.

16th March 2012

Today has all been about my endurance levels and how well I can balance and walk without tripping or slanting sideways. Martine started me off with a ten metre walk which she timed, at first, I used two crutches and my AFO. This was easy because using two crutches stopped me from relying on my left side for support whilst walking.

After a small break I had to repeat another ten metre walk which again was timed and this time I used one crutch and my AFO. This time round I felt the difference, I was more alert, I started using my hearing a lot more to ensure no one was behind me or too close by. I was watching what was in front of me or the direction I would need to turn into because with the support of one crutch I felt it sometimes slid forward making my balance a little poor.

My posture in this type of walk was not too great either because I started to slant towards my left side a little more for support to make sure I would not fall. I could feel the muscle in my hands tense up too because I wanted to make sure that I perform this walk as confidently as possible and to prove to myself that I am ready to move onto the support of one walking aid instead of two as this will be the next step into my recovery.

After a very intense, morning physiotherapy session, I was happy to join my friends in the day room for lunch, where some of them talked about how they had seen me walking in the morning and that they felt confident that I would do well.

It was so lovely to hear such positive comments from other patients.

After lunch, I was joined by Martine again, this time to walk the distance of ten metres with two crutches and no AFO. I must say this was the most challenging walk to do. Even though I was balancing with two crutches, I was unable to walk much without my AFO. My right leg would manage a few steps then suddenly I would feel a tremor as there were strange sensations below my waist, which would make me trip forward. I was unable to complete this walk as I did not feel confident moving forward without the support of my AFO supporting my right leg from my knee to ankle.

After my assessment I was told that for my safety, using an AFO all the time might have to be my way forward when I return home, because my leg was not fully capable of managing on its own. Surprisingly, I did not feel sad like I thought I would. In fact, I am happy that I have come to terms with the fact that life will never be the same, as before I had this condition. I am just grateful to be standing again and to be more independent again.

I knew right from the beginning that there are a group of people with this condition, who recover fully within the first month of being diagnosed with this condition. Then there are a group of people who end up living with a few deficits and finally there are some who do not make any recovery at all.

I am only glad that I do not belong the latter group. It has been a difficult few months but being positive and embracing and accepting the changes is the best way forward. I just have to manage this condition now and I think I am ready for this.

During the afternoon I had another meeting with the 'living with change group'. We decided as a group that we would benefit from receiving information about the topics before the meetings took place, as this would give us a chance, to have structured discussions in the follow up sessions. We would have questions to think about and anything that might be bothering us. It was agreed that this could be a possibility if everyone had the same opinion to run these meetings.

I finished my day with OT, in the kitchen where myself and Carol worked on our ironing techniques. I found out that I am getting better at sitting down and reaching across the ironing board. I still do not feel happy with all the tingling that keeps running across my arms and fingertips, but again, like the walking I know that the sensations when touching different surfaces and textures is another thing I would have to manage in the long run. As the scarring from the inflammation on my spinal cord has damaged some of the nerves, and that is something that is extremely hard if not impossible to repair.

I just need to accept all these facts and work on how I will help myself live with these feelings. If I just think about it and feel sad, I will only end up having a panic attack which then has a counter effect on my whole body, instead I need to see the positive side and convince myself that I will not be doing certain tasks for the entire duration of a day.

So, I just need to use a timetable like how I do in the RRU, when I return home. This is so that when I feel too much discomfort when doing a certain task, I would be able to stop and only return to it when I feel better. Only then I will be able manage to get things done and I am happy to have this plan in mind. It makes things clearer, and I do not feel quite so anxious or worried.

17th March 2012

It is a Saturday; a lot of the patients went home last night for their weekend visit. It has been such a quiet start. On the bright side I was given my suppositories early in the morning, so I was all clear before taking my shower.

One of the rituals of the weekend is to provide our weight details so that it could go on our chart for managing our nutrition. So, I decided to walk up to the machine instead of being wheeled over to it. This was very satisfying because previously my chair had to be weighed first, then my wheelchair with me on it was weighed then the chairs weight had to be deducted to find out how much I actually weighed. I used to feel like such a bother because the whole process involved a lot of time. Whereas now I can go and stand up onto the scales straight away with the HCA making a note of it.

I returned to my room and took off all the sheets from my bed and placed them inside a plastic clear bag. I walked up to the end of my room and placed the bag where the person collecting the laundry would notice it.

I then walked up to the cupboard where all the towels, bed sheets and pillowcases were kept. I returned to my room to swap my crutches for my rollator frame. I could not carry all the items back with my crutches as my hands got too full. So, I decided to use the rollator frame, which acted as a rail, I walked back to the cupboard and placed one clean towel, two pillowcases and two bedspreads onto the centre bar of my rollator frame.

I slowly walked back to my room ensuring the items did not slide down as I walked. I came back into my room and had to take a ten-minute break as I was starting to feel a little shaky from all the walking back and forth from the laundry cupboard. This is another area I need to work on, I feel tired after every little task I do, I need to try and push myself to manage more than just one or two chores.

After my short break, I made my bed in standing and managed to do quite a good job, the sheets looked straight and the top cover also looked neat. Once satisfied that I had made my bed neatly I took my shower and got dressed. I took my time doing this as during the weekends there are no physio or OT. Plus, there are hardly any patients in the ward as they are all on their weekend visit. Only a handful of us are in the ward as we are not quite ready yet for our weekend visits.

I had lunch all on my own in the day room, so I decided to use the television to give me company. I watched a wildlife documentary for about an hour after lunch, then returned to my room. I called my mum to see how the children were doing then quickly filled EH in, with how I was progressing this week.

After my phone calls, I sat in my chair for a while, looking around to see how I could keep myself occupied. I looked at my book collection and realised I had finished reading them all, so I decided to stroll over to my favourite part of the hospital. I picked up my crutch and walked to the library which seemed quiet today as no one there.

I read a travel book on Japan and just could not stop admiring their cherry blossom gardens. I sat on the chair, imagining myself in the middle of the beautiful pink and purple flowers. I felt relaxed and calm, it is amazing how a book can capture one's mind, almost making them part of the book itself.

Realising that I had been in the library for so long, I decided to make my way back to the ward, as the staff would be getting worried why I had been taking so long to get back. I got up and placed the book back on its shelf.

If I had brought my wheelchair with me then I could have taken the book back with me, as I would have been able to rest it on my lap and wheel myself back. However, as the book was too heavy and it was a hardback copy, it was impossible for me to walk back with it, because my arms are that strong yet, to carry heavy objects from destination to another.

I quickly scanned the shelves by the font desk and found a book I really enjoyed as a child. The 'Just so Stories', by Rudyard Kipling. There are so many stories in this book which tell you some amazing stories, about how certain animals got a specific feature, such as 'How the Camel got his Hump'. Cbeebies came up with a TV show similar to this book, called 'Tinga, Tinga Tales'. Again, it's great fun to see how they came up with such fantastic and funny theories of how an animal got its specific feature that it is known for. I decided to take the book back with me, as I could not find the fourth book from the series I was currently reading, which is the 'No 1 Ladies Detective Agency'.

I happily walked back to my room and put the book on my desk. I then took a good look around my room, tonight will be my last night here. This room has helped me so much in terms of my recovery for the past month and a half. However, I am happy that I will be moving into a bay with some of the other patients, I will not feel quite so lonely.

I started to pack my things in my little trolley, it was a strange moment where I felt both happy and sad. Happy because I will be amongst people and can take part in normal conversations. But sad because I will miss having my privacy maintained only amongst me and the staff, now I will be around others, and if I have any embarrassing accidents, then it can really affect my motivation.

Nevertheless, I must remain positive and only look ahead, being part of a group is also part of the recovery process. We all went through something similar so they will understand and not feel bothered by these little problems. I reassured myself.

After finishing with the packing, I still had a few hours to spare before bedtime, so I spent the remaining of my time in the PC room typing my diary accounts.

18th of March 2012

I woke up early and got ready to move into my new room, I wanted to move into bay B4 before the girls arrived this evening. This would give me time to unpack and make myself feel at home.

I have been given a bed next to Kathleen, as we both require the assistance of a hoist when things get really bad for us, but fingers crossed, we will both rise beyond our condition and only move forward. Opposite my bed is Dina and next to her is Melanie, both who joined Kathleen a week ago when three others moved back home.

I was waiting on Carol to be discharged so I can have her bed after she left. I will miss Carol a lot, she was a lovely lady who had a lot of wisdom, I will especially miss watching the Chase with her. I loved the way she knew most of the answers on the quiz show, it will never be the same again without Carol. But I am incredibly happy that she can now move forward in her life again. I wish her the absolute best and pray she has good health and the support from her children to help her with some of the tasks that she finds tricky.

As I was getting ready to be given the thumbs up to move to my new bay, I was surprised that the staff came into my room and moved my entire cupboard, along with my side chair and desk into my new room. I thought I would be moving to my new room with only my person belongings, but I realised that I did not have to do any actual packing, except for the things in the bathroom, because all my furniture was being moved to my new bay. All I had to do was put new bedding on the bed, which had been washed and sterilised by a member of staff. So now I just have to put all my clothes back on their hangers.

I am happy to be in a room with others again, at least morning breakfasts will be brighter. But what I fear is the routine, none of the others need bowel management in the morning but I do. "What will I do about the smell?"

I know I should not worry about being the only one, who still needs to use the commode in the bathroom, but it may cause a little discomfort for the others as it will come in their way. I have to find a way of making this sharing opportunity a positive one. Morning times are particularly busy, and everyone is in a rush to get ready and head over to the gym.

I have thought about it many times, since I found out I was going to be moving into bay B4, it has concerned me how I can make the best of this situation. Though, after a lot of thought, I have come to the conclusion that, I will tell the others to go and shower before me in the mornings, so I am not in anyone's way, yes that's a good plan, I told myself.

I unpacked my things and decided to put all my stuff neatly in my cupboard. First most importantly I walked over to the basin and filled lots of paper towel with soap. I came back to the cupboard and wiped everything clean, I wiped my desk and portable tray, as it was a good time to do so. Last time I cleaned it, I was having to do everything from sitting position, now I had the advantage of being able to stand and do things. Finally, I rearranged everything in my neat and tidy fashion. One thing that has not changed with my condition is my habit of cleanliness and staying neat, I cannot stand things being placed anywhere just for the sake of it. I believe everything has a place and needs to go there. I arranged my books, my water jug, cups and finally all my toiletries on my desk and asked Aiden to move it all to the corner next to the cupboard so I can have my armchair just next to my bed. I asked for my wheelchairs to be placed by the side next to the cupboard and all my walking aids can just go next to it. I looked around my station and was pleased with how my bay looked.

After lunch I watched a little telly and went down to the garden to just think about how I was going to save myself from embarrassment. I really did not want to have any embarrassing accidents with the girls around me. Till now I have managed to get over and done with the embarrassing part of the day in the morning and none of the other patients have witnessed anything, but now, up until my bowel management is over, I am going to feel very humiliated every morning.

As I sat on the bench under a large tree, thinking and rethinking everything over and over again, I felt the warmth of the sun on my face. All of a sudden, I started to feel a lot more cheerful, it is great how the sunshine and beautiful greenery works as the perfect solution for any sort of low mood swings I have.

I decided at once that what happens in the future is in no ones hands, but how we deal with a situation is something that we have some control over. Allah has given me so many wonderful things to appreciate, such as my parents and siblings support, both physically and mentally, I have a lovely house even though small in size, but it is the perfect combination of cosy and bright. I live in a lovely neighbourhood, in a lovely part of the town. Most importantly

I have my husband and children by my side, a lot of people do not even have that.

What I am feeling now are just pesky worries. Everyone who is admitted here at the RRU, is dealing with their own set of tests, like me they do not have to go around discussing everything, but inside they too may be dealing with something that is big for them. I need to stop worrying about being judged.

Starting to feel so much better I came up with the plan to remain confident and face every day as it comes my way. I decided to call EH, so that the next time he comes to visit, he brings with him a few bottles of air freshers, along with the top up of my usual toiletries, this way I will feel confident after my morning routine. But for now, my body sprays will have to do the job.

It started to get a little breezy, so I decided I should return to the ward, I strolled up to the room to see that Kathleen had arrived earlier than expected, I walked over to her and offered to help her unpack. It was quite nice to bond with her, we actually had so much fun just talking about so many different things. Suddenly what will happen in the morning did not worry me anymore. Everyone has a story, and I am not alone in fighting a lifelong disorder.

Melanie and Dina are to arrive early tomorrow morning, which is good in a way, as my first day in a bay room with only one friend who is right next to me is great, as long as she is not bothered by what happens in the morning, as she is the one right next to me.

One other thing I will have to consider, is when I write these diary accounts, I usually wait to write these just before going to sleep, but now that am sharing a room, I must remember to use the light over my bed and have my curtains closed so that I am not bothering anyone else who wants to sleep.

"There is so much to take into account, but I will be okay I am just going to be fine."

19th March 2012

I was very anxious about the events that took place today. First, I had to go through the bowel management process, luckily it was not too bad, and I got over and done with it quite quickly. Straight after my shower I had an intense working out session in the gym with the circuit group. We went through the team exercises first such as using the bicycles and treadmill, which followed with our one-to-one focused exercises, like the sit to stands, stretches and using the steps. Even though I was a little exhausted from the morning physio session, I was okay.

However, what threw me today, was the thought, of going on a home visit this afternoon. I knew this was coming up, but I did not know if I was ready to go through with it. This is because at the end of the day, I had to return to the regional rehab unit again.

Nikki and Martine accompanied me on this trip, as they had to make various notes of any adaptations required in the house, plus looking at ways I would manage when I go back home for good. But at this stage it was a general assessment to see how I will manage, when they start sending me home for weekend visits which is coming up soon.

I was told that I would have to sit in my wheelchair, which will be secured to the taxi I will be travelling in, because my car transfers were still not complete, and until I am assessed on how to go in and out of a vehicle from standing position, I would have to travel in my wheelchair for safety purposes.

Plus I would always have one of the team members taking me in and out of the taxi.

When the time came, Nikki came into the room to pick me up. Martine entered soon after who carried my walking aid, for me to use once I was at home, but for now, Nikki pushed me in my chair to the ground floor and into the car park, where a big taxi was waiting for us.

The ride home felt awkward. I was happy to be going home, where I knew my family would be eagerly wating for me, but I also felt sad that it was only going to be for a few hours and then I would have to come back again.

Driving into Luton after so many months felt unreal, I could not believe I was finally seeing the buildings, houses, and traffic of the town. Since the virus had attacked my body, I was being moved from one hospital to another in an ambulance, therefore I could not see my surroundings, but today I was able to see my town after almost three months. I admired the landscape around me as we drove past the chaulend area.

I was particularly nervous though, as we started to drive up towards my road, we passed my doctors surgery, which was literally a minute walk from the front door of my house. Martine looked at me and smiled, she told me I was very lucky to have my GP right next to me especially with my condition now, it would be of great convenience. I nodded in agreement and watched as we took a left turn into my road, passing a little bend before driving down into my driveway.

My house door was already open, EH was standing there with Zara right next to him, I waited for the taxi to park and then for Nikki to take me out. It was an emotional moment to be wheeled into my own house, where most of my family including my mum and siblings were waiting for me.

As soon as I came out of the wheelchair, I walked over to my sofa, but before I could sit down, Nikki had to check how low down it was from the furniture at the RRU. So, that when I sit down, I do not go down too quickly. She helped me to sit down carefully before walking up towards EH so that she could discuss the plan with him.

Once seated safely on the sofa, I was greeted by an overly excited Zara who wanted to show me everything in her toy box. She run back and forth taking out one thing after another and putting them on my lap, just like she used to most mornings. I joined in with her, showing my enthusiasm in her little game.

Once I had given some of my attention to Zara, satisfied she was okay, I turned towards my mum and eldest sister who were there too. My mum had Jannat on her lap, who I had seen for a short while just over a month ago, when EH had taken her to visit me, because she had stepped into a new milestone in her life which was starting on her solids. Today she looked all grown up and different from when I had seen her last. For some reason she seemed a little distant from me, I could understand why, as she was only four months when I was taken into hospital, when she did not really understand much about what was happening in her surroundings. Now, she was spending all her time with my mum, she only knew my parents and brother well. In addition, the past two months have been essential in her personal development. She is more aware of the different people who she knows as her family. For her now, I am like a new person, and she does not really know who I am. This realisation was a painful one, I had a lot of work to do, to build a relationship with my daughter after I come home.

This is going to take some time and effort.

Zara visits me in the RRU, so she has that connection with me, but I feel Jannat is little alienated from me. I felt sharp pricks of stinging tears waiting to come out from my eyes. I held on as best as I could because I did not want this visit to worry any of my family members of how sad I really was from inside. I missed being part of my family, I missed my life.

Whilst I was busy catching up with everyone else, EH showed Nikki and Martine around the house they made notes of how I would need to use the stairs, how I could manage in the kitchen, things that I will need, which have to go in the bathroom to help me in the mornings. Measurements were taken of the space inside the bedroom.

Nikki explained to EH that coming here, I was helped into the taxi using a wheelchair, as the taxi is big enough for the chair to go inside, but as his car was not adapted for that purpose, I would have to get in and out of it using a different method.

I am unable to lift my legs high enough, to go inside a car, as they feel heavy, and I just cannot not manage with balancing properly as it has been noted from all the assessments that they had done on me back at the RRU.

So, when I come home, for my weekend visits, I must hold onto the car door then using my sit to stands, sit method I will need to sit down first and lift my legs, the right first followed by my left with my hands and slide them into the car, then take my walking aid place it next to me. To come out of the car I would need to take out my quad stick first and using it to keep my back straight I will have to lift my left leg first and place it onto the ground, using the same method to take out my right leg. Once both legs are safely positioned on the ground and I am sitting on the side of the seat, similar to the side of a chair, I have to firmly hold onto my stick with my left hand and with my right-hand use either EH's hand or another member of the family's hand to stand up straight onto my feet. EH listened carefully and said that this would be fine.

The remaining of my stay was a lot of talking and catching up on what I had learnt over the few past months.

When it was time to leave, I took the spare bottles of air fresheners from the cupboard. I hugged everyone and told them not to worry for me, knowing that it was pointless telling them this because they know how I am, I always hide how I feel, especially when I am sad.

I was helped into the taxi with the aid of my wheelchair, I pulled my seat belt across and could see Zara look out from the window. It was an incredibly sad moment, my mum and siblings waved goodbye, and everyone looked happy, but I could see the sadness behind it all, just like they could see how I was putting on a brave face, they too were doing the similar thing for me.

The drive back to hospital was incredibly quiet, I could not stop thinking about my family and that look on their faces, as they waved goodbye to me as the taxi reversed out of the drive. I could still hear Zara crying, demanding for me to stay.

Coming back into the room was also difficult as the girls were all eagerly waiting for me, they wanted to know how I was feeling about going home. They wanted to know about my family and what their reaction was to see me home after such a long time.

Even though it was difficult for me, I spoke enthusiastically as I did not want to reveal how sad I was feeling from inside. I just carried on as normal. It is good to spread positivity as it is contagious, and what we definitely need in this room is a lot of positivity. It will help all of us get on the path to go home again.

Soon life will get back to the new normal for me, I will be with my family. For now, I just cannot take the expressions my children had on their faces off from my mind. I can still visual, at how sad Zara had looked when I was leaving. There was so much disappointment on her face, that I had not stayed at home, and Jannat looked as if she did not know who I was. It pinches me that one of my child is so close to me and the other so distant. I have so much work to do, to fill in the gaps in our relationship once I return home.

Oh Allah, please give me the patience and strength to be able to mend this bridge that I have between me and my girls. You listen to every prayer, please accept my dua (prayer) and help me overcome this calamity in my life, you are the most kind surely you will listen to a mother's call.

20th March 2012

During my morning physiotherapy session, I used my crutches more often, instead of the rollator frame. I know now I must double my efforts to build up my strength. I need to work towards my leaving date. For that I must be able to stand with as less restrictions as possible, it is going to be hard to move around with a wheelchair and rollator frame with two incredibly young children running around me. They are too young to understand that the slightest disbalance can cause me to fall.

Therefore, I must build up my endurance levels now. Using the crutches feels less restrictive than the rollator frame in terms of space, but it uses up both my hands, so I must ask to start training using only one walking aid that will give me more freedom to pick things up etc.

After an intense beginning to the morning, I decided to take part in the quiz group, which up until now I had been avoiding because of the feeling of claustrophobia. But I have told myself that, when I get back into the real world again, I will have to face different gatherings, such as going into the doctors, shops and with family visiting me.

Even though I felt my heart pumping fast and my throat feeling no air was going in and out. I stayed behind, to play a game of bingo, then I decided to leave. I am going to take one step at a time. Today I played one game, next week I will try to stay a little longer.

In the afternoon, more preparations were on the way to prepare for me leave the RRU soon. Nikki came and took measurements of my wheelchair so that she can order one for me to use at home. Just how will this be possible for me to utilize the wheelchair, taking into consideration the space that I have at home? With the dining table, sofa, Jannat's travel cot and walker already in the only room we have, how will I even mange to move around with my chair? I will not be able to even turn the chair around without feeling worried that the children might be behind me.

I had a lot of worrying questions, constantly creeping up on my mind, but I decided it was best, not to let it bother me too much. Right now, I had to build up my strength, so I had to focus on my goals. I looked through the sheets on my desk, which outlined what my goals were. Once I reminded myself of what was important to me at that precise moment, I knew what I had to do.

So, to make a start after that little pep talk to myself, I decided I wanted to spend my OT session in the kitchen. With Carla, observing me, I decided to tidy up the top cupboards in the kitchen. I was standing for almost forty minutes with three rest breaks. I had to use my left hand and arm throughout the whole process because I was unable to lift my right arm much. This is because of the pain that just run through my whole body every time, I tried lifting my hand above my head. This is another reason why it took so long to tidy only two cupboards, which only contained spices and dry ingredients.

I am exhausted now; but the girls cannot stop wondering why I settle down each night, to write down all the things that I do throughout the day. I explained to them that it makes me feel good, to be able to write my experiences down and then read them to see how I have been managing.

When I take all this back with me, I can remind myself of how I fought through this difficult time. I would never have thought that I would be back on my feet after how I had started off in December.

I am so grateful, for all my achievements and I can only thank my lord Allah for accepting my prayers and keeping me believing in my faith by making the changes possible for me. It was to Allah, who I used to make prayers and still do make prayers every night to make a miracle happen. For me that miracle happened, in the form of me being able to stand again, move again.

I also have no words to describe, how to thank and praise the dedicated team right from the beginning in Luton to now at the RRU, that have been involved in my care. I have watched them attend to all my needs and making me feel great about myself. I would have never managed if they had not been so kind and caring not to mention the efficiency that they worked with. Managing a group of four to six patients per member of staff be it in the morning, afternoon, and night. I just cannot imagine how they are so patient with changing, washing and dressing us every day.

21st March 2012

I did not feel like writing much today, for starters I felt quite upset walking around the RRU and not seeing the usual faces of the patients I used to see every day, and secondly my hands are quite sore from all the training at the circuit group.

Today has not been an overly exciting day. I was in the circuit group for morning and afternoon sessions, so I just got on with my usual exercises. Later on, I decided to try and walk a little more. I spent most of my afternoon in the garden reading my book till it was time to come up for dinner.

The day room is not the same anymore, many of the patients that I had started my journey here at the RRU with, have now been discharged. It's only Kathleen, Melanie, Dina, and I from the old group who are left now, it feels very strange. Soon Melanie and Dina will be discharged too. It is going to be very lonely without my friends.

22nd March 2012

Martine came early into the room, in the morning today, as she came up to my bed side to greet me, it was only one look at her face, and I immediately knew what I was in for. I know it was me who had asked for more intense training. Hence, Martine was making sure that I was really concentrating on the exercises I was not particularly good at. We started off by walking up and down the first-floor stairs which was great fun because my balance and strength in standing is getting better day by day. However, the pins and needles feelings just does not want to go away, and it bounces around my whole core and legs as I stand for too long. I did need two rest breaks between the climb up and getting down.

Things from here, were a little different I had to do the lovely floor exercises (which I so dislike). I looked like a penguin trying to balance on stilts waddling from side to side as I did some mini squats whilst balancing on my knees.

To follow on from the mini squats, was the lovely superman action/pose exercise, which are incredibly difficult to do, because of the constant wobbling while trying to reach out with one hand and lift the opposite side leg.

I was so happy when I was able to come off the floor and go onto the treadmill, it felt so much nicer to be standing. After the treadmill I went to join the circuit which was mostly exercising on the bike. But then I had to go onto the parallel bars to do my hip and knee extensions, I did not enjoy that at all because I still could not see my legs lifting off the floor very much, but I definitely felt the stretches inside my legs along with the shooting pains and pins and needles.

Martine stopped me when she saw the level of discomfort from my facial expressions. It is really strange and nice at the same time, at how the therapists know, when a patient needs to stop what they are doing. I had not mentioned anything to Martine or made any sounds to express that I was in discomfort, but she just knew just from my facial expressions that I could not go any further. I thought that was sweet of her to understand.

Miranda joined me for afternoon physiotherapy. We walked down the stairs, passing the café and shops on our way outside into the garden. Where we sat on the benches for about five minutes before proceeding forward.

On my way back to my room, Miranda assessed me on how I would shop for a few items. I went into WHSmith's holding onto my crutches, as both my hands were occupied. I knew I couldn't buy anything that would fall out of my grip easily, so I bought a newspaper by placing it under my arms. I then walked up to the till waited in a steady standing position whilst the person in front of me paid for their items.

Once I was at the tills, I asked the lady for a bag so that I could place the bag's handle onto my crutches handle and that way the newspaper would not fall out from my arms as I walk back up to my room. I took the money out of my trouser pocket and gave it to the lady, I waited for my change which I put back into my pocket. I was quite pleased with myself. Miranda thought I did great too. But in the real world it would be more than just a paper, I may need something like a rack suck or shopping trolley for more items, but I will think about this more in the days to come.

23rd March 2012

Today has been a day full of positivity, I feel I am a new person. To begin with my bed statement changed. Like the other girls in my room, I can now go down to the shops or cafeteria on my own whilst using my crutches. I do not need supervision if I walk downstairs, it is such a great feeling to feel that extra little bit more independent. I still have to use two crutches though depending on how tired I feel. If I am using the stairs then I can use one crutch, but that is only when I am feeling hundred per cent confident and safe.

I will be sensible, I will not push myself, I have waited this long to start doing more and more on my own. So, I shall not spoil it by over doing it. Even though right now I feel like I can do anything, but my body always feels differently to what my mind feels. So, I need to be careful.

To top up the good news today, I have been informed that my bowel care will be managed every other second day, so that's great news too. I will not be needing suppositories every day. But there is always a but, I have been told that if I do not empty fully every day then I will need the suppositories every day. So, I must drink a lot of water and make sure I am not eating anything that can cause problems for me.

To help me out a little, I decided to do some research on different eating habits that help manage conditions such as mine. Fingers crossed when I am checked every morning, I would be clear, which in the long run will mean *bye, bye* to suppositories.

After receiving two sets of good news, I was actually quite happy to see Martine. I knew she was going to make me practice floor exercises, but I now know this is all going to help me, and my body react in the correct way to do things.

Martine was pleased that I had actually practiced my exercises today without complaining about how much I disliked the clams and reach and squat. She felt I might be ready to do some exercises independently without supervision in circuit group. I am now allowed to do my floor exercises without anyone watching over me to see I am doing it properly and I am also allowed to go on the treadmill on my own as long as I do not use a high speed and remember to take into consideration all the safety requirements.

That is three pieces of good news all in one day. I am going to make sure that I do all my exercises properly, even if I find it difficult. I do not want to let my therapists down, they have shown faith in my abilities and I must do everything properly so that I can keep hold of this independence. If for any reason my body gets too tired or if I have any falls, then all these privileges will be taken away again.

So, rule number one, make sure to carry out every exercise in the way I have been shown and practicing in the last few weeks. Rule number two stop as soon as I feel wobbly, or the pain and pins and needles get too uncomfortable.

24th March 2012

It has been an incredibly quiet day today, the girls have gone home for their weekend visit and I was on my own again, it feels strange now that I am sharing a room to be on my own. I miss the morning chatter and the wait for the shower rounds.

I watched television during the morning and went for a walk after. Then this afternoon my husband came with Zara, along with one of his friends. We sat in the cafeteria, I played peekaboo with Zara, which was hilarious, because she kept pulling my hands away from my face, every time I covered it and then she would giggle for having stopped me. After our little game, I read her a book that she had brought with her, I have missed doing this for so long. I wish at that moment Jannat was here too, so she too could have been part of our game.

EH told me that he was going to stay here in London today at a friend's, with Zara that is why Zara had her little backpack with her with a few of her things.

I asked EH about how Jannat was and any new things she had been doing. Later, I shared all my achievements, and it was quite exciting for me to be able to mention so much that I was improving with, except for the improvement with my bowel care as his friend was there and I did not wish to talk about that.

Soon enough it was that time again, for my family to leave, once they left, I was on my own again. I practiced my floor exercises and did all my bed exercises. Even though I find some exercises exceedingly difficult, I am satisfied with how I feel towards doing them now. It is almost like a new me to just get one with them, without listing how uncomfortable some of them can be.

I did try something new; I clipped my nails today and it was so difficult, the nail cutter kept falling out of my hand. And for some reason I just could not press the clipper part, my fingers are not strong enough. So, in the end I just placed the nail cutter on the edge of my palm and then used all four fingers to press down together. Finally, I managed to clip my nails in a different way to how I would normally do it. Realisation hit me that if my fingers do not regain their full strength, then this is something that I might have to always do in the future.

I must speak to Nikki, to ask if there anything I can do to get the strength back in my fingers. I told myself.

25th March 2012

It has been yet another incredibly quiet day today; it has been so quiet that I can almost hear the drop of a pin. I made my bed twice just to give me something to do. Every room was empty, hardly anyone around except for the selected few of us waiting to be granted permission to spend the weekend at home.

I did catch up on a lot of TV programmes, I love watching the nature documentaries, it is absolutely amazing to watch the birds flap their big wings and fly far, far away to wherever it takes them. The splashing of the whales, deep into the clear blue ocean, it makes one feel how free these species are they can go and do whatever they want until they are preyed upon, which is the really upsetting part. It is almost as if freedom comes at a cost whether it is for people or these amazing species on TV.

After my binge TV watching session, I decided to exercise my legs, I walked down the stairs to the cafeteria and out into the garden. It was a little cold to read my book in the garden today, so I decided to come back upstairs. I practised my floor and bed exercises so I can show Martine tomorrow that I had not been lazy during the weekend.

26th March 2012

In circuit group I was able to do the floor exercises, two point and four point kneeling. I was pleased because my therapists praised me for carrying on with practising during the weekend. This was a merit moment for me, it has been a long time since I received any kind of praise for anything in my life.

Sometimes I feel there is a void in my life. I love my role as a full-time mum, but honestly when I search into the depth of my heart, I do feel the emptiness of not being able to interact with others at work. It makes me smile when I remember the good old days when I would walk into the CHSC department in Barnfield and everyone in the different teams would be having a great banter with one another.

I miss aunty Lily and Deena; they are the friends I have made who will always have a special place in my heart. I was baby of my team, I started off shy and extremely introvert, but Deena, aunty Lily and the lovely Childcare team girls, soon got me out of my shell. I left Barnfield, confident and loud.

I still remember how I got teased for having moments where my hands would be on my hips, to show everyone that I was being serious, and things needed doing. They would tease me saying, if that was the best I could come up with, for everyone to take me seriously. It was lovely I loved those moments. Life was good when I was at work, I was among those who really cared for me and my feelings. The whole department protected me from any kind of negativity that would go round. I felt protected.

I was a different person at work, always valued for who I was. I had to give up my job after Zara was born and things just changed from then onwards. I lost my self-confidence, I have started living in a bubble, always trying to please everyone.

It is hard at times, trying to always be patient and sacrificing my wishes and feelings for others, who do not always appreciate me. But anyways, I am happy that I am a great mum to my children and I love them, so I would never hope to change that part of my life. But I just wish that I were more valued, and my feelings are not always crushed with dominance. Anyways that is enough of me feeling sorry for myself, now I need to pull my socks up and just look forward to all that I can do to achieve my goals.

I did not have an OT session today as Chris was off sick, so I decided to utilise my time by working on my hands using the thera putty.

27th March 2012

It was an exciting morning today, my new splint arrived. It is made from hard shiny plastic, it is a little bit rigid especially on the ankle section, but it is supposed to support my leg in a better way compared to the soft splint.

Today, I also received the news that I have been waiting for such a long time, but funnily enough when I did receive it, I did not expect to react in the way I did. I was told that from this week on I should go home for my weekend visits.

Suddenly I felt something deep down in my stomach. What if I don't want to come back to hospital again after being at home for two nights? What if my children are affected in a negative way by the change? For starters I will not be the same mummy that had to leave them suddenly, and what if it does not make sense to them that I must go back to hospital after the short stay?

But the main issue I have is that how will I manage being at home where I do not have the space to manoeuvre my walking aids? What if I have any accidents? How will I use the bathroom? there were so many questions that I had in my mind that I was scared.

My housing issues are still complicated, still no luck with them, plus how can I persuade EH that moving to Milton Keynes is something that I do not want, how will I get all the help? I have my whole family in Luton, who can help me with all my day-to-day chores. But that is another topic on its own,

I can never win when it comes to getting my point across, and the last thing I want, is to hear how because of me our family has been affected financially, because my long hospital stay has meant that EH has not been able to go to work.

Nikki came to see me in the afternoon to find out what was really worrying me and why I felt reluctant to go home during the weekends. I could not be completely honest with her and tell her what was really worrying me. I will just cross that bridge when I must face it later on. That is why I love writing my feelings down, I can just say anything without worrying how it would make others react.

Anyways, Nikki explained to me that going home would give me a chance to make a note of all the difficulties that I will experience, and upon my return to the RRU, they can work on how to manage those problems that I would face at home. It is all in the package of trying to repair me as much as possible before I am discharged from the hospital. I am a good student, so if my teacher has advised that at this stage it is good to test the waters, then that is what I will do.

On the bright side I have been using a walking stick to practise my walking with. This is great especially when practising my stairs. Plus, I am now going to be like the rest of the girls in my bay they all use just a walking stick. Now I just need to try and free myself from the splint and I will be completely like them. This is getting exciting. But I still need to keep both the crutches just in case I have a bad day.

28th March 2012

I had to write a letter to DVLA today, informing them of my condition. Nikki provided me with a template, which I edited and emailed to her to check if everything was okay. Next step from here onwards would be to wait to hear back from DVLA and surrender my licence, which they will freeze until I am deemed capable and fit enough to drive again.

In circuit group I made sure that I was putting in all my effort to perfect my balance exercises. Soon I will be going home in the weekends, and the last thing I want is to have an accident because of poor balance. I really thought I would be so excited to go home, but now I feel it may be too soon just now, I am okay with walking and all my exercises. But reality really hit me hard when I went for that home visit. I realised there is just so less space to move around in, everything seems close knit. Here at the RRU I have ample of space, to use my wheelchair, when I am walking, when I do wobble, I am not in anyone's way. But at home, what if I trip and land on my girls?

Nikki has explained to me that unless I go home and get a feel for what life is going to be like outside the RRU I will not be able to make a list, of areas that I need to improve in or try to manage as best as I can because it could be that the stage that I am at with my condition is what I will remain like for the rest of my life.

I am worried, the pins and needles are always running up and down in my body. I walk as if something is always pulling me from the back, I feel so tired just after a short period of time from standing. My balance and posture are still not perfect. "How will I remember how to do things when I get home?" Here someone is always there to remind me to do my exercises properly.

I know that when I go home, I cannot reveal how scared I am, I cannot share how I feel with anyone, the feeling of possibly becoming a burden to my family scares me. Even though I have always put on a positive and brave face, ever since the first time I had been attacked by this disease. I have never complained that I am in pain, discomfort etc. but I still, have had to hear taunts that I am responsible for our poor financial circumstances, that I need to try and get better. I cannot explain that it is not in my hands to recover fully, it is just a matter of time.

I am under a lot of pressure I just do not know what is right and what is wrong anymore. I cannot share this worry with anyone from my family because of past events, I do not want to worry my parents or siblings. They are doing their one hundred percent to support me and my family. My mum is making sure that she is cooking regular meals for my husband and Zara, she is also a fulltime carer for Jannat.

I cannot let my worries and fears stop me from progressing. Nikki is right, let me go on the weekend visit's and make a note of where my weaknesses are. After we work on those weaknesses, I will be more prepared for when I am discharged.

29th March 2012

A few days ago, I developed a painful red spot inside my right nostril, I have been prescribed with antibiotics and I have been applying an ointment. However instead of getting better, the redness has now spread across my right cheek, my face feels painful, and I struggle to wash my face.

Today the ENT doctors came to see me right in the middle of my physiotherapy session, where I was pretending to use a flowerpot in place of my six-month-old daughter, I was trying to wrap and unwrap a tea towel around the pot pretending, that is how I will be changing my daughter's nappy when I go home. It was such an embarrassing moment to be caught at because only myself and my therapists knew why I was doing this exercise, but the doctors had arrived from a completely different department. I could feel my whole face turn red, my cheeks were burning, and I struggled to straighten myself up and get up. After wobbling a little I managed to pull myself up and explain to the doctors the story about my red nose.

The doctors pressed the area and it really hurt, they told me that the infection had to completely come out, in order to fully go away. So, they prescribed me with IV antibiotics, "Oh gosh after quite a while now, I am going to, have to have a canula attached to my hand once again, I really do not like these, it restricts my movements and just feels uncomfortable. But now for the next five days I must have this treatment to see if the infection will go away!"

During OT I dramatized the mornings events to Nikki to express how embarrassed I had been in front of the doctors. We laughed for a bit and then it was back to work, I had to complete the letter to DVLA, which is now ready to be posted.

I went shopping for Melanie and Dina in the evening. I wanted to push myself and see if I could manage shopping and money handling on my own. I took a carrier bag with me, which I used like basket to bring back all the shopping.

I bought two packets of wotsits and two bottles of Lucozade for Dina and a bar of galaxy chocolate for Melanie. I paid for Melanie's chocolate bar first and put the change into my right pocket. I then paid for Dina's items and placed the change in my left pockets, touching notes and coins at the same time did not feel extremely comfortable.

I placed everything in the bag and walked up the stairs. I am now using my single walking stick, but I think to come shopping I should have come with my crutch as I could have used the handle to hold my bag more comfortably. I came up to the room and gave both the girls their items and their change.

I then went to tell Nikki that I had shopped for the first time unsupervised. My bed statement was changed again, I am becoming more and more independent. This is good news.

My happiness, however, was short lived, firstly because today I have found out that Nikki will be leaving the team to join another department in the hospital. My new occupational therapist will be a girl called Eleanor. I was just trying to get my head round this piece of news when Dani came into my room, to insert the canula in my hand in preparation for the IV antibiotics. I must have an hour's treatment, and during this time I will be unable to get off my bed, because I am going to be attached to the IV stand. I took on board all the instructions and got ready for my first session.

The machine made lots of loud noises after the hour, this was to alert the nursing team that my treatment had been complete. The process is not comfortable, even though its only fluid that is going inside me I felt a lot of pain and discomfort. Funnily enough it does not feel the same to when I had the steroid IV session's, during that time, I did not feel pain. But with the antibiotics, it almost feels like the canula will come off with all the pressure.

After my IV antibiotic treatment all my worries came flooding back to me. How am I going to manage without Nikki? she has been my keyworker as well my OT. Now I must get used to a new therapist all over again. Every time something changes, I find myself repeating all the events that led me, to come here. But that is not all, every time a new person is introduced in my care then I have to have all those physical checks all over again and I really do not like going through all that repeatedly.

Well, this is no time to feel upset Yasmin, just snap out of it. I need to carry on pushing myself, until I have achieved the goals on my target sheets. I reminded myself.

Ouch, I cannot write anymore the canula is poking into my skin, it makes it difficult to write and I am little worried the pressure might make it come out. I placed my pen on my desk and made my prayer to Allah, to give me strength and patience to face the new changes coming my way.

30th March 2012

It has been an incredibly stressful start to the day today. Firstly, I was put on the IV antibiotics early in the morning at 7.30 a.m., just after the hour when I thought I could make a start on my day. I was told by Charlene that today I had to have the bowel treatment. I was given the suppositories. I am hoping that my bowels will be in a better routine soon, I really do not like having to wait for check-ups every other day, I am embarrassed and sometimes it really knocks my confidence that I am the only person in the room who needs to have this done. It is not a nice time of the day for anyone in the bay when I need these sessions.

After all the stress, I did manage to sort myself out and get ready before lunch, I had my shower and joined my group in physiotherapy. I mostly practised floor exercises and the parallel bar exercises, as I needed to improve on them the most. Also, when I go home for my weekend visits, these exercises will come in handy more. I repeated the same exercises with Martine in the afternoon session.

During OT, with Nikki, I mentioned that I wanted to start going on my weekend visits from the coming weekend as it is the easter weekend and with the girls gone home I would be too lonely in the ward. Miranda joined us and when I expressed my thoughts, both Nikki and Miranda thought it may be a good idea as I had mentally prepared myself for these visits now.

After dinner I was put back on the IV antibiotic, but this time round the canula did come off from my hand because of the positioning of the canula and the pressure of the flow in which the fluid was going through into my arm. It was very painful, and the area of my skin that was exposed to the fluid just stung, Kylie came to my rescue to wipe my hands down and took me off the IV. I was told that a new canula had to be inserted, I was not too scared, because by now I am so used to having these sorts of procedures.

The new canula is better positioned it is just under my elbow area I can now bend and move my hands more easily, previously the canula was placed on my forehand just past the knuckles, so every time I tried to eat, brush my hair, I felt a pulling sensation.

31st March 2012

Another early start today, my day started with being put on the IV antibiotics at 7.30 a.m. followed by having my breakfast. I waited for the girls to go and have their shower before me, whilst I went to fetch the new sheets and pillowcases for my bed. I took my time making my bed as neatly as I could.

Once I was showered and dressed, I went to have my physiotherapy as usual. I did not do anything different just the same as yesterday. At six p.m. I was put back on the IV antibiotics. It is strange how I am not actually taking these antibiotics orally, but the taste that is being left in my mouth is more stronger than taking the meds orally.

I am glad to be in bed now, I think all the stress of worrying about being a nuisance to the others in the room is tiring me out. The machine makes a lot of sound once the hour is over and until someone takes me off the drip the sound just continues. This is the same in the morning and the evening I feel bad that the others will soon get fed up with me. First, I had to worry about how my bowel treatment will bother the others in the bay, but now this noisy machine is not making this easy for me. I cannot wait till the treatment is complete.

1st April 2012

Another quiet sort of a day. I started the day with being put on the IV drip, after which I had my breakfast, later, I went to have my shower, and get dressed. I made my bed after having my shower today, as the clean sheets in the laundry cupboard needed restocking, so I waited till that was done.

EH and Zara came to see me in the evening, luckily it was a lovely day to sit in the garden. I watched Zara run around and coming back to me every time she found something like a leaf or pebble on the ground. It was beautiful to watch her so happy. However, it was heart breaking saying goodbye, but at least now I can console myself that soon I will be able to spend two nights at home with my family.

I was put back on the IV antibiotics in the evening. For the second time the canula popped out of my hand, this time the discomfort was more than the previous time. I just hope this is the last time the canula comes out, my hand already has numerous needle marks, right from the beginning from when my treatment started. It is not an extremely attractive look.

I must ask for a bottle of bio-oil to get rid of all these marks, I want to start feeling confident about my skin and looks again.

2nd April 2012

According to my timetable today, I was supposed to have a busy day, plus I was going to meet my new OT. However, because of the situation with my nose everything on the timetable had to be cancelled. I have been informed by the ENT doctors that I will need a little surgery to drain the nose as the infection is not reducing much.

I had been put on a drip and I was told that I would not be allowed to eat or drink anything until the surgery was over.

I was scared, I did not want to go under the general anaesthetic. What if it affects my limbs and I am unable to move them after I wake up? my trail of thoughts was interrupted by the ward manager Sue, who reassured me that the anaesthetic should not have an effect on my limbs, like with any anaesthetic, there would be the short-term side effects, but it should wear off soon after the surgery.

I am going into surgery at three p.m., but I will make a quick call to my family to inform them.

I tried to be as brave as possible whilst speaking to mum, giving her a lowdown of all that was going to happen and why. It was hard to hide how scared I felt from someone who meant so much to me. But I needed to stay as brave as possible otherwise mum would have got worried and that would have affected her health. Mum put Jannat on the phone, it was amazing listening to her babble and giggle, I felt like a burst of energy run down my body. I put down the phone feeling positive. I then called my husband to inform him of what was happening, I quickly spoke with Zara and then I was prepared for what was coming my way.

I could not write how I felt after the surgery on the day of my surgery, so the next part I wrote the day after.

When I entered the operation theatre all I could see were the lights above my head. The doctor told me what was going to happen, then he placed an oxygen mask over my mouth and inserted the general anaesthetic through my canula. I felt a very strange sensation and before I could count to three my world turned blank. The next thing I remember was opening my eyes in recovery and being wheeled back to my bay. The girls all greeted me happily and asked how I felt. At that point I could not speak because the little drainage pipe was in my nose and I just could not move my mouth because that whole area was in pain. I just wanted to sleep. I was constantly on the drip plus I had to continue with the IV antibiotics. I just did not feel my usual self at all, all the medication made me feel so lightheaded and nauseous.

3rd April 2012

The ENT doctors came to see me in the morning, they told me that for now I still had to continue with the IV antibiotics. Then later on one of the nurses will come and remove the stitches and take out the drainage pipe.

Renita came in all prepared I was scared at first, looking at all the tiny tools she had on her tray. I had seen something like that on TV, but never had I imagined that I would face a situation like that in real life. Renita could see the worry on my face and reassured me that it would not be as bad as it looks. I just had to trust that everything will be okay. I was talked through the procedure and all I had to do was concentrate on another thought for a few seconds, whilst she cut the stitches. She told me that I would feel a little pulling sensation when she first snips the stitches, then there would be a little discomfort when she had to pull out the tiny drainage pipe, which was attached to the stitches.

Once I was ready that I understood everything, I closed my eyes tight and imagined being in my living room with Zara running around and Jannat babbling in her bouncer next to me. My thoughts were interrupted a little when I felt Renita snip the stitches, as soon as she had done so, she told me to hold my breath as she pulled out the pipe as quickly as she could. It was not so bad when she actually pulled out the pipe, that was more like a very thin, hard plastic short piece of straw. But then there was a little string like part attached to the pipe, it was when this was pulled out that I felt a sharp sting in both my eyes. For a few seconds it left behind a very painful sensation, almost as if someone had pulled something out of my eyes. Despite the pain I kept my calm composure, as I knew the infection was out and I could continue with my treatment as normal from now on.

During the whole nose infection issue, I had missed two days of my morning physio session because of all the assessment and the IV treatment. However, luckily for me today, Miranda had come in to see how I was feeling after the surgery. After speaking with Renita to see what my condition was like, she asked me if I wanted to do some exercises. For me that was a wonderful thing to hear because I had been so bored the last couple of days.

As there were so many patients timetabled for the gym one after another, Miranda told me that she would walk me to the gym straight away. I was not allowed to go the gym on my own just for the morning session because the team thought it would be best that I was supervised. To make sure the effects of the anaesthetic had been worn off properly. The last two days had been quite slow, in terms of me having to spend most of my time tied down to a machine next to my bed. So, I did not really feel bad that I had to go to the gym being accompanied.

Once I got up from the bed, I did feel a tiny bit lightheaded. Renita handed me a cup of water to drink and told me to gently put my legs on the ground. As I did that both Renita and Miranda helped me put on my splint and trainers, as I was unable to bend down too much at this point. They handed me my walking stick, and each gave me a hand to hold onto to come off the bed and stand straight for a few seconds, just to get my balance sorted. Miranda asked me at this point to take a couple of steps and see if I can hold myself upright as I did that. If I managed then we could go the gym, however, if I wobbled then I would need to take further rest.

I closed my eyes once more and before taking a step forward I made a little prayer.

Bismillah hir Rahman nir Raheem (In the name of Allah the most gracious and the most merciful), please help me take a few steps, to reassure my team that I am okay and that I would be able to complete my exercises.

Confident that Allah would help me, like he has been through this whole process, I opened my eyes and slowly took a step forward. At first, I did feel the steps were a little difficult to take, but that was mostly the fear in my mind that I may not be able to do so. However, my balance was good, and I did not wobble, so I was told that I can go for my session.

Thanking Allah, for his continuous blessings, I started to walk into the gym, with Miranda's help. I held onto her arm with my right hand and used my left hand to use my walking stick. That way I was walking in a safe way Miranda was very patient as I took my steps slower than usual, but she understood that I was nervous because of the previous day's events.

I did not have time to wash and dress, hence I was still in my surgery outfit. I did feel very awkward at first, for being the only one in a surgery gown, but I was glad that I did not have to miss any of my sessions today. As I started my session, I forgot how I looked and enjoyed doing my exercises, it felt like a breath of fresh air, to be able to stretch my arms and body into different directions. I felt a burst of energy run down my entire body.

Miranda did not want to overwork me, so she asked me to slowly demonstrate my floor exercises. Which I gladly did. As I was enjoying myself so much, I had not realised how quickly the time had gone. By the time the session finished I was able to stand strongly on my own.

Once I had finished physio, I asked Miranda if I can walk back to my room on my own, as I felt strong enough to do so. Seeing how well I managed through the whole session, she felt confident that I would be okay, hence gave me permission to walk back on my own.

The first thing I did when I returned to my bay, was take out a fresh pair of clothes, socks, and a hijab (a head covering Muslim ladies wear). I laid everything on my bed, which had been already made today, maybe by an HCA staff. I then took out my gown, toothpaste, toothbrush, flannel, shampoo, and shower gel with a clean towel from the lower shelf of the cupboard and placed everything in a large supermarket shopping bag. As I am now sharing a bathroom with three other people, it was best for everyone to take their personal items as and when needed to, just to avoid any confusion.

I did not want to go back and forth from the bathroom to take my things, therefore the bag helped to take everything all at once. Before going inside, I placed my comb, hair ribbons, toiletries, and moisturisers on the little side desk, used for placing our lunch trays if we decided to have lunch in our room. This helps me organise everything and it is within reach, from my armchair before I come out from the shower, which makes me a little tired after all the movement. Plus, with the extra task of ensuring to take off the splint and putting it back on straight after my shower can exhaust me a little.

I called for assistance before I went into the bathroom, as

I am still not allowed to wash and dress on my own unsupervised. Niyah one of the HCA, answered my call, she guided me, as I walked into the bathroom and placed my gown and towel on the rail next to the shower. With the shampoo, flannel, and shower gel on the flap next to the shower seat. I then walked over to the sink and took out my toothbrush and toothpaste and spent a good few minutes brushing my teeth. For some reason, my mouth felt heavy after the surgery and I just needed to make it feel fresh again. I noticed my face had become a little puffy and my nose looked as if it has been squished inwards a little. The redness was still slightly there but not as bad, as it had been before the surgery. I placed my things back in the bag and placed the bag by the shower, this allowed me to put all my things into the bag, from sitting position once I had finished my shower and I could return to my room all at once without having to go back and forth from the bathroom.

Once I finished taking my shower, I felt really good, I was energised and I felt good from within, it is such a nice feeling to be clean and be smelling of soap. Niyah, who had been waiting outside for me, helped me to come out and sit down on my armchair. It then took me a further quarter of an hour to moisturise and dress myself, as I was tired Niyah helped me with most of it. Once I was dressed, she was able to go back to attending other patients, who also needed her help.

Whilst I was left to sort out my hair etc. I rested my hands a little before putting on my socks and footwear. Finally, I brushed through my long, thick, and tangled hair. I first put it into a braid and then twisted it into a bun and held it together with a big scrunchy. To finish off I wrapped my hijab around my head and clipped it to position. Satisfied with how I looked in the mirror, I put everything back in its place, with my dirty laundry in a laundry bag, ready to give to EH, to take home and wash.

As I was getting ready to join the others in the day room, I heard loud voices and laughter from the corridor. I then heard a familiar voice, which instantly made me smile. It was Jenny, one of the patients who used to be in this bay, had come to visit. She had been missing everyone here at the RRU. So, she decided to pay us a visit and told us about how she was managing at home now. With the patients timetabled to do various activities, Jenny could not stay for long, but her visit has been very inspiring and motivating, it made me look forward to my weekend visits at home.

I managed with the rest of my day as usual, Melanie had been taking extra care of me to make sure I was not over doing it. She accompanied me to most of my sessions, just to make sure I was okay.

I have to admit it has been an eventful day and I started to get very tired by the time we had finished having dinner. When it was time to take our medication, I was informed that my IV antibiotics would be changing to oral ones.

This is great news; as I would not be causing a problem for the others in my room. The sound of the machine can get a little annoying towards the end. Finally, I can stop worrying about the discomfort and noise caused by the IV antibiotics process.

4^{tth} April 2012

It was good to be back in my usual form today, I did not have to wait for the IV antibiotics, which saved me time, I was able to get on and off the bed as I pleased. My nose still feels a little sore and I am scared to touch around that area just in case it gets infected again.

I had an OT wash and dress session today, which was not our bathroom but the OT bathroom. Their bathroom has a bath instead of a walk-in shower. I had to use the bath board, which is a seat placed on the middle of the bath, making it easy for someone to sit down and have a bath instead of standing. The use of the bath board was to ensure my safety as I went in and out of the bath.

The whole point of this exercise was to train me to use this tool when I go home, because in my house we do not have a walk-in shower and because of the current issue with housing it is not possible to adapt it. Therefore, my therapists decided, it would be wise to start getting me used to the idea of using a bath board. Whilst the situation with housing gets sorted, so far it does not seem like that the issue will get sorted before my discharge date. Due to the waiting list and obviously the possibility of moving out of town. To be honest this method is a little more tiring as the space feels smaller and sliding my legs in and out the bath was not comfortable, particularly because my legs feel heavier after they have been in the water. It is difficult to describe, but that is what I felt.

During physiotherapy I walked up and down the stairs and finished with my floor exercises in the circuit group.

Today I spoke to Joe about benefits because my family's financial situation in worrying me. Things have not gone as I had wished for them to be and there are some issues with the type of help available to me. Joe reassured me that he would be chasing things up for to see what was happening and for me not to worry.

After Joe left, I was hit with more worries, I realised that life is going to change so much for me from now on, I do not know how well I will manage on my own without my therapists, I don't know if the housing association will transfer us to a two-bedroom house soon enough. For now, I can share a bed with Zara and my husband, but in long term I do not see how I will manage, especially if I need to go to the toilet a few times in the night. What worries me more is, I am extremely uncomfortable with the different touch and movement close to my body, the pins and needles just get worse. The tingling feeling increases too. Jannat will stay in her cot in the nights, but the cot is almost stuck to the bed, the space is very tight.

Then there is the issue in the actual living room, it is too small for me to comfortably move around with my aids. *How will I manage my life like before? How much control will I have with my balance, posture and household duties?* The questions to myself just do not seem to stop.

5th April 2012

Today I went into the gym with Ashi so that she could do an assessment on me for her course. I had to do a lot of moving, walking and stretching, all the things that I had been assessed on many times before. However, I did not mind being part of a study, as I want others to be aware of how a neurological condition can change someone's life.

After Ashi had finished with me, I was joined by Eleanor, my new OT (after Nikki had been transferred) and Chris. They were going to assist me with a new task today, which was to help me with my car transfer practice. This was all in preparation for me to go home for the first time over the weekend. Eleanor had read the notes left by Nikki, and realised that my weekend visits were due soon, therefore the car transfer was essential.

I had a delayed shower today because of all the practice exercises I had to do. I was a little wobbly by the time I reached my circuit group session. It only made me think harder that my endurance level are still not what I had hoped it would be, because I can feel my lower body especially my legs feel shaky after a thirty-minute session all in one go.

After lunch I had a little nap before organising myself to go into the afternoon occupational therapy session in the kitchen.

I was quite excited about my cooking session today; I had picked out a lovely recipe from the BBC website, for chocolate brownies. I really enjoyed weighing the ingredients and mixing them together. The batter for brownies is a little more stiff, compared to a cake batter. I had a lot of fun pouring the chocolatey mixture into the baking tray. Once in the oven, the whole kitchen started to smell wonderful, the warmth of the chocolate flavour was so delightful. When I took them out of the oven, they looked perfect. I waited for it to cool down before taking a knife to cut them out into nice square chunks. I tasted one, as I could not help myself, plus I do have this weakness for chocolate. It is one my most favourite sweets to eat. I can eat chocolate all day and not feel sick. Back to the brownies, they turned out perfect and I was confident to share them around the ward. It felt really good to receive so many positive compliments.

Towards the evening however, I did start to feel nervous again. This is because Dina and Kathleen had been picked up by their families for their long weekend. Melanie and I are going to be picked up tomorrow.

When we finished for the day, Melanie and I talked about our plans for the weekend, Melanie knew what to expect as she has been home many times before but for me this is the first time. I am not sure what to expect. I really do not want to be a burden on my family members. I just hope I can prove myself to EH, that I will not be a bother to him when I return home for good. All the time I was talking to Melanie, I had so many thoughts, running around inside my head repeatedly.

It is now almost nine p.m., Melanie is ready to go to sleep, I have pulled the curtains around my bed, so my bed side light will not bother her as she tries to sleep. I am not sleepy, I am worried, I know that I am doing well in the hospital and I have almost achieved all my goals. New goals are written up for me as I achieve the old ones. But I know that at home, life is not going to be as easy as doing a timetabled exercise routine at the hospital.

I will be amongst two incredibly young children; I need to stay safe for my own self as well as making sure that the children are looked after properly. I need to manage myself around their equipment and toys, as well as making sure that none my aids are on their way. I cannot let EH think that I cannot manage. I do not think I can take any further criticism about my condition and how it has changed our family life.

Sometimes I wish I can just be honest about how I feel when my self-esteem is pulled down. I have always taken every situation that I face in life with a pinch of salt. But this time round it's not as easy as just getting on with it. My physical abilities will really come in the way of how I manage things from now on. The most concerning thing is that this condition is lifelong now. I might not get any better from this stage forward. It is all about managing things from here onwards. I must perfect my exercises and I will get through.

Okay now it is getting late, I better put all this away and go to sleep, I need my energy for tomorrow.

6th April 2012

I had a very restless night, because I was both nervous and excited about going home. Melanie was picked up early in the morning straight after breakfast around eight a.m. I knew I was not going to get picked up in the morning, "If I am lucky, I will get picked up just after noon," I told myself. I then made my way to the shower and got ready as slowly as I could.

I tidied my bed and avoided looking at the clock, it was almost as if the clock hands had stopped. Also, the HSC and nurses kept coming into the room asking me if I was okay and how I felt about going home. I decided to go downstairs for a walk after lunch just to take in some fresh air. I made sure my phone was with me just in case EH called to say he was on his way.

After sitting in the garden for an hour till about 1.30 p.m. I thought I better get upstairs to make sure I had all my things together, one of the nurses will give me my TTO's (to take overnight) medications once my husband arrives.

Finally, at 3.30 p.m. I was picked up and for the first time in over three months I sat in my own car, it felt very strange. We arrived in Luton around 5.45 p.m. I was taken to see my mum first; my mum had suggested that till I managed to familiarise myself with being at home, Jannat should continue to stay with her. So, I can just get used to being around one small child and that way I would be able to get an idea, of how much effort I would have to put in to look after my children, when I come home for good. I did not disagree with mum, because I was already beginning to feel a little wobbly from all the anxiety built up inside me.

I was actually relieved that mum had suggested this idea. After a quick catch up with the family I came to my house. Suddenly, I started to feel that whirling feeling inside my stomach, I was nervous and scared at the same time. I was distracted by Zara, who excitedly took me inside, happy that I was home with her. I was glad to see her so cheerful.

Things were already hugely different this evening from how things were at the Regional Rehab Unit. When I got home, I wanted to freshen up, but first I had to face my first obstacle, which was the stairs to go upstairs. At the RRU all the stairs cases I used had the railing on both the right- and left-hand side so I was able to grab hold of it using my right hand and then with my left hand I used the walking stick or crutch to take my step up. This is because my left side is stronger than my right, therefore I must make my left side do more of the hard work with the right side following what the left does.

However, at home my grab rail on the staircase is on the left side and I do not have anything to hold onto from the right. Therefore, I sat on the first step as a precautionary step and used my arms to push me up one step at a time until I finally got up the stairs. I felt completely shattered after that, my arms ached, and my back felt a little sore from the rubbing affect as I pushed myself up the steps. I am glad that going down should be much easier as its always easier going down than climbing up.

I felt a little lost trying to find my clothes, as I was not used to the chest of drawers. Everything seemed alienated, I found it hard where things were kept. After which, I had my shower and went to eat my dinner so that I could take my medications on time, not really on time though, because at the RRU we have dinner by six p.m. and get our night medications before nine p.m., but today I had my shower by eight p.m. and dinner around nine p.m.

What I was shocked by was to see how late Zara was having her dinner. It was almost ten p.m. before she ate and got washed and dressed for bed.

This is one of the things I will sort out as soon as I am discharged. I will get Zara's routine back to normal like how I used to have it before I fell ill, right now everything is all over the place with her routine.

I made my way upstairs once again, using the same method as before, I could feel how sore my back felt, I knew straight away that this method was not going to work out in the long run because twice I used this method, but my back felt the pressure. I will have to learn to walk up and down the stairs. I must speak to Eleanor about this when I get back.

As I struggled into the bedroom, I crawled up to the bedside and pushed myself up to sit down. My heart was racing, and my breathing became heavy. I was in a great amount of pain. I was panting, my arms ached, and I felt strong sensations of tingling running up and down my whole body. I tried not to make a fuss and calmed myself down to avoid any kind of awkwardness.

As everyone got ready for bed, I looked around the room, trying to familiarise myself with where things were kept. I started to work out a way in my mind of how to avoid bumping into anything. I was absolutely exhausted by the time we got to bed, I was barely able to keep my eyes open, mostly because of all the medications I am taking, but also because the night before I hardly slept.

7th April 2012

The night was not comfortable at all, the bed was hugely different to the hospital. I could not adjust the position for one thing and secondly getting in and out of bed was difficult, because the cot was stuck to the bed. I had to slide in and slide out which was not extremely comfortable. But I did not want to make any comments otherwise I would be given a lecture on being too fussy and ungrateful.

I came down at 6.30 a.m. to have my breakfast, I knew EH and Zara would not be up any time soon. Finding my way around the kitchen was yet again another challenge, the heights and positions of the cupboards were different to the ones I used at the RRU. It took me almost half an hour to take out the plates and cups from their places and then make my breakfast. I cannot believe how hard it is to make some tea and toast. Am I going to be this slow all the time? I am scared how I am going to manage in the kitchen in the future, without bumping myself into the appliances and cupboards.

After eating my breakfast, I took my medicines and then cleared away the dishes. Then came the second most important thing I hard to do in the morning, which was to continue with my bowel treatment. I have been told that I need to continue to use the suppositories at home to make sure that I do not spoil the routine. As much as I felt reluctant to carry on with the bowel routine, I knew that if I did not do as I was advised then I can make things worse for the future hence I went ahead and used the suppositories to help me. I was glad to get over and done with this procedure before my family woke up.

At 8.30 a.m., I thought I should check on Zara to see if she was awake so that I could give her breakfast. When I went into the room, I found Zara was up, she was so excited to see that I was still at home, she jumped out of bed and followed me into the bathroom to wash her face and brush her teeth, she then went downstairs. She went down with great enthusiasm whilst I sat own on a step and went down one step at a time in sitting position. I am not used to the staircase at home, so, till I familiarise myself with it I shall not walk down just in case I fall.

We went into the kitchen where she excitedly showed me what she wanted to eat, I laughed pretending not to know what she wanted. I knew it would either be toast and milk or Weetabix, because she always alternates between the two. We talked in our childish language as she finished her breakfast. After I washed the dishes, I came into the sitting room and sat on the floor. I watched Zara get out all her toys and we played for what seemed like hours but, only twenty minutes had passed. But because my body is not used to so much excitement, I was exhausted. I told Zara that we should stop playing on the floor and get up on the sofa to watch some TV and that her toys could join us as we watched CBeebies together.

I cannot write much today because this is something, I do to feel relaxed, and I will not be understood if I tried to explain why I keep this journal of my experiences. Hence, I do not want to use up my energy in that area. That is why I am just summarising my today's experience.

The spaces around the house feel enclosed and I am

constantly worried I am going to fall. I just need to keep practising and soon I will be okay. It was good to be with my children though it is all worth it for them, to see how happy they are to see me, and playing with me. They are full of sweetness, innocence, and enthusiasm and that is what is going to motivate me further to not give up, coming this far. I can break this barrier of feeling worried and anxious. Zara and Jannat will be my driving force.

8th April 2012

I wanted to try and cook a simple meal today, just to test my level of endurance in my own home environment. I have to admit, it was a very satisfying experience. The only one thing that was challenging was getting all the equipment together and moving around the space that I have here.

In the RRU all the cupboards and equipment are at waist level, so I did not have to bend down to get anything out. Things will be a little bit challenging to start off with, but I need to keep practising and soon I shall get the hang of it.

In the RRU it takes me about thirty to forty-five minutes to make a pan of soup. Today it took me more than double the time to make a lentil and tomato soup, mainly because I had my excited daughter going in and out of the kitchen and sometimes, she was remarkably close to where I was standing so I had to keep in mind not to make any sudden movements otherwise either of us could have got hurt.

The other challenge is the types of equipment I have here at home, at the RRU most of the pots and pans have a different grip and the knives and chopping equipment are also different the handles etc are more easier to grip. "I must make a note of everything that I am having trouble with here, so I can speak to Eleanor to overcome these problems."

As I am so excited to be at home, I wanted to try different things to see how well I can do in my tasks. Hence, I tried to load a machine of clothes. I needed EH to pour in the soap powder for me, because I cannot pick up the box and pour it into the compartment without my hands constantly shaking. One more thing to work on, I need to practice lifting and pouring action in a balanced manner.

After the machine was done, I needed help from my husband to take everything out, but I managed to use the drying rails to hold onto and one by one placed the items on there. This is the key; I need to use all the furniture and anything that I can find, to stand and balance with using them, as my walking aid. Using the AFO is a must, but I cannot wear it when I am on the floor as it digs into my skin.

The children will play on the floor and when I am playing with them it will be hard to get on and off the floor. Especially because I need the bathroom after a while because I am very conscious about having any embarrassing accidents. My list for things to work on is getting longer and longer, but I am so happy that I am actually able to feel how life is going to be like, when I am discharged. But before that happens, I will have time, to improve on different areas with the help from my key workers at the RRU. Suddenly, I felt relaxed about being at home, at least I am having a practise run of things, it is much better than suddenly coming in and just getting on with it.

Now I will also have lots of things to talk about, from my weekend, to the girls back at the hospital.

We went to see Jannat at my mum's house after lunch, my siblings all came too. It was lovely just talking to everyone face to face after such long time. We had dinner there as I wanted to spend as much time as I could with both my children. I was excited to tell my mum what I had done in my day. Mum looked relived that I was happy. The most painful part is that I must go back to the hospital in the morning.

9th April 2012

We woke up early and got ready for my return to the RRU. My husband made the breakfast whilst I showered and got ready. He helped Zara to have breakfast and get ready. I gathered all my things and waited in the car with Zara, whilst EH loaded the car with my things.

I have packed some of my home clothes from my wardrobe, as I want to look the way I would at home, in the hospital from now on. It will make me feel more ready to come out of the hospital on a permanent basis.

I waited in the car with Zara, whilst my husband loaded the car with my things to take back to the RRU. We dropped Zara to my mum's house, so that she would not feel upset when I would have to return to the RRU. It is difficult for a child to understand what is going on in a situation like this.

Zara has had to see so many changes in her surroundings in the past eight months. First, with having a new baby in the house permanently. Just when she got used to sharing mummy and daddy with another baby, her mum had to go into hospital with no certain time of her return.

Since my admission to hospital Jannat has been living with my mum, but as she was only four months old, she really did not have an idea of all the changes happening. Zara on the other hand, is understanding things, and with two people that have always been living with her up until now, are not there together now, must surely be causing some sort of confusion inside her.

I feel incredibly sad just at the thought of how my child must be feeling with everything that is happening. At first everyone used to console her that mummy will be back soon, now it's been almost four months and there is no consolation that can be given because my family too are uncertain of how soon things will start getting back to normal again.

I returned to the RRU with so many more questions in my mind, which I was trying to resolve as I sat in the car. When I came back into my room, I noticed that the girls were still on their way. I decided to unpack my things and go for a walk just to find answers to the questions that were whirling up inside of me.

The fresh air helped and looking into the sky brought lots of hope to me. I knew that Allah would help me like always. I would not have come this far if it were not for my faith in my lord. I have been very blessed that everything I wanted to achieve since my admission to the hospital, I have been able to achieve, and this would not have been possible if Allah had not answered my prayers, surely, he is the most generous and most kind. I felt hopeful and positive because I knew that my lord does not burden a sole more than he or she can bear.

Suddenly, the greenery around me and the bright blue sky gave me a big boost. Everything was so full of life. Everything looked healthy and happy. A thought came into my head, that just like how the weather changes, where some days are bright, sunny, and full of life all around us, birds, trees, flowers, and insects doing their part for nature. There are other days where it is dull, cloudy, windy, and full of rain everywhere.

My life is going to be like this. I will have good days where I will be full of energy and strength and on other occasions, I will not be so strong and might not be mobile enough. I know this from everything that I have read, up on my condition, the online forums of other survivors and from my doctors.

I have decided that I will embrace this change with an open arm. I cannot let any niggling worries get to me, as this will only slow me down. I feel grateful now, that my mindset has managed to stay positive, even though sometimes I stumble.

Tomorrow is another day, so I will start with what I have learnt from my weekend experience. I am really excited to tell Miranda and Eleanor all about what I have learnt, I just hope they can guide me on how I can overcome these issues. Okay now I am feeling tired from all the excitement. I shall rest now; I can catch up with the girls after dinner. Saying this to myself, I shall stop writing for today.

10th April 2012

Straight after breakfast I had my early morning physio session with Ashi. We worked on balance exercises. We then used the tera bands to lift my toes up and down. Miranda and Eleanor were occupied with other patients today so for most of the day I did tasks independently.

Previously, when I had moved into the room which I share with three other ladies. I was not allowed to shower and dress on my own, because of the bathroom being wet and chances of soap being left on the ground. Therefore, someone from the team had to supervise me or I had to have my shower in the OT bathroom, for my own safety. However today I was given permission to use our shared bathroom on my own, as long I used my AFO and have it close by me when I have to take it off, just for that short duration of time.

I was advised to wear the AFO as soon as I have dried myself. I then have come into my bay in my dressing gown, so that I can safely moisturise and dress myself. I must admit this task did make me very tired indeed. Firstly, having to walk into bathroom with the AFO on, so that my balance was always strong. Then the whole process of undressing, taking off the AFO. Having my shower, straight after drying myself putting on the AFO in the bathroom, whilst sitting down on the shower seat. It was all very strength consuming. There were many movements involved, my hands tingled and my whole body just ached with a burst of pins and needles dancing inside of me because of the way I was moving.

It took me ten minutes after I came back into the room, to rest a little before taking off the AFO and getting ready. Then completing the process by putting the AFO back on again. But I cannot complain, I am the one who wants to be very independent, and if that means being sensible and taking all the precautions then that is what I will do.

I tried something new today, finally I went to the quiz group for the full duration, which I used to be very apprehensive about, because I feel claustrophobic sitting at proximity to others. However, I wanted to challenge myself and see how well I do. Whilst in the room, I tried hard to blend in with the atmosphere, even though at times I felt my heartbeat racing fast, and I felt nauseous I stayed in the room and participated as best as I could. It was a pleasant surprise that I won two cups on the board.

To finish my day, I cooked some noodles in the OT kitchen on my own, as Chris who was supposed to supervise me was off sick. But I was given permission to go ahead with the session on my own, as I was told that I could be trusted to stay safe and follow all the safety rules. It felt incredibly good to be noticed as someone who will follow the rules. The noodles tasted great, and I felt proud sharing it with my room mates.

11th April 2012

It has been another very eventful day. My day started by getting ready, the morning was combined physio and occupational therapy, as Miranda and Eleanor prepared to take me out in the community again.

I went into an actual big supermarket today after months and months. I was extremely excited and anxious at the same time. Both my keyworkers helped me get there by pushing my wheelchair as the Sainsbury's was just a fifteen to twenty minutes' walk from the hospital. Once I was in the supermarket, I asked to walk around using my crutch. It was quite nerve racking as I had to read off a list and then check for the aisle to go into and get my items.

There were only five items on the list, but it took me a long time to figure out how to get from one aisle to another. It was almost as if, I had forgotten how to read with lots of people around me, trying to get past etc. even though Miranda and Eleanor were always around me protecting me from the crowds, I felt I would fall, or have a black out. There was a burst of mixed emotions inside me. However, I knew that unless I passed the community test, I would not be ready for discharge, because when I go back into the real world again, I will have to at some point face crowds, lots of people and tight areas.

My legs wobbled like jelly, I held onto one of Miranda's arms as she took me around the aisles to pick up the items, that

I needed to put into my shopping basket. After what seemed like hours in the supermarket, we made our way to the tills, and waited patiently to be served. I gave the money and received the change. I could see the queue at the till as I was trying to put the change back into my purse. One of the coins had fallen down as I tried to take it from the shop assistant. It was difficult to pick the coin up, because my hands are still unable to grip small item properly, all I felt at the time was I was holding up the queue. However, Miranda reassured me that I had just as much right as anyone else and that they would just have to wait for their turn.

Turning bright red like a strawberry, I could feel my cheeks burning hot. I finally managed to take the coin to one of the corners then slide it up to the edge and then finally pick it up as the coin had more height from this angle. I carried out my shopping and sat on the wheelchair for half of the way then I asked if I could try and walk the remaining half of the way with the shopping to see how my body manages walking back a little distance more than usual, with some shopping.

It was worth the try, I managed to walk some of the way then sat back down on the wheelchair as the surface below me felt different to the hospital grounds. The pavement had lots of bumps, there were tree that came in the way, some of the slabs moved up and down. Therefore, I decided it was safer for me to sit down again.

I did think of how many areas I still needed support in as we came back to the RRU. It was easier to achieve goals in the RRU because there were not any real hazards on the way, but in real life there are hazards in every corner, from people, objects, trees cars and many more things. "I have to work really hard now; I can't let my fear of claustrophobia hold me back from facing the real world. Maybe I should make an appointment with Bianca to let her know what is making me so afraid at times. Yes, that is what I will do, once I get a chance." Saying this to myself I felt a burst of positive and hopeful energy run inside me.

After lunch I did some more work on my balance with Ashi supporting me, later this afternoon I went into my circuit group to practice all the usual things. But all that time many things were going round and round in my head. I just wanted to come back to the room where I would be left alone with my pen and paper so that I can make a list of all the things I need to work on before the second of May.

There are only a few weeks left now, I need to make most of all the therapy, and if there are any areas that need further working on, I need to make a start now. But how will I know how many areas there are? today I only found out how difficult it would be in a large store because I went into one, but there could be many more things that I will face where I will struggle. How will I mange then?

I have made a list of things for example, attending an appointment at my GP surgery, which is about thirty steps from my house door, but the street starts going a little uphill as we get to the GP's door. The actual doors are heavy, and they just close quickly with quite a force if it is not held open fully. Right now, my arms are not strong enough yet, to hold onto something and to let myself in at the same time. There is also the issue of going into local grocery stores, the layout is very tight, and people sort of bump into each other all the time because of the tight space.

As I was busy making my list of things to brush up on, I was interrupted by Joe. I had completely forgotten that I was supposed to go to his office at four p.m. We had to discuss the issue with my benefits. I told him that my employment and support allowance had still not been sorted out. It has been over three months; my husband has not been able to go to work because of childcare and we were now at a very tight spot with our financial circumstances. Joe noted everything down and reassured me that he would chase this up, as a matter of urgency now. He also told me that he would come and see me again to complete my disability living allowance application before I left the RRU, just to make sure that payments were not delayed too much after I went back home.

Right now, I fear everything, there is this whole situation with our financial circumstance and how we are going manage as a family because EH is the only person working. I had to leave my job after my maternity period finished during Zara's time, then I was expecting Jannat not too long after that. So, I have been a full-time house mum ever since December 2009.

I am going to have to take care of the children as EH goes to work, but the how will I manage with two such small children on my own, with all my health difficulties. Mum and my sisters can help me out with all my chores, but what will I do when it's evening time. I cannot expect my mum or my sisters to stay over, as I only have a one-bedroom house. EH works evening shifts as he cannot work during the mornings because he prefers working late.

How do I speak to him about changing his shift around? If I say I am struggling, then he will not really understand me. I have always been a person that puts others first before me, I have got on with whatever has come my way. But this time it is different I am physically impaired. How can I fight with my own body? I cannot and that is the truth.

It has not been long since; I spoke about how I will manage when I go back home. That EH wanted me to make an application for my younger sister-in-law to come over from Bangladesh, as my carer. I was really hurt at the time, because since being admitted in hospital I have shown so much bravery, even though I have been constantly scared inside, I have never let it show on my face. I have been positive and hopeful mostly for my family members so that they will not have to worry about me. I am not completely hopeless, I can do most things on my own, I just need a little support along the way that is all.

Already we are struggling for space in the house, now if we have additional member, I will feel out of place, especially with my incontinence issue. I would be absolutely humiliated.

No, I cannot ask him to change his shift around, I will just have to manage with my mum and siblings helping me out. I just need to sort out Zara's routine then I will be okay. I need her to wake up and put her to sleep at proper times then she will eat and drink at the correct times. Yes, that is what I need to try and figure out, without my parents or siblings getting any ideas of my struggles.

I cannot even speak to the doctors or therapists here, then they will try and speak to my husband to try and make him understand, but I do not want that. He will only get upset with me, which will make things worse for me when I go back home. I do not need to be reminded that I am a burden. I know that already.

It is so nice that I can write all these feelings down on paper, I feel like I am conversing with an actual friend, who is just there as a listening ear. I am so glad I can let out what is inside me on paper, at least it is not bottling up inside of me. I feel lighter and happier.

I can speak to my siblings and parents if I wanted to, but they will only worry and try to resolve things for me, but that might not go down well with EH, therefore I cannot involve them in my matters.

Sometimes pretending just works fine with me. I do not have the energy to face any awkward situations right now. Let things just be the way they are. I can only be hopeful that one day things might change for the better, when it comes to the relationship that I share with my husband.

Okay it has been a rollercoaster of a day today; I need to get some sleep now.

12th April 2012

Right, we are now heading for the end of another week, tomorrow evening I will be going back on my weekend home visit. There is just so much that needs doing.

Chris is still off sick, so the planned OT session did not go ahead. After circuit group in the morning, I was joined by Miranda to work on my balance exercises. But this time round she changed things a little, she gave me twenty pounds of weight, which I used to move around on the mat. It was okay to move forwards and to move towards the left-hand side. However, moving backwards was a challenge and it was almost impossible to move towards my right- hand side.

This is something that I must come to terms with on a permanent basis. I need to accept the fact that I will not be able to move my right limbs as well as I could in comparison to my left limbs. It is hard because sometimes I just do not think. When I am given a task, I feel I could just get on with it and do what I must do. Then reality hits me straight away, when I am stationary and even though I can feel some twitching sensations inside of me, I am not actually moving from my positions.

Anyways, Miranda was lovely, she patiently waited whilst I tried and tried to complete the task properly. She also told me not to be so hard on myself. She explained to me, that eventually my health condition will start to make sense to me, and I will learn live with it as part of me.

It is strange how when all this is explained to me, I know and I can understand the logic behind it. Then why does it disappoint me when I try and sort of fail at my task. Am I expecting too much? Is there no chance of a hundred percent recovery? No, I must be grateful that I have come this far, I cannot question myself over and over again. It will only slow me down. I am strong, I will learn to accept this truth.

After lunch I started organising my things to take home for tomorrow. I have one bag full of dirty laundry, and this time I am going to challenge myself to start and finish a washing cycle myself. My thoughts were interrupted by Miranda, who now after Nikki leaving, has become my keyworker, which is great because I feel comfortable discussing things with her, as I have a certain level of comfort talking to Miranda. She understands what I am feeing and what is worrying me. I do miss Nikki a lot, but I am so glad that Miranda took over from her as I did not want to start discussing my situation with someone who really has not seen me progress over the months. Miranda has seen me at my worst and now she is seeing me at my best.

In key working session, I talked about how I felt this week, about going home and the types of challenges I am going to try out. Miranda mentioned the use of different types of equipment I may need to settle in properly. I already have the bath board, the raised toilet seat, but I will need grab rails and stair rails to support me further. I may also need a commode, all this information will be passed onto my local adult social services, who will put things in place when I return home permanently.

I am tired today, even though I have not been as active as yesterday, I can feel myself feeling tense and there is a strange tightening feeling around my chest. I just cannot stop worrying about how I will manage in the future. I want to do things for my family, I do not want to end up becoming a burden on them.

Last week when I went home, I had the best time being with the people I loved. The comfort of holding my children, being able to feel their tiny hands in mine. However, I spent a few hours during the day, to rest my body too. I found the whole experience so overwhelming, and my body just did not manage to keep up with my mind.

The most important thing for me is to not let my husband notice that I am getting tired, I need to show that I will be fine once I am discharged from hospital. Once he notices that I am still weak, it will not take him long to make me feel guilty that things in our lives have changed so much because of me. Already I have had to hear remarks about paying for hefty parking tickets, to come and visit me every other second day. After which I told him to only come once a week, it does not matter that I am here all on my own without any family. I have my health care team and my patient friends to keep me company.

Though, to be honest, it does hurt me so much every evening when all the next of kin would come to see the other patients in the ward. Whilst I have to pretend that I needed to go to the library or the garden, just so I did not have to be present in a room, being the only one with no one there for me.

Why is everything so complicated? I wish I can just shake this horrible feeling off. However, I need to remain positive, I have to understand that I am not a burden, it is the duty of a spouse to look after his or her other half, relationships are not a one-way thing. I cannot let the traditional norms scare me, not right now. There are so many husbands here that are travelling a far greater distance, compared to Luton to London, yet they come everyday and with all the necessary things that their partner needs. They never utter a word that would make their partner feel guilty.

Although, no matter how much I console myself, the truth is throughout this whole process, our communication has been broken down even more than before. I am scared, I cannot talk to anyone about this, I just wish there is some way in which I could make him realise that even though I have been through a life changing transition. I have remained optimistic and full of hope.

I have not complained about my situation or been grumpy about it in front of family or guests. Even though deep down inside of me I am scared, very scared. I have not let these fears show on my face. I have been positive and always smiled whenever I have had visitors. Surely this must have been noticed. I deserve some credit, don't I? for not being a pessimist or being depressed.

I have always worked on myself to remain hopeful by holding onto my faith. Why can he not notice these things, I know that he has had to come and visit me at the hospital every week and take my dirty laundry home to wash, but that was a choice he made as he did not want me to wash the laundry here at the hospital. When I found out that the frequent visits to the hospital were becoming burdensome to him, I asked him to come once a week only, just so he can bring me clean clothes and toiletries.

He has also been doing the house chores for the last few months, but he is only taking care of one child, my mum has also taken on board full time childcare. Jannat is always with my mum, and a little baby needs much more attention than a two-year-old.

In addition, my mum is also cooking for EH and Zara every week sending cooked meals in containers to last the whole week. All he needs to do is just warm it up and cook some rice to go with it. My family are lending their support a hundred percent, surely, he can see how they will always be there for me.

What is most upsetting for me right now is, I spoke to my mother-in-law on the phone a few days ago and after asking me the usual things about my health, she started telling me how she felt sorry for EH, who now is having to look after a child all on his own along with doing the household chores. As he had never had to do any house chores whilst growing up in Bangladesh, someone always attended to all his needs, and now here he was being a full-time dad.

As I am writing this, I cannot stop the hot tears from falling down my cheeks, I mean I am going through so much and yet indirectly I am being told that I am responsible for what is happening.

Why am I not able to stand up for myself when it comes to this weak marriage of mine, for the last six years I have compromised, changed, adapted, and tried to mould myself the way that is expected of me. I even gave up a job that was bringing me good money home, not to mention the people that I loved to work with, they always reminded me of my self-worth. Yet today I am the one that is being made to feel responsible for our circumstances. I did not choose for this to happen, things have led for my body to suffer this shock, and now here I am suffering the consequences of something that was not my fault. But am I complaining? In fact, I am constantly looking at the bright side, motivating myself, finding reasons to be happy about.

Lost in my thoughts, I was suddenly, startled by Joe's entry into our room. He noticed that I had been crying and immediately sat down on the chair next to me to ask me what was going on. Like always I just smiled and came up with the perfect excuse that because I had not managed to complete my tasks at physio session today, I was really upset, especially with my discharge date coming close by.

As I spoke to Joe, I hid the pages I was writing on as I did not want him to accidently take a glance at what I was writing. We discussed the situation on housing and my benefits. I was told that we were still waiting to hear from the job centre on the status of the application. When Joe left the room, I carefully took the pages I was writing on and hid them inside an envelope.

I must be more careful not to get carried away when I am writing, I need to be aware of my surroundings. The last thing I want is the team getting a hint of what I am really worried about, then they will have word with my husband and that would make things worse for when I return home. Because there is one truth that is bigger than anything else right now and that is, I need to keep my family's unity. I do not want the children to suffer from any more uncertainty. They have been through a lot and I cannot make things worse.

13th April 2012

During physio session today, I had to use flowerpots and move them in different areas of the mat, sometimes on its own and sometimes using a towel to wrap around it. The idea behind this exercise was to see how I will manage on my knees using my balancing skills, whilst bending forward to move the flowerpot, pretending that the flowerpot is one of my girls. Obviously, children do not sit or lie still on the ground, they fidget and move, so I had to see how quickly I get tired trying to keep up with a moving child, especially when it comes to changing nappies etc. I am glad I have done this exercise because I really got the feel of how tingly my body feels when I am on my knees whilst trying to do two other things in that position. I can see it will be a challenge, but I need to practice my floor squat exercises in my own time, so that I can build up my stamina.

I joined everyone back in the room to get the rest of my packing done for the weekend. The girls got picked up before lunch, so I was on my own during lunch. I watched little bit of TV to keep myself company. After returning to my room, I read my book for an hour. I then went down for a walk in the garden, today it has been a little bit breezy, so I had to hold onto things like bench tops, tree branches to keep myself up. It is strange how a little wind can take me off course. But at least that is something I now know, and I can take that feedback, back to my therapists.

It is as if I am discovering something new each day, that makes me vulnerable for when I am ready to go back into the real world. I am more grateful now than ever before that I am learning things and appreciating them much more, sometimes we just get on with life without thinking twice that if our health is compromised in any way how will we manage?

I was picked up around four p.m. to go home, one of the nurses came and handed me my medicines to take home.

Once I came to Luton, I wanted to see the children first, so I went to my mum's house to see Jannat and to pick up Zara at the same time. I did not sit for long at mum's, she had already laid out my dinner because I had mentioned that I want to keep to the RRU's eating routine for now otherwise it causes a problem for my bowels.

I spent some time with Jannat after dinner, then mum took her from me to make sure she eats her dinner on time. I was pleased to see that Jannat has a timetabled routine; I want to start getting Zara used to a better routine too. This is one of the first things I will explore after I come home for good.

I said goodbye to my family, Jannat will be staying with mum up until I come home for good, as we do not want both children having to deal with uncertainty for now, plus I am still trying to get used to the lack of space we have in the bedroom. It is going to be extremely difficult with three people sharing a bed with a cot bed almost stuck to the bed.

I need to speak to housing association to rehouse us as a matter of urgency, otherwise I might just end up hurting myself if I were to lose my balance. There is just so much to do, to get life back on track. I think I might need to make a list of things to do and start ticking off what I have done and what I need to do and prioritise them accordingly.

Okay Zara has just come into the room she looks extremely excited to take her things out of the chest of drawers. I better go and help her.

14th April 2012

I woke up at 6.30 a.m. and completed my morning routine, I came back into the room and woke up Zara, as I did not want to eat breakfast on my own today. I helped her to make sure she brushes her teeth properly and washed her face. After we both moisturised our faces, we came down. I switched on the telly for Zara and went into the kitchen.

I asked Zara if she wanted to eat toast and butter, or Weetabix. As usual she chose Weetabix. I made myself a cup of tea and two slices of toast. I had to bring in every item one by one to the table, as I have to hold my stick with one hand, so both my hands are not free at the same time whilst I am in standing position.

After breakfast I wanted to sort out the clothes that were on the drying rails. I dragged the rail and placed it near the sofa. I then sat down on the sofa so that I could use both my hands. It is simpler doing it this way as I can get all the folding done into different piles and have them ready to go into their designated areas.

I used one of Zara's clear plastic toy box to place all the items so that I could use it as a trolley to move around the different areas of the house. I am glad that this method worked, otherwise all my folding would have gone to waste if I had just left them on the sofa as I have a very inquisitive Zara following me around. It is quite nice because she finds it funny when I drag the box to different parts of the house.

After an eventful start to the day, I sat down to watch some telly with Zara, she talked me through every program, and I had a lot of questions to answer. I then rested until 10.30 a.m. once EH woke up he had his breakfast whilst I went to take my shower. After I was done, EH gave Zara her shower and then went to have his own shower. It was lunch time by the time everyone had finished getting ready.

After eating lunch, we went into town to see if I can handle some shopping, I have to admit it was a little adventurous at this stage, but I am glad I tested the waters to see how it would be like. I must admit usually I would do anything to go shopping, I love looking around the home and children section. However, today I just wanted to come home as soon as I could. The crowds, the feeling of being lost in a circle of people, was constantly on my mind as I went from shop to shop.

I was really exhausted by the time I went to my mums, to see Jannat. I told mum that I would be leaving for the hospital early tomorrow morning, so I will not be saying goodbye in the morning. I spent as much time as I could with Jannat because I will not see her until next week now.

I had dinner at mum's, to maintain my routine, but EH and Zara came home to eat theirs later. I have come upstairs now to write my account for today. Zara will be up soon, as soon as she has had her dinner. I am going to watch something on the laptop with her once she gets changed for bed. I just hope I can stay awake; I am really tired, and it is only 8.45 p.m. right now.

15th April 2012

It is beginning to take its toll on me, that I am coming home to my family only to go back to the hospital again. I do not like to create uncertainty for my children anymore, Zara keeps asking me if I am going to stay with her. It is hard for me to give her an answer, I do not know what to say, because every time we see each other, it's only for a short time. I know I need to complete my treatment and I have so many areas to work on before I come home permanently, but I do not like seeing my children sad. It is because of them that I have managed to come this far.

I have always focused on, that the sooner I get better the sooner I can come home to my children. I miss their touch, the warmth of their body next to mine as we cuddle down to read a book, or to watch the telly. For now, I am on my own when it comes to reading or watching the telly.

My thoughts had slowed me down today. I have so many questions which I know have no actual answers to, because no one really knows how my condition will affect me and my life. It all depends on my will power and my attitude to living with and accepting the fact that I now have a permanent neurological disorder. That will influence the way I live for the rest of my life.

I did not do many tasks at home today, because I felt overly emotional, and I was trying to put up a brave face for everyone else so that my worries did not show on my face. I had the mask of a permanent smile on me, I talked as if there was nothing bothering me. I spent the morning collecting all my things and preparing myself to return to the hospital.

16th April 2012

I woke up early, had my shower and headed for my circuit group session. It was only me and Kathleen. Melanie and Dina will not be scheduled for all the circuit group sessions from now onwards, as they are due to be discharged before me.

Chris is back at work, so I did have OT session with her today. I filled her in on what I had been doing in her absence. I asked if I could focus on bending and lifting today. As this is what I find most challenging when I go home for my visits. My balance is quite not there yet.

We headed into the kitchen, I tried where I could, to not use the grab rails when I bent down as far down as I could. It was very tricky because after a few attempts my legs started to feel wobbly which resulted in me losing my balance.

After an exhausting OT session, I had physio with Mick, where I had to practice my floor exercises. I bent down towards the ground balancing on my knees, picking objects up from the mat, such as bowls and cups.

By the time it was evening I was shattered, these days I am mainly aiming to perfect my floor and balance exercise, as the reality is, that I will be running around after two small children when I return home, so I need to build up my muscles.

17ᵗʰ April 2012

The morning was extremely exciting, I had the orthotics clinic, where my walking was examined with and without my splint. Moulds were taken of both my feet, as I have an arch shape beneath my toes which makes it difficult to put pressure on the ground when I am standing. The moulds taken will help create insoles that will help me put that pressure on and hopefully I will stand more firmly once they go into my shoes. I need to wait a week for them to arrive.

Today I really enjoyed being in the quiz group as we quizzed the quiz masters with our questions. It was Melanie's idea because today's quiz session was her and Dina's last time being in the group.

In the OT kitchen I made some delicious jam scones, following a recipe that Sheena (one of the HCA who had been watching over me for the last few weeks in the kitchen) had brought in for me, it was her mum's recipe and a good one too. The scones were appreciated very much by my friends and the staff. I was grateful that Sheena shared the recipe with me. It was kind of her to bring it in after the conversation, I had with her last week, when she was helping me putting on my splint.

After OT I was timetabled for physio straight after, where I was working on my balance exercises again. I used weights to move from one part on the mat to another. I then had to hold Ashi's hand and walk bare foot across the gym.

I had time for a quick rest break which lasted half an hour

before I had to head in for my OT session with Chris. We decided that today we will focus on perfecting my ironing skills, I reluctantly got all the things together onto the table. I do not particularly like ironing as my hands tingle a lot especially when I must hold on the iron for a long duration of time.

I find it difficult with holding and sliding an object from one side to another. It is not an extremely comfortable feeling. Today I tried ironing from both standing and sitting. Both methods were a little uncomfortable, but I felt more safe by sitting, as the iron did not balance on the iron board, but on the table, which is more sturdy.

After lunch I had my meeting with Joe who updated me on my benefits situation.

18th April 2012

Eleanor and I went into Sainsbury's today. I volunteered to do some shopping for Melanie, who has a cooking session on Friday. As the weather was not nice today, Eleanor thought it would be best if I did not try to walk to the supermarket today. As well as being cloudy it was quite windy so taking my safety into account, Eleanor used the wheelchair to take me there.

Once we got there, she parked my wheelchair to a side, and I was allowed to walk inside the market. I had brought a list with me, I took things from the shelves and placed them in the trolley. I was using the trolley as my walking aid, like a rollator frame to help me stand up straight and balance. I had placed my walking stick inside the trolley, this is to teach me ways to use my aids correctly once I leave the hospital and if for any reason, I was to go into the supermarket, I could feel independent whilst I shop.

Today we decided a different method to pay for the items, last time I queued at the tills and felt a little nervous. So today Eleanor decided that I should try the self-checkout. This not only saved time as the queues were shorter and moved more quickly, but there was space around me, I was not directly facing customers after me. The fact that they were behind me and I could not see them helped me because the last time I could see them whilst I was packing my bag. Which made me nervous, as I felt I was holding up a big queue.

Eleanor pushed me on my chair back to the RRU, when I

returned to our room, I found out that Kathleen had been taken in for her operation. I put the shopping inside the kitchen cupboards and informed Melanie all her ingredients had been put away, ready for her to use on Friday. I then had a quick half an hour rest before joining the girls for lunch at the day room.

After lunch, I went to find Ashi for my physio session. It was a successful session today; I had finally managed to do my sit to stand exercises without using my hands to help me lift from the chair. I also did my knee raises on the mat. When I finished my session with Ashi, I joined the circuit group. I did some cycling on the bike, followed by walking up and down the steps. I then did the extension exercises on the parallel bars and finished on the treadmill.

I had to take a quick nap before dinner this evening as I felt over exhausted with the increasing number of exercises I have to do these days. It is getting so much more intense now. There is always a full timetable and I always have the exercises that I dislike and find most difficult, scheduled more than often.

19th April 2012

Kathleen is still recovering from her operation yesterday. As I would have been on my own in circuit group today, Dina was asked to join me. We worked through everything we had learned. We both knew where we needed to practise a little more and where our strong areas were. I am now taking notes every time I have a session just so I can discuss options with my therapists.

In my OT session I requested to do some more of the bending exercises, as my wobbly legs, is a big concern for me. Especially with the room that I have in my house, I need to make sure that I manage to bend and get up in tinier spaces.

Eleanor was pleased with the progress I have made with my hands; I am able to hold on and pick up objects better than I had in the previous months. She has now moved me onto the next colour of the thera putty, I am now going to use the pink putty, which is quite a bit more tougher than the yellow one I was using previously. I am only to use my right hand, as my left hand is stronger than the right, so I need to work out the right hand more.

In my afternoon physio session today, I really enjoyed myself. Mick gave me a tray and asked me to walk slowly around the gym, pretending that the area we were walking in, was the area in my kitchen. I then had to place objects on the tray, pretending it was food and drink. To make the role play session a little bit more difficult, Mick placed skittles in some of the area. I had to make sure that I balanced the tray with the objects and walked past the skittles holding the tray. Making sure that I did not trip or drop the tray.

It was quite amusing because the skittles were supposed to be my daughters, when I told Mick that in reality the children would be moving around me and not staying still, he reassured me that once I got the hang of balancing and holding things in my hands, we would move onto the next step. At this stage we had to make sure that I was really strong in the exercises that were given to me.

I am so happy that my therapists have really considered all the feedback I have given to them after my home visits. This way my exercises are now being structured for my individual needs. I suppose this is what is happening with all the patients who are going on their home visits. I now understand why it is so important to have these visits, it is the final preparation before we are discharged permanently. Then we are on our own to deal with all the challenges and hardships.

I feel incredibly grateful that we have this opportunity. The staff are simply remarkable. They are putting in so much hard work and time, to cater for each individual. I just want to thank all the NHS staff across the country, as it is not always easy to see how much they are doing but staying in hospital for so many months now I can see exactly what they are doing.

One member of staff is having to attend four to six patients in an hour. Right from the start of day, lifting us from when we were completely immobile, to changing, washing, and dressing us. Giving us our medication on time, making sure we are completing our exercises. Sometimes due to the nature of the patient's mobility level, two members of staff are required to attend to them, at the same time like when having to do the transfers, giving showers etc. The list goes on, once one shift finishes, the evening staff come in and work throughout the night. The most amazing part is that the staff never get flustered, they always have a smile on their face and reassurance in what they say. It makes staying in hospital a less scary experience.

I finished my day with key working session. I spoke to Miranda about the situation with DVLA, my housing issues and generally how life would be like returning home.

20th April 2012

It was a very emotional day today. It was Melanie and Dina's last day at the RRU. I am really happy for them, but I will miss having them around. It is only a couple of weeks before I, myself go home, but I will really miss my friends. I will especially miss discussing the Apprentice with Melanie every Wednesday night.

It has been quite funny actually, at first it was only me watching the show as it has been one my favourite shows since 2007. Melanie asked me one night what I was watching, and I explained the format of the show to her. From then on, she joined me to watch the show when it came on. Sometimes it would clash with the football, some patients would want to take over the remote as they wanted to watch the footy, but after much debate and discussions, myself and Melanie managed to persuade the others to try watching the Apprentice and see how entertaining it actually was. To our surprise four others have joined us to watch it every Wednesday.

From now on 'You're fired' has become our favourite phrase we have a laugh and joke about it when we are in the gym. Even the staff who follow the program join in our conversations, we are all extremely excited to find out who will win in the end.

I helped Melanie make breakfast in the OT kitchen, we all enjoyed this last breakfast together and exchanged gifts with one another. It was agreed that we should try and stay in touch.

We understand how busy life could get, but we want to try and keep each other updated on our progress.

After sharing an emotional group hug, laughing, and crying at the same time, we made our way to the sink to wash up and dry all the dishes ourselves. As we had made the breakfast, it was up to us to clear away everything after us. I washed the dishes whilst Melissa dried them. After we had put all the things back in their right places, I headed off to my physio session at 9.30 a.m.

I was on the treadmill to start off. I then went to do my balance exercises. I sort of had an idea where the main focus would be today after my previous session with Mick. I had to walk with a tray in my right hand which I balanced on my waist, by placing my right hand beneath the tray from centre position. This method ensured that the tray did not wobble, like it would have if I had just held it from the side. Plus, it was more comfortable for me, as the weight of the tray was divided on both sides. The only one obstacle I faced was I could not see my toes, which is something I always look at when I take steps, it helps me see what is in front of me. With the tray balanced on my waist, my toes got covered, so I had to take baby steps to move forward.

To make the workout even more difficult, I was asked to place a ball on my tray and walk from the gym into my bay. I had Mick on my side at all times but being watched as the ball rolled from one side of the tray to the other, also made me nervous. However, I did manage to come into my room and impress the girls with my new completed challenge. They all clapped for me, which was quite overwhelming.

The time had come when, Melanie and Dina said goodbye to everyone, it was a happy and sad moment, happy because they could now return to their routine. However, I will miss them so much, the last month we had grown even more closer to one another because we were sharing a room together, and we were known as the loud and noisy room, because someone was always laughing or telling a joke. Our room was so lively. Now things would be different, I know Kathleen will miss them even more, as she has been with them longer than I.

After the girls went home, I got my things ready to go home for the weekend. As I was packing, Joe came to see me to update me on the situation with my benefits. He told me he had spoken to someone in the jobcentre regarding my claim. He told me he would send a letter to them to put things in writing, regarding why he thought that the amount I was currently receiving is incorrect.

After lunch I had to have another full assessment led by Miranda and Eleanor. It is good that I am improving every time they come and do a new assessment.

Finally, I was picked up 5.30 p.m., for my third visit home. I am excited and looking forward to what I can do tomorrow. I want to try my tray and balance exercise, let us see how I do.

23rd April 2012

The weekend did not pan out as I had planned, Zara had caught a cold and she was not feeling very well. I spent most of my weekend taking care of her. This is the first time in months she has had mummy to take care of her when she has been feeling under the weather.

Hence, I did not come back to the RRU as I was supposed to yesterday evening, I spoke to the management on the phone and asked if I could stay one more night. I was allowed but told to return before my afternoon medications were due today. We are only given a limited amount of medication to take home for the weekend so returning on time is particularly important. However, as my daughter was unwell in front of my eyes, I did not have the heart to leave her when she needed me to be there for her.

I have to admit though, as we have a timetable for everything here at the RRU, I am so used to this routine. Before going home for the weekend, I had made a mental timetable of how I was going to utilise my time. Nevertheless, what I have learned is sometimes, things will happen, which is beyond our control and we must face these situations in the best way possible.

I also had to divide my attention between both girls. I felt that as I was giving a lot of my time to Zara to see if she is okay. Jannat would look at me with her big eyes wondering why I was paying so much attention to Zara.

Just before I fell ill, I had worked out a way to make both children feel they were equally important to me, but back then Jannat was still a baby, and I was getting Zara used to having another child in the house. However, fast forward four months, Jannat has grown up a little bit more and she understands what is happening around her. So, I must be careful of how divide my attention between both the girls. Plus, I need to be more careful with Jannat's feeling because she has been with my mum the whole time, since I have been in hospital, so she needs to feel the same love and attention when she is with me. Therefore, my biggest challenge has been to reassure both my girls that mummy loves them both, but mummy is struggling just a little for now. "No matter how much we plan, or have timetables in place, sometimes things beyond our expectations, will take place. I just need to be ready to incorporate those moments as they come my way."

I came back to the RRU at one p.m., just in time for my medication. I had already grabbed something to eat before I left the house. I felt terribly upset when I came back today, for many reasons, firstly because I had to leave my children behind, secondly because Melanie and Dina would not be in RRU anymore, thirdly because when I arrived, I was told I would have to move beds and go to where Dina was, which is good in some way because the bathroom is right next to it. But all I can feel right now is the cards and messages she used to have on her bedside. It feels odd being in her place. Kathleen is still recovering so it is incredibly quiet.

All of a sudden there is so much silence all around. The new patient who arrived tonight is similar to the way I was when I first came to the RRU. I think this is what is scaring me even more. I am placed opposite to her and all I feel is if I am looking into a mirror of the past. What if I go back to being like that again? What if I cannot move, walk, or do things properly again? I am scared it is only a matter of days before I get discharged and I have this scary feeling going round and round at the bottom of my stomach, making me feeling sick.

I found dividing my attention between the girls was the biggest challenge, because I did not want to hurt neither of their feelings. On top I am not always feeling a hundred percent. How am I going to take care of myself to make sure I do not fall ill again and manage the emotions of my girls? Till now I have not been hit by this realisation. However, the experience of being home this weekend has brought forward new challenges. Till now I was only focussing on physical strength, physical ability to get things done. What I have missed is how am I going to face the mental and emotional needs of everyone in my family.

I went to do some more research on my condition and looked through the support forums of people who are now living their normal lives yet facing certain challenges. All the research has reassured me that there is always help out there such as adult social services, the council, doctors etc.

However, the one thing I was hoping to find more information on, was how a parent such as myself manages with a health condition as well going back to looking after two incredibly young children. Unfortunately, there was not much information on that side, because most people are either over fifty, or between eighteen and twenty-three. So, most of the people either had children that had grown up and are able to look after themselves, or some do not even have children. I do not fall into either category I am twenty-nine with two young children.

Well, I must not despair, next time I will do more research on people that have similar condition to mine and see what I can find. There are many support forums on the net. I just need to persevere and focus on my search. I am sure I will be able to get some sort of help.

When I speak to the doctors and nurses here, they all tell me the same thing, that every patient is different and every patient has a different lifestyle, so it is difficult to categorise patients and their recovery levels. I do understand all this, yet I am panicking from inside.

I need to stay strong and positive; I will leave as planned on the day planned and I will manage my life as best as I can. I am stronger than I believe. Right, I cannot write anymore. I am tired now and I need to rest.

24th April 2012

I did a hot and cold test today. It was interesting because I have had this test when I first came here, and certain areas of my body can feel the different temperatures but certain cannot. For example, I can feel temperature from my elbow down to my wrist, yet the inside of my hands and my fingertips struggle to identify the different temperatures. Once the temperature test was done, I had the 'feel' test. Different types of objects and materials were stroked against my face, neck, arms, and hands. I am still struggling to cope with smooth materials like silk, marble, and plastic as the feel of these things on my skin, make me feel very tingly and the pins and needles starts dancing around inside of me. What has surprised me though is, I can cope much better with the prickly and rough objects on my skin. The best way I can describe the feel of those is like having one of those massage machines, that vibrate on the surface of the skin. I was told that my body and skin react in this way because of the level of nerve damage.

For my physiotherapy we tried something new, I walked on grass, again this was like a 'feel' test. I am and have been managing to walk on tiled floors, concrete floors, and carpets. But grass is a little different from the above. Sometimes grass is dry and non-slippery, but sometimes is moist because of the rain and could be slippery, the issue is sometimes it is long and sometimes cut short. With this experience today, I realised that I do not struggle as much to feel the harder surfaces beneath the splint and shoe. But the grass is very tricky, I am not sure when I have placed my foot down without looking at my feet.

25th April 2012

During the morning for both my OT and physiotherapy session I had to go through more assessments. These are the same assessments that were done upon my admission to the RRU. The assessments were necessary to compare the strength of my limbs for before and after being treated here. The good news is the left side is a lot more stronger, the right side still needs working on, and it is a matter of continuing with the discipline to exercise regularly and make sure the muscles get their workout. I have been briefed on how I can fit in my exercises in between my busy schedule of being a full-time mum.

The rest of my day has been pretty much the same as before where I have focused on my stretches, balancing, walking, and cycling.

In key working session, my discussion on the housing issue continued. Miranda made all the notes and reassured me the housing association will be updated on my situation, however the possibility of getting housed into a suitable property for my needs. All depended on what the housing association have available in the areas I am wishing to move into. The main obstacle that I have in my head at the moment is how safe would it be for me to move to Milton Keynes?

26th April 2012

It has been like a revision day today. I started with transfers from bed to chair, then sit to stands without using my hands to help me. Then we went through all the hip extension and stretch exercises. I had to do my balance exercises, moving on the mat picking objects up and down as I did so. I tried to tip toeing, which was one of the harder ones that I still am not able to do. Even when I am holding onto the parallel bars, I am telling myself that I am going to tiptoe. However, when I look down at my legs, they stay where they are, the good news is I can feel the tremor in the legs, which means the message is getting there, it is only the strength in them that is preventing them to do as told.

OT session was also the same, this time focussing on the upper limbs. I had to push my hands out, pull them towards me again, followed by some other moves, such as wrist flexion and extension, where I had to move my wrist up and down, whilst Eleanor tried to move it inwards and outwards as necessary and I had to try and stop her from doing so.

I had to also do some finger flexion and extension. This is where I stretched open my hand then closed it again into a ball shape. The most difficult exercise was where I had to touch each finger with my thumb, this still feels tingly and uncomfortable, but I managed to touch each finger for both my hands. Each part of my arms and hands, were given a mark, and these were compared to the marks given to them upon my admission to the RRU.

27th April 2012

Today was just the same as the previous days, in terms of exercises. I did make some coconut barfi's in the OT kitchen and had quite an experience. Whilst shaping the barfi's and coating them in the coconut. I managed to knock over the bowl which had the desiccated coconut in it. It took me over ten minutes to clear away the mess. As all the little bits of coconut was really fiddly to pick up even though I gathered all of it into one pile I had to slide the whole lot to the edge of the table where I held a plastic plate with my left hand, and I used my right hand with the cotton cloth to sweep all the coconut onto the plate.

However, as I tried do this, I lost my hand coordination. For a second, I lost my balance and my hand moved away from the edge of the table, but it was too late as the right hand already made its move, which resulted in all the mess to fall onto the ground.

As this point it was too difficult for me to try and pick up all the little pieces without tripping. So, I had to call for someone to help me clear up the mess. It was quite a drama, I felt very embarrassed at the trouble I had caused, but if that was not all, when I started to clear away after I had finished making the barfi's. I went on to make a bigger mess when I did the washing up.

I had put all the bowls, utensils, and trays inside the sink, just so I could clear away the rest of the table and then come back to the sink as that would only leave me with the washing up. In my past OT Kitchen sessions this has worked perfectly for me. But today I forgot to take out some of the things from the sink and place them on the side. So, what happened was, I turned on the taps with a little too much pressure and the water came out and hit the object inside the sink causing it to splatter everywhere.

As soon as I realised what happened I turned off the taps, but because for a few seconds my mind went into shock of what was happening the tap was left on for longer than I had thought. So, all of my top was wet along with water dripping down the sink onto the floor. Luckily for me, Lindsay was going past the kitchen and saw what had just happened. She straight away took out the hazard sign and left it at the front of the kitchen so no one else would go inside. She then carefully walked me back to my room to get changed out of the dripping wet clothes.

Whilst I did that, Lindsay went back and cleaned all the mess I had made. I sat on my bed feeling terribly upset, without making any sounds, I could not stop crying. Tears flooding my face. Lindsay must have informed Eleanor and Miranda of what had happened, so it was not long before they both came to see me to find out what was going on as I am normally not that clumsy. I explained that I could not really tell what had happened, but it just did, it was almost as if my brain was sending the messages, but my body was not cooperating very well.

I was reassured by both of my therapists, that all the stress and anxiety I have been building up inside of me, might be a cause of what had just happened rather than me losing my strength again. They told me it was normal to feel anxious and worried about the future, especially one where we have to cope with a health condition. After a while I started feeling better again and soon cheered up. I went to find Lindsay to thank her for cleaning up for me, I then went back to my room to pack my bags ready to come home this evening.

28th April 2012

After the day I had yesterday, I was incredibly happy to be home today. It is the 28th of April, my wedding anniversary. My goodness me, it has been six years, how time flies by, I cannot believe how much life has changed in the past six years. I started my day making breakfast followed by doing the house chores. I washed a machine of clothes and managed to put them on the drier rails myself.

After lunch we went to Asda with the children to stock up. It was very tiring as walking in and out of the isles was exhausting. When I went shopping with Miranda and Eleanor back at the RRU, I only had to find a few items on a list. However, today we bought nappies, wipes, baby milk and all the other household shopping.

I held Zara's hand with my right had whilst I held onto my crutch with my left hand. EH pushed the trolley with the shopping, with Jannat sitting on the trolley seat. Zara moved me from one side to another excitedly, I had to make sure I always maintained my balance. It was so tiring, usually I love shopping, but now I just seem to despise it. I was so tired; I can still feel my legs wobbling from the experience.

I went to see my mum after shopping so that I can leave Jannat with her again. Whilst at my mums, myself and Zara had our dinner there. Mum could tell I was really tired and suggested that I have dinner and feed Zara too, so all I have to do when I come home is get into my pyjamas and go to bed.

That is exactly the advice I am going to follow, so that is all for today dear journal, see you again tomorrow.

29th April 2012

It has not been a hugely different day today. I woke up and had breakfast with Zara. I made EH's breakfast and covered it up so that when he woke up all he had to do was warm it up. After my shower I helped get Zara ready so that we could have lunch and go and see Jannat before I came back to the RRU.

30th April 2012

As it is my second last day here at the RRU all my exercises have been repetitive. In circuit group I was with Martine going through all my floor and balance exercises. With Mick I went over all the sit to stand and transfer exercises.

During the afternoon I made vegetable and bean kebabs for everyone. It was quite emotional as all the staff praised my cooking skills, they told me that they would miss having me cook and share the food I made.

I went into the computer room in the evening, as I wanted to leave the RRU with the satisfaction that I had thanked everyone.

I have been able to say goodbye to most of the staff members. But there are a lot who I will not see now. Hence, I decided to write a letter to thank every person, that I came into contact with whilst getting treated here at the RRU. It was an emotional roller coaster as I remembered how each and every one of the staff at the RRU involved in my care had taken the absolute best care that they possibly could have.

From being there for my physical needs, to helping me calm down when the nerves got the better of me. I was never left feeling alone, I was always encouraged that I should make good recovery. In some ways this was the family I had supporting me in the last three months, it is going to be hard to say goodbye. On top of everything I am a little bit of a drama queen, so it's going to be a loud, crazy goodbye. I want to leave with the satisfaction that everyone remembers me as a strong-willed person.

1st May 2012

I went and returned all the books I had borrowed from the RRU library. I looked at the small room one last time. This had been my area to relax and destress in the last few months. I do not know how I would have passed my time if this library was not here. There were only a limited number of books, but I enjoyed reading by the little window and went through the journey of the characters in the books. It has been an amazing experience. Nowadays there are a lot of people who enjoy reading e-books and have many different apps to read them from. But for me it is not the same as picking up a book and going through the pages.

I spent most of my day taking off all the notes and cards from the side of my bed. My friends had sent me cards with motivational and inspiring messages which I want to take away with me and keep forever.

I returned some of the things that I did not need any more to Eleanor, such as the grabber to pick things up from lower down. I have practiced my bending, balancing, and picking things up from the ground and wish to continue to carry on doing so without any help.

I have been on a walk, around the ward to go and see all the patients that I have made friends with to say goodbye. I also said goodbye to a lot of the staff members.

It has been an emotionally draining day. I am not sure what the future holds for me, but I am leaving the RRU with big dreams and high hopes. To be as normal as possible and to accept the new me and move forward. Things will never be the same for me again, my whole life is going to get affected by my condition, but I must make the most of it. I can still enjoy my life if I want to. I cannot let negativity feed through my brain. I know there will be times when the going will get tough.

But I have full faith in Allah, that he will bestow his mercy upon me and guide me through the difficulties. I need to choose what I want. I cannot look back and wish what could have been. I need to look forward and see what can be.

2nd May 2012

I woke up and did my final bit of packing and then spent the whole morning going and saying goodbye to all the staff who were here. I gave my thank you letter to Sue and told her to read it at the staff meeting after I left.

It is funny how I felt that instant. When I first came to the RRU I was crying because I did not know how things will work out for me. But today when I am leaving, I feel sad to leave behind all the people who have cared for me unconditionally. I shall never forget the kindness and love these staff members have shown me. It is because of their love and care that I am able to be a part of my family again, who I am finally reunited with forever hopefully.

I waited till noon before I was picked up for the last time. I walked out of the building being escorted by Eleanor who helped my husband take out all my belongings and wheelchair. The car boot was packed with so many things, wheelchairs, walking aids, medication my suitcase.

This is it from here a new journey begins and this time I am on my own.

I did not say much in the car as I did not know what to say. I was happy and sad at the same time. Happy because I can be with my girls forever. Sad because I did not know if my disability will be seen as a burden.

"Phew, finally I have managed to read through my scruffy handwriting and provide you, who is reading this book. With an insight of what I had been feeling and went through when I was in the hospitals. It has been a long journey. But I am glad and grateful that I lived through that. It has made me stronger than I could have ever imagined."

As I started getting back into the normality of my life and routine, I was unable to write a daily account of what I had done or achieved, but I used to write every now and then of anything new I felt I had been through.

May 2012 - March 2014

My struggles did not end with the Regional Rehab Unit (RRU). I went through the real ordeal when I was back at home. I did not manage to keep a journal after my return to home. For several reasons, I jumped into full time mummy mode and started picking up the pieces from where I had left.

The first biggest task for me was to rebuild my relationship with my girls. There were so many things that I needed to know and understand about their routine to help me figure out where I stand with them. It was easy to start getting close to Zara again because she knew who I was and she also visited me at the hospital every week, until I started coming over for the weekend visits and we spent more time together.

Jannat on the other hand was finding it difficult to be without my mum. She was only four months when my mum had taken charge to look after her for me till I got back from the hospital. But in all this Jannat did not really know that I am her mum. I feel she had started to think her gran was her mum. I spent weeks building the comfort level between myself and Jannat. She was not used to waking up and seeing me in the morning. She would look around the room and at the door. I could understand that she was looking for my mum. On days when my mum would visit. Jannat would almost run towards her and forget that I was waiting for her.

The next problem I faced was trying to divide my attention between both girls, I tried hard to be as fair as possible, but during the initial days it was more than hard. When I sat and played with Zara and asked Jannat to join in, she would want to do something else. If I tried to please Jannat and do as she wanted, then Zara would get upset. It was a task and a half, but after couple of weeks when the dust had settled. The children got into a routine. They were happy to see me around all the time and they had started to get into a routine that worked with mine. This is because initially even though I felt really strong when I left the hospital, being at home and doing the chores and looking after two children was proving to be quite the challenge.

So, I had to make up a routine where I would wake up by seven a.m. and have breakfast by 8.30 a.m. Then I would take a quick twenty-minute rest before starting the showering rounds. After everyone was clean, I would prepare a quick snack with fruits, just as I used to before I was taken ill. Around twelve thirty I would start making lunch, as I had to always keep in mind that I was taking my mediation on time.

After lunch, from about two p.m. till four, we would play games or watch telly and I would also fit in a thirty-minute nap for myself as I could feel my body asking me to slow down and rest. I did not want to ignore these messages. Then I would catch up on my chores such as folding clothes, ironing and starting the washing machine.

Finally, at 6.30 p.m. I would wind down and start making dinner, feed the girls, eat myself and leave some food aside for EH for when he was ready to eat. After dinner was done, I would take the girls upstairs, get them changed into their pyjamas ready for bed. I would then make sure that they were asleep before taking my night-time medication and falling asleep.

That was a typical breakdown of what I used to do normally on any usual day. However, there were days where I had to fit in so much more. Such as when my physiotherapist would come home to help me with my exercises. My living room was the only place where I could exercise, but the space was a big issue. I had to watch out for the sofa, the dining table, Jannat's travel cot and walker. Some days the kids would be running around whilst I tried having my session. It was quite overwhelming really because I wanted to make sure that I am following the instructions, but my mind would be wavering to what the girls were doing at that precise moment.

On other days, there would be extra tasks such as shopping for groceries and essentials. I learnt so quickly to adapt to the environment around me as I had no other choice. If I did not try to fit in well then, I knew I may be considered as a burden. Hence, I went with the flow on every occasion.

Life went on as usual for months after leaving the hospital. I found I did not really have time to focus on myself as I had fully dedicated myself to my household responsibilities. I had my fair share of struggles too. There would be days when my bowels had to embarrass me, and I would have an embarrassing accident.

Some days just trying to get out of bed was a massive struggle. I could feel pain and tingling in my muscles. On those days I knew I had to be sensible and listen to my body and rest. My mum continued to send me cooked meals every week, which helped me a lot because I did not have the strength to stand and cook.

As well as struggles with my health, my plight to find suitable housing continued for months. It was beginning to become exceedingly difficult with the space I was living in. I was always scared that either I would trip over something or the children will get hurt because of all the equipment I needed to help me mobilise.

One fine day, my prayers were answered, and I received a call from Jephson Housing Association saying they had a property in Milton Keynes. That was ready for tenancy. I had mentally prepared myself to make this move to Milton Keynes, so that my husband did not have to travel for work, and he would be living near his eldest sister. I knew that he had been wanting to move to Milton Keynes for a while now, that is why he had started work there.

However, before the situation had been different, I did not mind moving because I had my health on my side. Now things were different. I had my whole family here in Luton, who would drop anything and come to help me out if I needed them to on my struggling days. In Milton Keynes, I had no one. I did not have that comfort level with my sister-in-law, so I was not sure what I would do on my bad health days.

Despite all those worrying but true issues, I decided to move to Milton Keynes just to make my husband happy. In spite of my family members and relatives opposing to our decision. The move happened quite quickly with my mum and brother helping out, to decorate and moving all of our belongings to our new home.

In October 2012 we moved to Bradwell in Milton Keynes. I started getting used to a whole new life, I did not have my mum round the corner to jump into my aid. I had to figure out a way to cope with my daily struggles, hence I decided to find ways to help me reduce the amount of extra work I was doing.

For example, changing dirty nappies of two children was much more hard work, because of the number of times the wipes and labels of the nappies would give me troubles. I found it difficult to pull thin items out of a tight case, like the wipes in their pack. Which were all securely put in together. My fingers did not feel the number of wipes I was taking at any one time.

The same issue I had when I tried taking out the Velcro tab from the nappies. For some reason it was hard for me to put my fingers close to one another to pull out the tab. The tingling pins and needles sensations in my hands hurt me so much, that I used to be worried when the girls needed a change. That is why I decided, to toilet train Zara, number one because of my hands and number two, we were thinking of sending her to nursery now as she was almost three years old.

I started using my wheelchair in the kitchen, when I used to cook, just in case I hurt myself. I wanted to be safe than sorry. The good thing about the kitchen in this house was, that the kitchen was more than double the size of the kitchen in my previous house. The living room was also much bigger in comparison to the previous house.

Just as I started getting used to my life in Milton Keynes, I was taken ill quite seriously a week after Christmas. I am not sure what it was that triggered it, but I was sick, I started vomiting, getting a high fever. The joints of my muscles ached, and the pins and needles just hurt me all over. I was unable to function properly. Deep down I feel it was the anxiety and stress built up inside of me that triggered my condition. As it was a year since I was diagnosed with my neurological disorder. Everything flashed in front of my eyes and I was in a daze. After a difficult week and with my sister-in-law helping me out, I managed to recover but I was very weak for a few days after the onset.

As soon as I was back on my feet, I took over my household duties. We started to get in touch with the nursery near our home to discuss when Zara can start. As the nursery was only a five to eight minutes' walk from our house. We decided that I would take Zara to nursery every morning because EH did not do early mornings, so he would pick her up at the end of the day. As the timetable was for her to go in two full days on Wednesday and Thursday and on Fridays, she would only go in for the afternoon sessions.

Zara starting nursery was good for her, as the past year had been a lot for her to take in and adapt to. She had started asking me a lot of questions regarding how long I would stay with her. If I would go back to the hospital. She had even started disliking the NHS sign, if a letter from the hospital, or even from places like the health clinics would come to the house. She would tell me that they are bad, they take mummy away from her. She would even start feeling insecure if she walked past places that displayed the NHS sign such as the opticians and dentist.

I had realised now that the extent of her fears that mummy would fall ill and go back to stay in hospital were so deep. That I had to do something to reassure her that I would be fine. I started explaining to her that the NHS does not take mummy away from Zara, in fact it helps mummy feel better so that mum's health is in good condition. I told her that all the letters that come home from the GP and hospitals, make sure that mummy is attending her regular check-ups and if someone needs to come home to help mummy with her exercises. Slowly but gradually Zara had started believing that mummy would be with her.

Starting nursery took her focus away from me a little. She

would talk more about what she had been doing at nursery, her friends. She would enact the games she played. It was lovely seeing her being worry free, she was finally beginning to enjoy herself properly.

Adult social services had provided me with an OT, who would come home and help me with my upper limb coordination. I had weekly exercises I had to complete and keep practising.

I started attending physiotherapy sessions at the local clinic. Everything was getting into a good routine. I started becoming remarkably busy in my new lifestyle, which was physically very straining. As I was always working extremely hard to manage all my household chores, plus giving time to my children. I made sure that each day I spent an hour in the morning and an hour in the evening before dinner, where I sat with the girls and played with them. This gave them reassurance that mummy was with them. I could feel their sense of relief when they were with me, as they would come up to me in between games and just give me a big hug or cuddle up on my lap for a while.

However, the physical strain soon started taking its toll on me. It was around May 2013, when I suddenly started feeling a lot of tingling around my face and it started feeling numb. I found it difficult to lift things, and I noticed things would just slip out of my hand. All the stress from having troubles with managing with the new symptoms, caused breathing difficulties.

After staying overnight at the hospital, I was referred to my GP, who then forwarded my details to the Neurologist. I was seen by a neurologist called Mr Bartlett at Milton Keynes hospital. I explained all my symptoms and he suggested that I be referred for an MRI and possibly a Lumbar Puncture to investigate what is going on. For which I would need to go to the John Radcliffe Hospital in Oxford. Where I would be under Dr Lane's care.

I Started worrying that this may be the start to another long-term treatment. However, I remained hopeful till my appointments came through.

It was quite a stressful ordeal attending several appointments back-to-back, but I still went through with everything as I did not want to get back to square one. When the reports came back to Dr Bartlett, he told me that there were no problems identified in the MRI of the spinal cord or the Lumbar puncture.

However, there was a possibility that there may be inflammation near the brain, to make sure that this was not the case I had to go in for an another MRI, this time of the brain. Thankfully, this scan also came back without any issues. But from here on I had to be referred to the John Radcliffe Hospital on a permanent basis. Where I would have regular appointments with Dr Lane who would be my new neurologist consultant.

For a while, things started to become normal again, and with a few alterations to the medication I was on, I started to get on with my life as normally as I could.

Things soon started to change again once winter approached. In mid-November I had an appointment at the John Radcliffe with Dr Lane, where I explained that I was starting to have difficulties with my bladder, which had not been a problem for me since I left Northwick Park Hospital. I explained that my bowel issue had never really resolved itself and I was being seen at the bowel clinic regularly for this.

I had also developed sensation changes around my face, I started finding it difficult to brush my teeth again every time I opened my mouth to put the toothbrush in, my hand will somehow miss my mouth and end up near my nose or eyes. Dr Lane explained to me that she had not known my case for long enough, to be able to summarise what could be leading to all these changes. I was advised to be admitted to the hospital so that my condition could be investigated, and I would need an MRI scan of the spinal cord and a CT scan of the brain, where a dye would be injected into my hand to help provide a clear image of any lesions etc…

For a moment, I sat still in my chair, processing all the information I had been given. "It's a Friday evening, I will have to go back home and wait for the hospital to call me, when a bed becomes available. How am I supposed to go out from the room right now and relay this information back to EH and my family? How long do I have to stay in hospital?" I could not hear anything else that was being said to me. I was lost in my own head, questions floating in front of my eyes. It took me a while to get hold of myself and think of the positive outcome this could lead to. I had to believe in the treatment my consultant was advising me, after all I did want to start feeling better again.

Dr Lane walked me out of the room and reassured me that we would get to the bottom of whatever was causing me to feel a little under the weather.

As I walked into the lift, I could just imagine the look on my children's faces. Zara had asked me time and time again if I would leave her, and I had promised her I would not. *Now how am I going to face her? She will start to lose her confidence in me again. What about Jannat? She has just started to get used to being around me and the family, EH will not be able to handle both the children on his own, but this time mum is not around the corner, she is in Luton we are in Milton Keynes. How am I going to figure this out?*

I went down to the car park, legs wobbling as I looked for our car parked outside. I approached the stationary car, every step seeming to drag itself, my legs were so weak, I was worried I might fall over. I slowly opened the door with trembling hands, knowing what I was about to say next might not go down to well with everyone.

I sat down in silence for a couple of seconds, breathing deeply and calming myself down, I turned towards EH and explained everything that had happened in the appointment. He was silent for a while and then told me everything was going to be okay. As he started the car and began to drive out of the parking, I picked out my phone from my bag and decided to call my mum to tell her that I might have to go back into hospital again.

I also wanted to ask if she would she be able to look after Jannat for me again. As I did not want Jannat to be left feeling isolated like the way Zara had, when I first was hospitalised. Jannat is familiar with mum and staying with her should not unsettle her too much.

After explaining everything as calmly as I could, I felt a sense of my mum's worry, but she reassured me that it was not a problem, and she would be happily expecting the kids when the hospital calls me. Deep down I knew precisely what she was thinking at that moment, this was the reason why, she and the family did not want me to move towns. They knew that my health could take an unexpected turn, hence having family around to support me was essential. However, I too did have my reasons for taking such a difficult decision, even though it was not mine, sometimes we just live for others and try to make them as happy as we could.

I sat in the car relieved about childcare, but I was not sure how I was going to tell Zara, this would be my third time going back to the hospital after leaving Northwick Park. I had told Zara that I would never leave her again, but here I was again, once more preparing to be admitted at the hospital. She would never believe me again. I sat in the car silently, sorting out a plan of what I had to do next.

As soon as I came home, I sorted out dinner for the children, happy that they were fed, washed, and dressed. I decided that I had to make sure that there was enough food in the fridge for EH and Zara just in case I got a call from the hospital earlier than expected.

I took out frozen meat, fish and vegetables and put them in warm water to defrost. Whilst that happened, I took out the onions, garlic, ginger, and potatoes to clean and chop them and leave them aside to start my cooking whilst the other items defrosted.

EH had left for work soon after dropping us home from the hospital, so I had to keep an eye on the girls whilst I cooked. I switched on the telly and put 'Hello Kitty' on YouTube for both girls to watch, as they were both going through the 'Hello Kitty' phase. Satisfied that they would be occupied watching that for a while I quickly wobbled my way into the kitchen to start cooking. All the time I cooked my brain was running a hundred miles per hour with so many thoughts, both positive and negative. I could not help worrying.

It was almost 9.30 p.m. and I had managed to cook four curries. I was exhausted and shattered, now almost dragging my body to move, I cleaned up the cooking surfaces and stored the curries in containers, at least that would be three to four days of meals sorted. After which, either my sister-in-law or my mum can send food.

Being mindful of the time I quickly took the girls upstairs to settle them down for bed so that once they were asleep, I could take a quick shower. My body was completely shattered, every part ached, I needed to stop and rest, I knew that, but my mind was ahead of me, I had to be prepared just in case that call comes. I finished praying my salah (prayer Muslim offer to Allah), after which I felt at ease and my mind started to feel peaceful. So, I decided I should sort out some clothes which I might have to take to hospital with me, that way I would be less burdensome.

I finally went to bed, not realising how tired I had become, my eyes closed as soon as I lay my head on the pillow, I did not even have time to worry anymore, my body just needed to rest.

I woke up early the following morning as I could not sleep properly, worrying about what was going to happen. I woke up the girls and gave breakfast to them. After which I gave them both showers and got them ready. Just as I was brushing Zara's hair, my mobile rang, I looked at the number, which was one I did not recognise, but it said Oxford at the top. My hands started sweating as I double clicked the dialling code, it was indeed oxford.

As I answered I was told that my bed will be available on Sunday evening and I was to report to the hospital by six p.m. It was Saturday today, that was quick, just yesterday I had been to Oxford for my appointment. I told the receptionist that I would be there and thanked them for their super quick efforts in finding me a bed.

I finished getting the children fully ready, I took out their toy box and asked them to play, I also put 'Hello Kitty' on the TV for them, which was their current favourite programme. I sat them down and made my way upstairs to inform EH of the phone call.

Neither of us had anticipated that we would hear back from the hospital so soon, but I did have a gut feeling from my conversation with Dr Lane that it would be an urgent matter. Hence, I had cooked as soon I came back from the hospital. I had just secretly hoped that I would get the call at least a week later, that way the children would not feel that mummy went to hospital for a check-up, then mummy ended up going back to the hospital again.

I took out my trolley and packed it with all my things. My hands shook as I filled the trolley with pyjamas, tops, trousers, toiletries, medications, and pads. I called my mum to tell her that I would be visiting her on Sunday afternoon to drop off the children then go into hospital by the evening. I Do not think even mum was prepared for things to happen so quickly, but for me she kept strong. Mum told me not to worry about the girls but just to concentrate on my health and do as the doctor advises.

After speaking to my mum, I thought it would be best to call my sister-in-law to inform her of the same. After listening to me, she said that it was great that my in laws would be here in a couple of months' time, as their visit visa had been accepted.

She told me that when my in laws come here, from Bangladesh my mother-in-law could look after the kids for me and make sure that there was cooking available, if I had to go back to hospital for further treatments. Apparently, this would take a lot of pressure away from my mum and the children would not have to travel between Milton Keynes and Luton.

I listened and was shocked at this response, I did not know how to reply to this, as I knew that early next year they will be here on their visit, but my mother-in-law does not stay very well in health herself, so it is not really going to make a difference to me. Looking after the children and cooking for the family would be out of the question for her. In Bangladesh it is different, there is always someone around to help with the chores, but in this Country, everyone has to manage all on their own.

I politely laughed and said, yes that would be great, but hopefully I would not have to go back to hospital again. As for the situation now, I knew my mother is my rock, she can stand through any storm and still stand strong for me.

I put the phone down feeling really disappointed with the conversation I had just had, no matter what I do to prove that I am not a burden on my family, somehow, directly, or indirectly it is hinted towards me. That is what hurts me the most, I do not even ask for any help around the house, even with this serious condition I am managing almost like a single parent.

But nevertheless, I cannot change the mindset some people have, it is their own view I suppose, but I know for sure that I am not a burden, right? I can manage with looking after me and my family without any support right? Then why am I feeling as if I am causing so much inconvenience? Is it my fault that I ended up having this condition, which does not even have a proper name, it is just a chronic neurological disorder.

Hot sticky tears rolled down my eyes, which I kept wiping with my scarf, the girls were playing beside me, I did not want them to see me upset. I carried on preparing my things, *my self esteem feels really low right now, I feel I do not have a voice, just to say what it is inside my heart. I am hurting from within, but I cannot do anything about it.*

It was another early start for me on Sunday morning, I got up and got the kids ready and packed a travel bag for Jannat, I also packed a few of Zara's things just in case she wanted to stay at mum's, but somehow deep down inside me I knew she was not really going stay at mum's because she has never been used to staying at mums without me.

After lunch we made our way to Luton, at this point I really dreaded my decision to move to Milton Keynes. I wish my mum were just a few roads away, at least I could have spent a few more hours with my family before going into hospital.

The move to Milton Keynes, has been really impractical. I am working twice as hard to keep up on top of things at home, look after the kids and do all my household chores, with almost zero help. If mum were near by at least she would have sent me cooked meals every week, and that would have been one less job for me.

I know what has made my health go down, but I cannot speak of it to anyone as it will cause problems for me in my personal life. Apart from my parents and siblings, nobody understands my condition and to what extent it affects my abilities to do things.

People usually look at me and think I am doing great just because I smile and talk positively all the time. I do not go around whining about my situation, or I do not act like a soggy sock in social gatherings which are mostly out of my choice as

I suffer from claustrophobia.

Instead, I go with the flow and just listen to everyone around me saying how great I am doing, and I practically do not look ill anymore. The only thing that gives away that something is wrong with my health is my walking stick and my moon face.

Just sometimes I want to scream and say, "I am not okay; my exterior may look ship shape, but my interior is a totally different story. I struggle to get up, I struggle to do my chores, I struggle to go to the bathroom at the middle of the night." But no one needs to know that, that is my private life.

I sat silently, cursing myself in my mind for being such a coward and not being able to stand up for myself. I wish I was a little bit more brave; I wish I could say no to people if I did not approve of something. I wish I just did not do things to please everyone else, even if it meant compromising with my own wishes and feelings.

I looked behind to where the girls were sitting, they were talking to each other in their baby language and looked so happy. My heart felt heavy thinking about how they would feel when I would leave them again.

Before long we arrived at mum's, my youngest sister had come to see me off, my brother came downstairs, to give me a hug and tell me it's only a short-term thing, I will be out of hospital in a matter of days. My mum embraced me with teary eyes and told me to be strong and not to worry about the children or my husband she would make sure things are okay at home.

I had a quick cup of tea and got ready to leave, my youngest sister, Naz, sat down on the floor to help me put on my shoes, and splint. At that moment all I could think of was how much she must love me to touch my shoes with her bare hands, trying to fit them to place without hurting me as I did not have the full strength to get the right feet inside. Without using my hands to guide my feet to go inside in the correct position. But right now, my sister was touching the soul of my shoes. The girl who would never touch the sole of her own shoe if it could not be helped, was sitting down and not caring about anything else right now but making sure I was comfortable. I felt incredibly grateful to Allah, for giving me such a loving and caring sister.

I got up and hugged everyone, after which, I slowly made my way out of the house to sit in the car, ready to go to Oxford. I did what I was best at, I smiled as happily as I could, then in a very jovial voice told everyone not to worry for me I would be fine just make sure the girls are okay. I went and sat in the car and looked out of the window, looking for answers I suppose. I know that Allah swt does not test anyone more than he or she can bear. So, if I am coping so well that means, I can go through this. "Yes, I am scared but at least I am not completely immobile like I had been at the onset from my condition. So, I am glad that I am in a much better position. Life has to have ups and downs to enjoy life fully. If things are rosy all the time, then we would get bored."

As soon as we reach the inpatients at the John Radcliffe, I was shown to a room on my own, it was a nice square shape room, with a bed, armchair all spaced out nicely, there was a toilet attached to the room, so I would not have to go out into the corridor. I got changed and sat on my bed. After my obs were done EH went home, and I sat down and looked through the window. It was completely dark outside. I carried on looking through the window for as long as I could remember.

I was woken up around nine p.m. to have my medication before I fell asleep again.

I woke up before breakfast was rolled out, I went into the bathroom to clean myself. I read Wudu (washing before performing salah or reading the Quran) and came back to my room. I sat on the bed and started performing my fajr salah (first of the five prayers, Muslims offer to Allah swt). I felt a relief, instant peace inside me as I started praying. It was soothing, I felt the pain inside me was easing with every action. It was a great way to start my day. I knew Allah will look after me no matter what.

Just as I finished making a humble prayer to Allah swt, to look after my kids and to not let them get hurt or lose trust in me. I was interrupted by an HCA to ask me what I would like for breakfast. I smiled and asked for a bowl of cereal, the most easiest to swallow, especially when you feel like you are going to cry, plus it has the milk element with it.

I sat with my cornflakes next to the window and looked out of the window. The world was beginning to wake up. I could see cars parked outside, there were a few people walking into the building. Birds were flying around, the sounds of their chirping sounded so refreshing it was like a beautiful conversation they were having amongst themselves.

Dr Lane came to see me during her rounds on the ward. She had a kind smile and she told me that I had to have various tests and scans to investigate what could be causing the deterioration of my condition. The whole week went by with me waiting to get all my tests done. The routine was pretty much the same as how I had in the RRU. Therefore, I will not go into all the same details.

I stayed at the John Radcliffe for a total of five nights and five days. On the Friday I was told that all my tests and scans had come back normal, there was no further inflammation, and the brain was all clear, which was the biggest relief. I was happy that I would be discharged and ready to go home. Why my health was deteriorating was a mystery, but I had to keep an eye out and let my consultant know of any further changes I notice.

At this point I knew why I was feeling poorly, it is something I cannot discuss with my consultant or with anyone else. It was all the stress I was going through at home. One day it would be to attend a party, or for hosting big gatherings at ours, or the next for making applications for my in laws to come over on a visit. How am I going to cope with so many people in the house?

I have an embarrassing condition where I suffer from incontinence. But this was a realisation that others did not see. It was almost as if my condition was being disregarded as a serious matter, I was being expected to be happy and normal around everyone.

Life went on as usual, another year came to an end and we stepped into 2014. A year where my life took a 360-degree turn. I do not wish to get into too much detail of what happened as it brings back a lot of painful memories. It was towards the end of February that I had an emotional breakdown, I could not cope with the way things were at home.

My in laws were here, but for some reason my father-in-law was staying at our house and my mother in law was staying at my sister in laws house, apparently, this arrangement was to help me manage everything at home. However, to me it was extremely hard to digest, the fact that no matter what everyone was telling me. There would be someone, in the family or relatives, who picks up on this arrangement and blames me and my condition, for my in laws having to split up and stay with us.

One evening I was so overly stressed by everything that was happening in my life, and the events led to something that was unbelievable, I slipped into a coma.

During which time, there did come a point where my family were told that I would not come out of it and that they had to be prepared for the worst.

My mum reminds me at times, that how all of our family, relatives and friends had united in making prayers for my survival.

The last thing Zara had told my mum was, "They have zipped my mum and taken her into the storeroom." Mum gets terribly upset even now when she remembers Zara's words to describe the paramedics and their ambulance van.

Luckily for me after a week I did come out of the coma and stayed in the ICU for a further few days until I was moved to the general ward before being discharged.

This was the last time I spent time in Milton Keynes. My parents moved me with them to Luton, the girls stayed with their dad until I started regaining my strength. Further events followed and due to unfortunate circumstances, my marriage broke down and I separated from my husband.

From here on starts the real journey of my story to finding myself. When I was in my marriage, I had lost my identity, my confidence, my strength, and my ability to make serious decisions about mine and my children's future.

Now I was on my own. Even though I had my whole family and siblings next to me, I had lost my companion. I was not sure how I was going to manage. We had separated amicably and decided that the children would stay and be schooled with me.

At first, I did not know how to make a start, some serious questions flooded into my mind immediately. I had no money, how am I going to the raise the children? What will I do about housing? I am staying in the small room at my parents' house, things are okay for now, but in a few months, Zara will start reception, she will need more space as she grows up. Jannat is only twenty months younger than Zara so they will practically grow up and need things together. Where do I make a start?

It had only been a few weeks since I was discharged from hospital and now my world had completely changed dimensions. I had barely got my strength back and I was faced by some exceedingly difficult challenges.

However, I had no time to mull over things. I needed a plan and I had to focus. I remember having a conversation with my eldest sister, Parvin, questioning the doubts I had in my head. She explained to me that things would take time, but eventually would fall into place.

I knew what my goal was this time round too, just like the previous time. Last time I had to get back to my kids, this time round I must give my children the best upbringing I possibly can on my own. I have to make the right choices for their life, education etc…

Initially, my sisters helped me to sort myself out, by helping me make phone calls to the Department of Works and Pensions to support me in getting financial help. They accompanied me to the banks to speak about savings etc.

This is because in the beginning, when I would make a call, I could not stop stuttering, I would get so nervous, emotional that words would jumble and mumble from my mouth. So, to help me out my sisters made the calls for me then pass the phone onto me after explaining to the person on the phone what I was going through.

Hence, I was able to get in touch with the jobcentre to sort out my ESA, after helping me to make a few other calls, towards helping me get started on the benefits that I could receive. My sisters told me that I would have to be confident and make follow up calls to chase how things were progressing.

They were not going to do it for me as I have to build my own self-confidence and I had to believe in myself. It was really hard, but I knew that if I did not try then I would never overcome my fears.

Prior to becoming a mum, I was a confident lady, working full time and managing all my finances. However, things had never been the same after Zara's birth. I slowly started to lose my confidence and stopped believing in my abilities to do things. Even if it were to be making a simple phone call to the doctors to book an appointment.

So, now here I am again, like how I was when I was sixteen years old, when I had to open my first bank account all on my own. I had to hold onto the ropes of independence by myself and now once again I am doing the same thing.

My siblings would attend the bank etc with me to support my mobility. However, when it came to talking to the customer service advisors, I was on my own, I would watch from the side as they would stand there and let me do all the talking.

Initially I hated it, I did not like explaining my situation because I felt like a fool and a weak person. However, once things started to sort themselves out, I felt confident that I can make a few phone calls and attend the doctors, banks etc I was able to talk and made myself be heard.

No one thought I was a fool. It was all in my mind. I was too worried. My siblings had returned back to me my voice, to speak confidently in public. That was my first hurdle passed. But it took a lot of practise.

The second challenge was sorting out housing and schooling. Once again, I found myself losing confidence. This time round I was helped out by a truly kind auntie, who got in touch with the local school, which is the same school that I had attended as a young child myself, to see how they can support me in finding the right kind of help.

The family workers, from what was then called 'Building Blocks Children's Centre' a few years back, got in touch with me. Two ladies came to see me at my parents' house, who took down all the details of my circumstances. One of them was called Clara, who later became my family worker, and with time, whose help, and support have been invaluable to me.

From here I started finding my feet, Jannat and Zara started attending the nursery. I enrolled on the 'Freedoms' course, a course that I could relate to. Where I met amazing people that had been though their own journeys. I learnt so much and I started applying what I had learned, to my life to get myself back on the right track.

Firstly, I had managed to go into the council office with my brother and make an application to go on the housing waiting list.

Secondly, I was worried about how the children were taking my separation from their dad; hence I went back with this worry to Clara, who told me that she could get someone to do some workshops with the children to see how they were feeling, without asking them anything directly.

Luckily for me the person who was going to lead these sessions was Karen my 'Freedoms' course instructor. Karen did some wishes and feelings work with the girls, through play, she manged to get the girls to draw pictures about different scenario's, the pictures depicted emotions of how they felt about mum and dad, then mum and dad not living together anymore. I felt these workshops really helped the children express how they were feeling. This was all recorded-on file.

As the children started to feel more settled with the move to Luton again, I started to feel more relieved.

I had, however become very hesitant about going out because for some reason something inside me used to stop me from wanting to step outside the house. I felt a whole bubble of emotions floating around me. I was scared that people would talk about me, laugh at me, or even ask me why I had made the choices I made. I felt safer and comfortable being at home. My travels were limited to just going to the nursery and back.

My family worker Clara used to come and see me at home in the initial days, where a lot of paperwork was completed. Some of which, put me into contact with various individuals from different organisations who supported individuals like myself to speak about our journeys and take things from there.

In September 2014, Zara started reception, but she got a place in a School which was much further away from where my parents lived. This was because I had made an application past the deadline, because of my sudden move to Luton, therefore I could not have a choice as to where Zara was placed. But I had to accept the placement that was given to her.

For the time being I accepted the place and did have in mind that when I make Jannat's school application the following year, I would ask for a transfer for Zara. However, I did not even know which schools I was going to apply to because there was still the issue of if I would get a house and where I would get it. But I decided to take things in steps, I had to deal with one problem at a time otherwise I would have had a meltdown.

As I could not take Zara to school myself, and I did not have anyone who could take her to school each day, I contacted the admissions team who put me trough to transport. They arranged for a taxi with an escort to make sure that Zara went into school safely each day and was picked up safely and at the end of the day was dropped off home again.

I attended appointments at the John Radcliffe at regular intervals and have been doing so, ever since then. My consultant Dr Lane is an amazing person who has helped me so much. With her words of kindness and reassurance I felt strong and still am feeling strong about how I can live my life positively and only look forward to how I can live a better, productive life.

I used to suffer from insomnia, hear voices when I used to try and sleep, that would keep me awake at night. However, with the correct medication management and exercises, I have overcome these problems.

I still do get nights, where I only manage to sleep for two to three hours without any disturbance, but then the pain and the pins and needles wake me up. I struggle to put myself back to sleep again because my arms and legs feel heavy to sleep on my sides, so I have to sleep on my back, which is not extremely comfortable because my back gets very sore from lying in the same position.

Obviously, I have had to make myself understand that this

is going to be an ongoing problem for me and no matter how many times my medication is changed, or the doses are altered these are all short-term fixes. The real way to tackle this was to train my brain to accept that pain and pins and needles as a part of me.

I had to start seeing the pain, pins, and needles and that feeling of heaviness as one of my attributes. It was difficult because I used to fall, trip and bump into things, since I used to lose my balance because of the persistent pain and pins and needles.

During the early days, it had bothered me a lot. However, I did not have the time to sit and mull over how complicated my life had become because of my health condition. I had two incredibly young children to raise. No matter how much I would be supported by my parents and siblings, ultimately it was my duty to raise my children and give them the best possible upbringing that I possibly could.

So, I started to do some research on single parents with health conditions and how they faced different challenges. It was very inspiring to read other people's way of coping and things that they had adopted to support their family.

It was more reassuring for me to read and relate to people's journeys, which were in some way similar to mine. I did not feel alone, it made sense to me that things would not always be easy going however they would not always be difficult either.

It cheered me up, so I started to organise a routine that the children needed to get into, starting from their sleeping, eating timetables to making time to play with them and to see if there was anything that may be playing on their minds.

Since then, till now I have always made sure that I take

the time to ask my children about their day, how it has been for them, if there was anything that they were particularly happy or sad about. This way the girls know that mum is always there for them as a support system for them.

I wanted to look at ways to improve my life further, I wanted to do something that involved supporting others and wanted to do something to help improve my own mindset. I spoke to Clara about doing some voluntary work just so that I can test my endurance levels and see how I manage working in an environment which was similar to the College I used to work for.

Clara arranged for me to do some hours at the Children Centre, it was a great way to interact with others and I did not have to worry about my good days and bad days, as I would be volunteering for people who were completely aware of my condition and circumstance.

Zara started to attend sessions with an organisation called CHUMS, that support young carers and give them some respite to deal with living with a parent who has a disability. I was hesitant at first, because I told CHUMs that my children do not actually care for me, but they are very understanding of how bad my health could become.

They told me that attending CHUMs would help them cope with certain elements of living with a parent with a disability. However, because of the age only Zara could attend for the time being and Jannat could join her the following year. I was happy for this to go ahead. So, Zara attended CHUMs where she was picked up and dropped off each Saturday to spend time with other young carers to just play for a few hours.

The following year I was still waiting to be housed, each week I would go online to bid for a house that I felt would cater for my family's needs, things did take time though.

In the meantime, I made Jannat's school application on time so that I would not have the same problem as I did during Zara's application. This time round I was faced with a different kind of dilemma, Jannat got her place in Beechill, for which no transportation was required because it was only a matter of two to three minutes away from where my parent lived. So, I would be able to take her without any issues. However, I did want both the girls to be in the same school, but I was told that I would have to wait, as Beechill was an oversubscribed school.

Just as the school year started to approach an end, I managed to successfully bid for a house. I was given the chance to accept the house which belonged to BPHA housing association. The only problem was it was on the other side of town to where my parents lived.

The one big advantage was that it was only a few roads away from the hospital. There were many disadvantages to move that distance. However, living in cramped conditions had started to get the better of me. I found it difficult to sleep in a double bed with two children who were growing up fast and they fidgeted a lot so sometimes I would get extremely uncomfortable sharing the same bed with them. It was not ideal at all. The other issue was my bowels would occasionally embarrass me and I did not like facing those moment's in front of my family.

Plus, I wanted more certainty for the children when it came to Schooling. I did not like the thought of them having to move schools in between the year, just to be in the same school as each other. So, considering all the pros and cons I decided to accept the house and move to the other side of town.

I then contacted school admissions where I liaised with a lady called Teresa, the same lady who had come to speak to the parents at Beechill, when we were making our applications at the beginning of the year, to ask if both the children could be placed in the same school, where transportation would be provided for them. After exchanging a few phones calls with Teresa, I was informed that both girls could start at Pirton Hill Primary school and a school bus with an escort would be provided for their safe pickups and drop offs.

If my auntie had not introduced Building Blocks Children centre to me and if they had not stepped in to help me when they had, then I would not have been able to come this far, especially when it came to making decisions. I still remember when used to have my sessions with Clara during the early days, I remember telling her my story and at the end I said, "Clara, in this journey I have lost myself, I have lost Yasmin. I would one day like to find Yasmin the same person before the Transverse Myelitis."

Today when look back, I can happily say that the grey clouds are moving aside, I can finally see the light at the end of the tunnel. There is hope and wonders ahead for me. I just have to carry on making wise choices.

Moving houses was scary because now I was on my own with the children. I had a lot of doubt if I could manage, would all the health and safety aspects be met. I contacted adult social services again, this time to inform them that I had moved and was on my own. Therefore, I would need assistance with managing my day-to-day chores.

An occupational therapist, called Jane was assigned to me who came and took notes of everything then made a note of how adaptations could be made to help me be mobile in the house. There were certain hurdles at this point because the bathroom of the house was located downstairs, which was a problem for me as I needed the bathroom a few times in the night. Going and up and down the stairs was risky because my body get so tired, especially in the evening. My lower limbs feel tight and numb.

Jane told me getting the stairlift installed would mean having to make changes to the walls, because the stairs led upstairs straight from the passage as you enter the house and there is no space for the stair lift seat to slide down to because of it would block the entrance to the living room. The other suggestion I had made, was to get an upstairs toilet made, but that too was a problem because of the space of the rooms. Hence, I had to wait and see what would happen when the request for the stairlift went through.

Days went by and I was still waiting to hear from the social services team in regards to getting someone to come and help me out with the chores. Here again I faced obstacles as I was told that I would not get anyone to come and actually do the washing and ironing for me, but someone can come and sit with the kids, and supervise for me to do the chores myself.

I did not find that extremely helpful, because my family were already sort of doing that for me on a weekly basis anyways. I just needed for someone to come and actually help me on a daily basis with the tasks I found most difficult to do on my bad days only when I become wheelchair bound.

When I was told that this would not be possible because that sort of service is not provided, a person could not just come in for bad days, plus there was no certainty when the bad days will take place. So, I had to accept the fact that I was on my own and I had to try my best to manage my chores and look after the children. I was lucky though, as I knew I had my mum and my brother as my main backup for if I had a sudden turn of bad health.

I started adapting to the house I used the furniture and the walls as my walking aid for moving around short distances. As it was not always ideal to wear my AFO when in the house. As I had to get on and off the ground a lot.

I started teaching the children who were now five and half years and four years of age to learn some basic independent tasks, such as going to the toilet, washing hands before and after meals, brushing their teeth three times a day, washing and wiping their faces and getting ready on their own for school.

I would place all the items on the bed for them and they would change by themselves. I assisted with brushing their hair as it was very thick and smooth which made it unmanageable. They had already learned how to take out and tidy up their toys. So, we had an action plan in place, and it started working for us which was lucky for me.

I gently had start making the girls aware that if I would have a bad day then they were to call my mum or siblings. I showed them my mobile to show them how it worked. I had stuck on a piece of paper with all my emergency contacts by the landline and I also stuck on a prescription with the list of all my current medication. So that in an emergency if my family had to call the ambulance, then all the information would be available for the paramedics.

I was hesitant to do this, but I knew that it was important for the girls to know that mummy could be a little unwell at times. I did not like talking to Zara about my health becoming poorly, as she had been scarred to some extent with me becoming unwell and going into hospital. However, it was essential that she knew that there was always a plan in place and someone from my family would look after them in my absence.

At first Zara was very reluctant to listen to me as she would start crying and ask me if I was going back to hospital, however thankfully with time she saw for herself how my good and bad days worked, so she was more comfortable with the whole process. Jannat would do as Zara did, so both girls were becoming more open to the idea of mummy's good and bad days.

I showed Zara the kitchen cupboard where dry food items, such as bread, croissant, biscuits, and cakes were kept. So that if I was to have a bad day and they had to wait for someone from my family to arrive, then they would not have to wait to have a snack they could get it themselves.

The school bus used to come anytime between 7.15 a.m. to 8.15 a.m. So I had to make sure that the girls would go to bed every day at 6.30 p.m., so that they could fall asleep by 7-7.30 p.m. and waking up in the mornings would not be too difficult. The girls were quite happy to go to bed early because they used to get so exhausted after such a long day at school.

I had to make sure though that I heard both girls read at home each day, in order to help them understand the books they used to bring home each day. Also, it was expected from the school that children were heard reading each day by their parents.

I found homework most amusing, it took me back to my childhood in school. We did not have homework until we were in year six, and that too we only had it during holidays. I started getting homework regularly when I started year seven. So, I was quite surprised that children from year R onwards had started getting homework. I did not however, mind sitting with the girls and helping them complete their tasks.

It gave us a special kind of bond. I talked a lot and the children listened. We would also play one little game together each night just to spend quality time together. I have found that this was one of the best things I had adopted. Because it is particularly important for us parents to give our children our time. That is all they need at times to feel secure and loved and know that someone is there always, to look after and take care of them.

My children even now tell me that they prefer to watch a TV programme with me rather than watch it on their own. Zara now makes sure that each weekend we do something together as a family, it can be anything from painting, playing with a jigsaw puzzle, papier mache to sewing. This is because during the evenings there is not really much time for us to do anything with arts and crafts.

Plus, evenings are my most difficult times. My body stops listening to me and it becomes a struggle to manoeuvre. However, that does not stop us from conversing with another. When I look back just six years ago from now, it was me who would ask the children, how their day had been? What they ate during lunch? If they were worried about anything? Or if anyone had upset them? What should we read together? Etc.

Today the roles have reversed the children would start asking me these questions as soon as they see me after school. Which is great because I feel so involved in their day and they feel involved in mine. It makes us a very satisfied and happy family. All praise and thanks be to Allah swt, who has blessed me with wonderful kids that take so much care of my wishes and feelings.

Had I not invested that time of mine back then. I do not think that today the children would be so connected with me. For me, it was all about nurturing our relationship right from the start. Just like a plant, the more time and effort you take to look after it since the time of sowing the first seed, the more it blooms with life. I am happy that even when I found it difficult to sit down and play games with the kids, I still tried, because that is what has made our bond so strong.

As I started to understand my condition more and how it affected my daily living, I was able to put strategies in place to help me out when I struggled. For example, sometimes I would be making a cup of tea. A simple task pre my health condition did not take awfully long, about four to five minutes using an electric kettle.

However, with the health condition I found that task a challenge in itself. Some days the cup would fall out of my hand over and over again because I found that I could not really grip onto the handle, even though I closed my fingers together to wrap it around the handle it was not tight enough, the same problem I had with the spoon it would just slide straight out of my grip. Hence, I had to be careful and use both my hands to assist one with the other.

On some days I would feel that when doing the washing up, I was gently placing the clean dishes to one side. When in actual fact the dishes were sort of being slammed down. It is difficult to explain but it was almost as if the hands were doing something completely different to what the brain was telling it to do. Hence, I had to practice and practice the techniques of lifting things up from anything big to small and placing it down gently. I made up my own exercises, to ensure that my hand coordination was good.

One of the things I found difficult, and still do till today is clipping my nails. As I am unable to hold the nail cutter the way I used to. I have to place it in my palm then use all my fingers and the thumb to clip my nails, if I try the old method of using my thumb and the first two fingers, I am incapable to do anything as the fingers do not have the strength to press and lift.

I started to train myself into thinking that it was best that I find ways to complete tasks, even if it is a little uncomfortable, it is better to try and do something, than to not do that task at all. Otherwise, the other option would be to rely on someone else to help me out. That would have compromised with my independence and it could have led to me becoming terribly upset and depressed.

I was worried that if I ever fell into depression because of not being able to be how I was prior to my Transverse Myelitis, then my kids would have had to bear the consequences. They would have had to been looked after by my family on more occasions than anticipated. Which would have been bad for their mental stability too. As they were already insecure about me and having to see me upset or out of action would have really had an adverse effect on their minds. This would have led to them not being able to live their lives stress free because they would have been unsure of what to expect from me. In the long run it would have affected their school performance too. Which was something I was extremely worried about.

I had to prove to myself to me, more than to anyone else, that I was fully capable of giving my children a happy and worry-free life. I wanted them to enjoy their lives like the rest of their friends. Therefore, I had to ensure that I understood my condition and worked together with all my therapists to manage my body.

I was assigned a physio therapist to come home and help me with my exercises. Coincidentally it happened to be the same therapist who had helped me after I left Northwick Park. This made things easy for me, as I did not have to repeat my story like I had been, every time when I met a new therapist because most of the time, they would ask me what it is and how it debilitated my life. This was due to the fact that my condition was sort of a rare condition nine years back, not many people had heard of it.

I remember when I first spoke to my physio therapist in Milton Keynes about how I felt a little bothered with the fact that I had to keep explaining myself over and over again, every time I bumped into people, whether it was in relatives' houses, the shops or Zara's nursery. When asked why I was using a stick to walk and why I walked funny. I used to tell people that I have a neurological condition caused by Transverse Myelitis. Straight away they would ask me what that was. From there I used to reiterate my story. Which had started becoming a little bothersome for me.

After listening to me, the therapist had suggested that when I met someone outside the medical team and if I did not want to go into a whole long conversation, especially with people I just happened to bump into, like in the shops. Then it might help me to just say that I had suffered from something similar to a stroke. From then on, I have started doing that.

My physio took down all the new details and asked me exactly what it was that I needed help with, and we would practise in those areas. I told him about the difficulties I had with climbing the stairs and I was getting a sore back from sitting down on the steps to go up and down on the days I felt weak and every night because during the evening I wobble more.

I also wanted to practise my walking as I felt very scared and worried when I walked outside, especially in confined spaces. As a result of these discussions, I would have sessions every week practising sit to stands, to make it easy, for when I cooked in the kitchen. As being able to get up and down from the chair safely was important because I needed the wheelchair in the kitchen to get from one side to the other.

But I did face some difficulties in reaching the cooker, it was a problem because the height was different from the height of my chair. Which was slightly lower down compared to the height of the cooker. So, I would have to stand up every time I was stirring or putting something into the pans.

We practised going up and down the stairs taking actual steps to go up, rather than sitting down on the step to push myself up onto the next step, which is what I had been doing. With time I had started to build up on my stamina and stability which was a relief. I had also started to become more confident with my walking.

I was managing quite well on my own, except for the occasional trips and falls at times. Which I did not pay too much attention to, as I knew I would have these balancing issues.

However, unfortunately the frequent trips and falls led to me fracturing two of my middle toes on my weaker foot. I would have done something about it if I actually felt the pain at the time. But because of the poor sensations I could not tell that something had happened. Not until one day when I felt sharp pains when I stood up.

I looked carefully at my toes and realised they were sort

of curled in and I could not straighten them out. So, it was when I actually saw the shape and structure of my foot change, that I realised that something was not right. I knew I had to show this to my neurologist the next time I met her.

When I did have my consultation with my neurologist, she examined my toes and told me that I would need to have an X-ray to confirm it was indeed a fracture. However, just by looking at it she could tell that it was going to be tricky to sort it out, because of the sensation issues I had. From there on, I was referred from one-foot specialist to another, with several X-rays being taken.

I knew that I was tripping and falling mostly because of my balance issues. Although, there was one other reason why this happened so often. It was due to the problems I faced every night with having to use the bathroom. That is when most my falls took place, I needed to use the bathroom frequently as I suffered from concerns with my incontinence.

More so, it was when I tried to get downstairs to use the bathroom that I would sometimes slip or roll down the stairs, as I was trying to get to the bathroom at the middle of the night, when my body would feel really heavy and numb from all the day activities.

It was then that I realised that it was not safe for me living in a house where I did not have safe access to the bathroom in the night especially with the bathroom being so tiny with extremely limited space to manoeuvre.

I was on the waiting list to be seen by an orthopaedic surgeon; it was looking likely at this stage that I may need surgery. That is when I thought it would be best for me and my daughters, to live in a house which gave me safe access to the bathroom at nights. Especially if I had to have surgery then how would I manage the stairs at night?

Therefore, I contacted Jane, my OT, who gave me an update on the stairlift issue, she told me that it had been agreed that I would have a stairlift, but it would take a lot of work to put the stairlift in place because of the layout and design of the house. However, there was no guarantee how soon all the work could be carried out.

After my conversation with Jane, I had to assess the practicality of living in a house that had a lot of issues when it came to making adaptations to suit my needs. Mainly being the facts with the way of how it had been designed. The walls came in the way of making any changes. So, I spoke to Jane again and informed her that I was going to get in touch with both the council and housing association to request for a transfer because the house was not practical for my needs, especially if I needed surgery. Jane backed my decision and agreed that this may be the better solution.

Although, I knew there would be delays before the house transfer happens because of the waiting list system. I was optimistic that the change would be beneficial for me and my family. It was in November 2016, that I contacted the council and housing association to inform them of my decision, the council put me on the waiting list again.

The housing association told me to let them know as soon as I was successful in finding a house. A few months went by and I successfully managed to find a house in March 2017.

Again, it was not perfect for all my needs, but much more accessible than the house I was currently living in. It had more space, mainly in the living area, where after having a sofa set and dining table in place, there was plenty of room to use my wheelchair. The passage was slightly larger too, with a sufficient place to store outdoor shoes and my splint and outdoor walking aid. The house was definitely more practical for my needs.

There was also the added bonus of the local school being close by, maybe it would only be a ten minute walk from the house. So, I had started to consider the possibility of a school transfer for the children.

The move was hectic, but my family made the transition from one house to another as stress free as possible for me. My brother Mo, youngest sister Naz and her husband painted the whole house for me, after which I had to arrange for the nets, curtains, and blinds to go up, which my eldest sister's husband and my nephew had put up for me.

One by one all the things that needed to be taken care of, to make a house into a home was done. Mo and one of my cousin brothers drove all the furniture from my old house to the new one, then they set and fixed all the furniture for me.

Whilst my family did all the physical work, I had to take care of all the admin side of things, such as a change of address. To fixing a meeting with the housing association officer to come and see the old property to make sure I had left it in a good condition and arranging for the school bus to come and pick up the girls from the new house.

After the move I had started to think about something which was particularly important for me. Currently my children were waking up an hour early every day so that they could be ready for the school bus, which was anything between 7.15 a.m. till 8.15 a.m. They would then be dropped off home after school, around 4.10 p.m. every day. I found that this was making them extremely tired hence I had decided to take a chance and apply for places at the school, near to my new home. I had assessed the distance and decided that I would be able to manage to take them to school every day myself.

I liaised with Teresa from school admissions, explaining to her my reasons for moving the children's schools. Who then helped me complete the relevant paperwork to apply for the school places. It took a few months, but both the girls finally got a place in the school that I had wanted them to get a place in. I informed the school of my disability and my circumstances. They were very understanding and reassured me that they would support me as best as they can.

Finally, once all the work was taken care of, we were settling into our new home nicely, I started feeling more confident in myself. I was beginning to get exercise outside of the house every day for about half an hour (that is taking the girls to school and picking them up, consisting of around fifteen minutes each way). Even though I felt very tired and needed to take a short nap after the school rounds, there was a strong feeling of satisfaction that I was much more independent and having the chance to socialise with other people really helped me mentally.

Nevertheless, it was not until the winter of 2017, that my body really surprised me once again. I struggled a lot more, especially in the mornings, getting washed and dressed had started to become a chore.

My mum had to cook for me, as I could not cope with standing for even a short duration of time. My entire body tingled, and the pins and needles sensations run up and down throughout my whole body with greater speed than usual, making it difficult for me to even balance properly.

It was then, I got the girls used to getting ready in the mornings on their own, as I was unable to help them. This did, however, cause a lot of agony for Zara as she found herself worrying about me all the time. Even though I used to reassure her that it was a temporary phase and after a few days I would be back to normal. It had become difficult for me, convincing her, that I would be okay. As she was able to see for herself how much I struggled, even just to make breakfast and wash the dishes.

As a result of the sudden deterioration in my health, I found myself unable to take the girls to school in the more colder than usual days. This was because the tingling and pins and needles sensation in my lower limbs completely stopped me from doing even the simple tasks. It was during this time, I started to feel quite upset, because I knew I had taken a big risk with changing the girl's school, I had lost the privilege of a school bus collecting the children.

Now if the children missed school, it would come down to me for making that big decision of moving them. Disheartened, I was unsure what to do, however, once I notified the school about what was happening, they were incredibly supportive. They arranged for the family workers to pick up and drop the children back home, on the days I was unable to do the school rounds.

With the school supporting me and reassuring me not to worry about my bad days, I started to feel relaxed once again. I convinced myself that with my neurological disorder, I would have to go through the good days and bad days with my body. So, every day would not be the same, I just had to be prepared, with how to manage things on different days.

Jane had completed my assessments and sent requests through to the council for the appropriate adaptations to be made to the house so that I can better manage my daily activities. With time a ramp was put in place outside my house to make it easier for me to go in and out.

Also, a stairlift was installed to make it easier for me to go up and down the stairs and some grab rails were put in different areas of the bathroom. Luckily for me the bathroom did not have a bath but a walk-in shower. So, a shower chair was provided for me to safely have my showers.

The winter passed and I started to feel a lot more energetic. Just as I was getting back on track with managing things again an appointment came through with regards to my toes, I had to go and see an orthopaedic surgeon at Stanmore hospital.

Previously I had been told that the only way to fix the shape of the toes was, maybe through surgery, but during my appointment at Stanmore, the surgeon advised me, he thought that surgery would not solve the problem in the long run because surgery would not only weaken my foot, but it could cause further interference with the sensations I had. Furthermore, there was no guarantee, to say that I would stop having falls, in the future, to prevent further fractures. Therefore, the best option may be to have steroid injections to assist in manually fixing the shape.

All the information from the appointment, was relayed back to my neurologist who advised me that the steroid injections may have helped if the problem had been brought to attention earlier, however at this stage it is too late to fix it with this kind of treatment.

I had a lot to take in, from there on, I realised that there was no permanent cure to sorting out the problem with the deformity of my toes. But like with my health condition, I would have to manage a way to stop any further complications.

I knew for sure; I did not want to take risks that would make my situation any worse. Hence, I decided that I would have to train myself to manage with my toes, the way they were. I started by buying a pair of shoes, from an online website, that especially designed different shoe types, for people who had a condition called hammer toes, which was how my toes were beginning to look. The shoes were great as there was a lot of space for my splint and insole to go in. One of the other great features, of the shoes were, that they were wide, and the straps were easy to use and grip.

With the issue of my toes taken care of, I started once more to carry on with my life as normally as possible. Thinking that there could not be anything else worse, possibly that could happen now.

However, towards the end of October 2017 my children came up to me and raised some concerns that they had, about how they felt when they went out to spend some time with their father. Listening to them I realised that the agreement that we had in place currently, which was mutual agreement between me and ex-husband, was not really working out for the children.

They needed more consistency for when they were visiting him and where they went to spend that time.

I realised the girls were not really enjoying themselves and they started to complain a lot more. Hence, I decided to apply for a child arrangements order which would provide a legal agreement of how often and where the children would have their visits.

It was quite a stressful ordeal getting everything sorted plus the costs to arrange for a solicitor to complete all the necessary paperwork was piling up on me and I started to feel really deflated as time went by.

I started to suffer from sleepless nights from all the stress and anxiety. It was at this point that I knew I had to occupy my mind from all the worries I was going through.

I did have faith, that now, that I had applied for the child arrangement order, things would be much nicer for the children. However, because of the amount of time it could take for a verdict to come through, was really nerve racking for me, a lot of stress and anxiety was building up inside me.

As a result, of me waiting to hear about what would happen, my self-esteem started to go down again. I started to feel worthless once more. I was constantly occupied with issues, either in regards to my health or something to do with the children.

It was during this time that one night, I was speaking to my elder sister, Parvin, crying about how worried I was about everything and how I felt worthless because I did not see myself as a strong independent person.

I still remember saying that, "I am a really good sister, a good daughter and a good mother, but beyond that I am not really good at being anything else. There was a time that I went to work, and I used to feel so satisfied at the compliments I used to receive at the end of the day from all my colleagues that I used to work with. However, now apart from my family members who I know would be biased towards me anyways. I did not really receive the occasional praise at times of how well I was doing at something."

After listening to my troubles, Parvin asked me to answer a few questions honestly, which would help me find the answers I am looking for, I just had to voice them. Firstly, what I expected from life now? Secondly, things had sorted itself out, one by one, what was it then, that was really bothering me?

I listened to the questions and took a deep breath, I told her that I really wanted to start working again, but with my condition and with how often my body just jumps between the good and bad days, there would not be an employer out there, who would take me on. *Previously, I had tried doing some voluntary work in the past but had to give it up when I felt overly tired. I did not manage well, to cope with sitting in one position for more than an hour.*

The way in which my body reacts now, I have to sit for a while, then have a lie down then walk around a little then sit back down again to feel comfortable. It is very tricky because of the pins and needles, the constant tingling, and the excruciating pain. Which make it exceedingly difficult for me to be in one position for a certain duration of time. I have to keep changing my position around to feel better.

In the real-life working world this sort of issue would not suit any employer. Then on top I have the bad days to deal with, where I become out of action for most the time, needing help and support to get by. There is also the problem of not knowing when a bad day will take place, anything can trigger it, I just have to manage with it as it comes.

My sister listened to me patiently, agreed with all what I had said, but then told me there was more to it than just that, with what was making me feel upset. She then asked me once more what was it that would make me happy and feel good about myself as a person.

At this point I knew what it was that I really wanted, so I finally plucked up the courage and told her I wanted to become a children's author, a dream I had as a child. However, I never pursued it because I felt I would not be able to manage to have my book published as I am not really confident with my spelling and grammar.

Then as life went by, I forgot the dream and just carried on going with the flow. It had not occurred to me till now that I had felt a void and it was this the writing that would fill that void. However, my confidence was getting the better of me. I felt scared that people would laugh at me for not being good enough.

At first Parvin listened to me, without saying anything but she only interrupted me when I mentioned the problem I was having with my confidence.

"I need to stop you for a minute, you are much more stronger than you think you are. Even though physically you are much weaker than you hope to be, mentally you are a lot more stronger. Look at how you are a strong role model for your children, they can see your struggles, battling with your condition on a regular basis, but yet you do not give up hope, instead you are giving them a very normal life. You are making sure that you are providing them with not just the material things but the quality family time that they need more than anything else to feel happy. So, what is stopping you? when it comes to doing something for yourself?"

She told me that I should take my writing forward if that is what I wanted. In regards to the spelling and grammar issue, there were editors and proof-readers out there to take care of that side of things.

I then replied, I did not know where to start, how would I go about finding a publisher? to which she very smartly replied back.

"You can always start by researching publishers on the

internet, come on stop finding excuses, if you have a plan then you must take action and do something about it."

After putting the phone down, I sat for a while with a world of information to take inside. On one hand I had the child arrangement order to worry about and on the other I needed to do something to stop myself from going into depression. I knew that writing stories would help me, as I love listening to and telling stories.

However, it was jumping into the unknown and out of my comfort zone. None the less I spoke to my youngest sister, Naz and repeated the whole conversation I had had with Parvin, the night before. To my surprise, even Naz thought I should go ahead and pursue my writing. It was a way to keep myself busy and stop myself from worrying about my health and other things.

Okay, so now that I knew I had to make a start with my writing, I decided to be more serious in my approach. So, one day, after dropping the children off to school, Naz came to pick me up. She drove me into the mall and took me WHSmith, where she selected a nice A4 writing book. It had a golden background with pink flowers going across. When the book was opened, one could see the lovely pink and blue floral border decorating the pages.

Naz turned to me and said, "A pretty book will help you to write down yours ideas more easily, the colourful background should inspire you."

I could not agree more with her, as I wanted to make sure that when I do start writing, then I do have a master copy that I can look back at, years later when I am in my sixties; so that I could show my daughters how I had planned my stories and characters, it would be fun to look back at all the scribbles and crossing outs.

"Look at this nice ink pen, it would go perfectly with the book, plus it would look much nicer than the ink of a ball point pen," Naz told me, as she picked up a pen, with the perfect shade of dark blue ink.

After paying for the stationery, we walked back to the car, as Naz dropped me home she said, "Now do not ponder over anything more, start writing down your ideas as soon as you get in. That way you will have a few ideas to work on to build your story up on. Good luck and I have full faith that you will write a really good story," saying this she helped me out of the car and walked me inside, before driving off.

That night, after the girls had come back from school, I sat down on my bed and took out my notebook and pen. I looked at the book on my lap for a while, I still could not believe that I was going to actually start writing a book.

Turning the first page, I started to imagine what it was, I was going to write about. I knew I wanted to write for a younger audience, but not quite sure about the exact age range. I also wanted the stories that I write, to provide some sort of a moral or motivational message to help the society as well as being fun. But I just did not know where to start.

It was then I remembered stories I use to listen to as a child and all the books I read from the library. Finally, I started jotting down points then I had to decide on a title. I knew exactly what the title would be, because I wanted to write about two sisters who would go on some sort of an adventure, and there would be a few books on the adventures that they went on.

Obviously, I was going to name the characters after my own two children. It is because of them that I have felt so strong and motivated to get a grip with my health and yet manage my family life as comfortably as possible. It is because of their love for me, which made me feel so good about myself. Every time I have felt weak, or upset, my children have always cuddled up to me, asking me if I am okay. Most importantly, not a single day goes by without them telling me they love me at least ten or more times in a day. Hence, I decided to call my books "Adventures of Zara and Jannat".

That was going to be my theme, once I started writing, the ideas just came into my head, I felt so good and happy. I was in an imaginary setting, where these two children were having so much fun and along with them in reality, I was having fun. This was because writing was something I loved, I dreamed to be an author and now it seemed like I was only a few steps away from making that dream turn into reality.

From then on, every day, after dropping my children off to school, I would start to write a little more. I realised that by indulging myself in my writing I did not feel sad or upset anymore. I was getting over this niggling feeling of self-pity, instantly I felt thankful, and I thanked Allah swt for giving me the strength, but more importantly, for giving me siblings that had so much faith and confidence in me that I could do something with my life.

It was as if I had my own personal therapists helping me overcome my worries and fears. Allah has been truly kind to me for giving me such a loving and understanding family.

A couple of weeks later, I had my story completed, so now for the next step. I had to wonder into the world of research to find out about book publishers and how they went about getting a book published. At first, I looked into the names I was familiar with such as Usbourne, Scholastic, Harper

Collins, Bloomsbury and Nosy Crow to name a few. It was one phone call after another.

This whole process was a big learning curb for me, what I had learnt from this experience was, some publishers were not taking in submissions from new authors. Whilst others did not accept work from the author themselves, but it had to go via an agent.

Once again, I was being faced with a new challenge and I started to feel that there was no way that I was going to have my book published because the whole process of finding an agent, then managing all the costs was too much information for me to take in. I found myself slowly drifting away from the idea of having my book published I just did not know how and what I had to do.

Just as I was on the verge of giving up, my children kept asking me, "Mummy, when is your book coming out? we are so excited for you. Mummy, we are so proud of you." I knew I could not turn my back on my dream now, not with my children dreaming the same dream for me. They were proud of me and I could not let them down.

So even though I was having to face so many rejections, one after another I decided to persevere with my journey. I changed the way I typed my searches on google, I started to search for publishers who would take on authors without an agent and someone who was completely new to book writing.

Finally, I came across Austin Macauley publishers. I called them up as soon as I got their number and spoke to a helpful lady who advised that I could submit my manuscript either via post or email. However, I would have to wait for at least twelve weeks before hearing back whether my work would get published or not and also how much it would cost me to do so.

After twelve long weeks had past, I had still not heard anything from the publisher. I started to think that maybe the time was just not right, and I had not been successful. I slowly began to give up but remained positive that at least I had made a start, and one day I would achieve my dream.

It was a week later, just as I was getting the girls to start on their homework, that I heard the post, not thinking much of it, I walked up to the front door to collect the post. There were many different sized enveloped on the ground, some were bills, others were junk mail. As I quickly sifted through the mail, I felt something a little heavier than the others, it was a white A4 envelope, my heart skipped a beat when I saw the Austin Macauley stamp.

With trembling hands, I opened the envelope. Inside there was a navy-blue file, which contained the publishing contract. At that moment I could not believe that I had actually made it. My book was going to be published and it was actually going to be available to the public. I screamed in joy as both Zara and Jannat looked at me. I handed Zara the file who then read the letter that came with the file. She too shouted in excitement.

"Yay! Mummy you have done it, you are having your book published, yippee!" she continued, then turned towards Jannat, "look Jannat, mum is going to have her book published."

"Well done mum, you really wrote a book, and everyone can read it," Jannat cried over excitedly.

Both girls came running towards me and we ended up having a family hug. Zara handed me back the file and turned towards Jannat, both girls happily got into a conversation of their own discussing when the book will come out.

I put the file down and called both my sisters to tell them that my work had been accepted and I was going to become an author.

My sisters were incredibly happy for me and they were more pleased that I did not let the worries and pessimism come in the way for me to go ahead and do something about my dream.

Things were moving ahead with both the publication side of things as well as the child arrangements order hearings. I started to feel myself stretch between two worlds, one which consisted of my dream and that dream to becoming a reality.

Whereas on the other hand, some decisions were going to be made in regards to how and how long my children spent time with their father.

So, I was happy and anxious for the months that went by, I suppose in a way they were both balancing out how I dealt with the different emotions. If that was not challenging enough, I soon received some other news on my health front which opened up a whole new can of worms. On the referral from my neurologist, I had to have a dexa scan which would identify any issues with my bone.

A few months after the scan I was called by my GP who told me that I had to go into the surgery to discuss my scan results as there were some abnormalities and we had to discuss how we were going to manage things from here onwards.

I went to see my GP two days later who informed me that for my age my scan results did not really tally up with how my bone density was. I had developed a condition called osteopenia, which meant that my bones were becoming brittle and weak. Which meant that as I aged further, I was at risk of developing osteoporosis. As I sat there trying to process this information, I was told that I had to have a few other tests to rule anything else out as to why I could have developed this bone condition.

A blood test was one of them, which I was not too worried about, but it is the name of the next test that threw me off my wagon.

The doctor wanted me to collect a bottle from the reception desk before I left and come back when I could, with a urine sample to do a Bence Jones Protein test. I had never heard of this kind of urine test. But I was in for a little bit of a surprise when the doctor explained as to why I needed to have the test.

The Bence Jones test is used to check for multiple myeloma. My mind went blank, and I could not think for a few minutes. "Was I hearing right?" I was shocked, stunned, and terrified. "Could it really be? Was there a possibility?" I was asking myself these questions and my mind started running ahead of me when the doctor told me stop and not to start worrying. It was only for a precautionary measure, because only then could she prescribe me with the medication I need for my osteopenia.

I was told that I should not start worrying about any sort of cancer related health condition as this was only a test to rule out any possibilities. But at that moment I could not think far beyond the word cancer. "What if the test came back and it showed something for cancer? What would happen to my children? How will they cope? What am I going to do with the ongoing child arrangements order hearing?" I was hit with one question after another.

As I came out of the doctor's surgery, I felt my world

falling apart once again. Just when all the worries were on one side, just when my children were beginning to believe that mum will be in good health and we would live forever as a happy family, I might have to have further treatments.

I came home and sat down, tears running down my face, the flow was constant, the more I tried to wipe it away the more it stung as it came down. Finally, I managed to get hold of myself and tell myself that a diagnosis had not been made. This was only a test to rule anything out, it was definitive.

I did not wish to share this piece of news with my family as it would unnecessarily worry them. However, I could not conceal the news from Parvin, as she knew I was going to see the GP in regards to my abnormal scan results. Therefore, she wanted a lowdown on what was going on.

With a brave face I told her what I had been told. I made sure that I sounded strong and not worried at all, but I could not hold the act for too long, because as I spoke, I remembered all the other things I had to juggle around with at the same time. On one hand I was really enjoying my writing and, on my way to having my book published, then on the next hand I had the child arrangement order. And now this. "How was I going to balance everything with my ongoing chronic neurological disorder?"

My sister calmed me down and although she sounded so positive and strong, I could sense the worry in her voice too. This is because in our family we have a history of different types of cancer. We agreed that I will not worry myself and feel unwell over something that might not be. Hence, I had to wait till the results came back.

I told my sister that I wished not to share this with anyone else for now, otherwise everyone will have to live in this cloud of worry and gloom until the results come out. Therefore, I did not wish to put them through that. Already everyone has suffered enough in regards to my health and this will really worry them further.

I went in for my blood test and provided my urine sample and then the wait began. I was living in complete fear and pretending to be okay.

For a while, from there on, when I went to drop the children off to school. I used to meet some of the lovely staff; and I used to have my normal conversations with them like I usually did. However, during this time, I felt as if I was saying goodbye, because I was not sure, what news I would receive from the doctors in the coming days.

It was hard to smile and to not break down when I met with the family workers by the gate of the school, who would always ask me how I was and how they felt my children were a credit to me. It was one of the most difficult things to do, was to smile and be so chirpy, when inside all I could feel was being worried. What was more difficult was the fight to hold back the tears from coming down which would then reveal the feelings inside.

A week later I was called back to the doctors to discuss my results, after what seemed like a yearlong wait. I was nervous but in a way sort of relaxed at the same time as I just wanted to get over and done with finding out what could have been the cause of my low bone density.

Plus, I knew from previous experience that if after a test you are not called almost immediately then "no news is good news." Convincing myself I walked into the doctor's room, who informed me that both my test results had come back normal. I instantly felt that heavy wait lifted of my shoulders as I sighed in relief.

I was told that the steroids could be a reason for my condition. At which I informed the doctor that I was on my way to reducing the amount of prednisolone I was taking for reducing the inflammation. But that was something that I was in consultation with, with my neurologists at John Radcliffe.

I was very grateful to the doctor for sorting out my tests so promptly and relieving me from my distress.

I walked out of the room and called for a taxi to take me home. I needed time to just process what had just happened. Just over a few hours ago I was feeling nauseous, stressed, worried, upset and so many more overwhelming emotions.

But now I felt like, I was on a hot air balloon, being lifted off the ground and just rising above the weight that was pulling me down. I came home and called Parvin, to inform her that everything was okay. I then called up my mum to fill her in on what had happened, and why I had been so lost for the last couple of days when she used to call me.

At first my mum was annoyed with me for not telling her, but she then did understand as to why I did not wish to make a fuss, before knowing what was actually happening. We were both very thankful to Allah (swt) for keeping me strong and helping me through this tough time.

As soon as the tension with my health was over, I had yet another big challenge to face and prepare myself for. In the coming month I would be attending the final court hearing for the child arrangement order. I just prayed the documentation would be complete and the judges would be satisfied with all the information they needed to make a decision that would benefit my children as to how and where they see their father.

At that moment all I could think of, was how I had just

come off one speed train of worry, then hopped onto another one straight away. My mind was always busy, and the worst part was that for every worry I had to put up a brave face in front of my children so that they would not be affected by my fears. I especially worry for Zara, who is quite sensitive, and she is easily worried.

Last week I was hiding my health worries and this week I was preparing for yet another life changing ordeal. For some reason I was going from one end to another end of the spectrum.

I hope in the coming days I can just sit down in front of the telly with a hot mug of my favourite green tea, which is the twining's salted caramel flavour, with a big bar of Cadbury whole nut. That would do wonders for my stress. However, for now I had to prepare myself and make sure that I do not fall weak.

When I was a young girl and when my mum use to fuss over me, telling me things like, what I should eat to keep myself healthy, how I should dress in different weather conditions, when I should sleep etc. I never really appreciated the worry or stress behind her telling me all this. I just thought she was finding it hard to accept that I was growing up and could take care of myself. But now that I have two children of my own, I want to make sure they eat right, sleep enough, dress appropriately for the different weathers etc. I understand why my mum worried, it was not because she was being fussy, but because she cared, so much that she was going out of her way to make sure I was okay.

Even now, I do not know what I would have done without my mum, she is like the sixth emergency service, always available seven days a week, twenty-four hours, three hundred and sixty-five days in a year. She cooks for me; she looks after my children for me when I am not well. She sorts out my house, sends me shopping. She never stops, this is because she loves me and would never stop caring for me. She wanted to and is still protecting me from any troubles that come my way.

Today when I look at myself and try to sum myself up as a mum, I feel like I am just like my mum, I would do anything for my children to be happy. I want to protect them from any worries, harm etc.

The fateful day had arrived, I anxiously went into the family court for the final hearing. Both sides were represented in front of the judge with all the supporting evidence. I felt my chest tighten as I had to wait for the final verdict. Luckily for the children the court hearing worked out in their favour, at last they would have much more consistency and reliability in the way they spent their visits, with their dad from now on.

Straight after the court hearing, I had to start preparing myself for the new school year. It was late August (2018) and I had not had a chance to buy the new uniforms due to the stress and anxiety of what would happen in the court hearing.

The new school year started in September and I started making myself busy in planning my second story. I had been interacting with my publisher on the progress of the first book and the first set of edits had been completed. The next step would be to discuss the cover and the illustrations.

Life became even more busy now, I was spending my time between, writing my book during the day and when the children got back from school. I was spending a lot more time with the girls making sure they were reading to me each night, we went through the spellings and from Wednesday to Friday I ensured that the girls were completing their homework properly.

Then in the weekends they needed to be prepared for their Arabic classes. Mentally I was feeling exceptionally good that the children and myself had a lot of different activities to keep us busy, interconnected, and happy with the variety of things that we were doing.

However, physically I was yet again beginning to feel a strain. I noticed that every morning when woke up I would suddenly just go down, like I was about to fall, I would then have to quickly grab hold onto anything like my bed, sofa or the walls to pick myself up. I had ordered myself a new walking stick just for using in the house, to the one I use for outdoor use. It was easily foldable and away from anyone's way when I was stationary.

With the winter making its way, once more I started to feel even more weak, hence I made an appointment with my doctor who told me that they had referred me back to the orthotics department just to see if there were any new issues with my limbs.

Once I went to see the orthopaedic doctor, I was told that the strength on my left leg now too, had deteriorated, hence they would have to order me a splint for my left leg. I sat there not knowing what to say, because I believed that I was just going through the bad day phases of my condition, I did not expect to hear that my strong leg now had weakness in it too. I took all the information in and waited till all the measurements were taken for a new splint.

I then met my Naz in the car park, who had taken me to the hospital and was waiting outside for me. I gave her a lowdown on the news that I had just received. After which I remained silent on my way home. I knew in my heart that this news should come as no surprise to me as I had been told at my many visits to the neurologist's clinic that after being stable with my condition for a while there will come a time when my condition starts to deteriorate slowly. But I had to stay positive and manage the condition well like I had been till now.

For some reason though, I could not reach an agreement with my heart. My mind felt powerful, and it took over my heart. "I have come this far, and this year of 2018 has been a roller coaster ride with all the things that have been happening, now I have to come face to face with this new reality. How will I do it? Where am I going to get the strength and positivity from?" I was in this conversation with myself which was just leading nowhere.

So, I decided to switch on the telly and just watch some feel good TV till it was time to pick up the girls from school. As I flicked through the channels, I came across a documentary about a young girl in India, who had somehow had this horrible accident where she came in contact with a running train that went over both her legs. Resulting in devasting consequences.

As she lay in the hospital bed surrounded by her parents and family, she did not say anything, she listened to the doctors and how they were preparing her, for getting back home and sorting out the adaptions etc they would need for her to get about at home. No one in that room gave her any hope of standing on her two feet again, it was all about how she had to take it easy and look after herself to not get hurt.

This young girl had so much hope and belief inside herself that she wanted to prove everyone wrong. So, one day as she lay in her hospital bed, she told her father that she wanted to climb the mount Everest. Her dad at first listened to her and then burst out laughing. "You cannot be serious my dear," he said. Her father reminded her that she would find it exceedingly difficult to walk with her new prosthetic legs let alone climb the Everest. He told her not to think about such things and just prepare to be discharged from the hospital.

The girl was adamant and full of self-belief, she then told the rest of her family one by one as they use to visit her that she was going to climb the mount Everest and not be a someone who everyone sympathised with all the time.

Not believing in her determination her family would dismiss the idea, but this girl had so much energy and strength mentally that she got in contact with the relevant organisations after she was discharged from hospital and finally, she was trained up and started her journey to complete this climb.

There came points where she almost froze, run out of food and oxygen but she did not give up. It was through her sheer determination and belief that she completed her climb, with her leg coming off at times because of the extreme minus temperatures. However, she did not give up. She wanted to prove to herself and everyone in her family that she was not going to be a burden, she was going to do something with her life even though she had lost her real legs.

As I switched off the telly, I wished I had, had the chance to watch the documentary from the beginning to follow this girl's journey. I felt so inspired and motivated, that all at once all the doom and gloom feelings inside me had shifted apart. It was almost as if universe knew that I needed some positive mindfulness.

Indeed, Allah test us with hardships, but then makes it easy for us to overcome those hardships, we just have to remain strong and have faith.

That evening Parvin called to see how I was doing because Naz had filled her in on what happened. She was expecting me to be sad and worried as to what will happen next. However, she was surprised that I was so full of energy and happy, like as if the news about my new splint did not really matter.

She had to ask me, "Are you okay, you are sure that you are not in denial? Come on if you need to offload your worries, then do so, do not bottle it up."

I insisted that I was fine, I then told her about the documentary I had watched earlier that afternoon, somehow it had given me a little pep talk.

"I watched this amazing story about a very strong girl, who did not allow self-pity to take over her mind," I reiterated as much as I could, of what I had seen to Parvin. My sister was glad that I had returned to my positive self and that I was not going to let a splint take over my life. I had seen so many ups and downs in the last seven years this was only another little speed bump.

Over the coming weeks I started to do some actual mindfulness exercises just to help me relax and sleep. I started doing some different stretch exercises along with my usual ones every morning after my morning prayer and before sleep. It prepared my body to stay calm and the pain was kept under control.

The day I went to pick up new splint was quite comical, when I went into the treatment room, I opened my shoe, and the therapist placed the splint inside. As soon as I was strapped up, I stood up after being instructed to do so. The most funny thing was even though I was holding onto my stick as soon as

I stood up, I fell back onto my chair, like how a mummy does in a cartoon programme, with my legs and arms facing out as I tried to stop myself.

The therapist told me that up till now, my left leg was helping me with my balance, so even though I was wearing a splint on my right leg I was able to balance because my left leg was free to position my body as it wobbled. However, now with both legs were being restricted by a splint each, the balance when I stood up would be tough because both the legs had to get used to wearing a splint and the upper half of my body hard to work hard to ensure a good posture was being maintained.

Finally, after a few failed attempts I managed to stand up, this time I could feel my legs shaking inside my splints. It was absolutely hilarious. I could not stop laughing at how I looked. I was then told to take a step forward and then a step back. As I did, I found it quite difficult, because now neither my right nor left leg were moving, I was just standing on the spot. When I asked why this was, the therapist told me that the signals were coming from the brain to move but the legs were finding it hard with the restrictions, before the left leg was doing most of the hard work, the right leg just copied the left leg's action but now with the left leg finding it hard to move with the splint the right leg just waited.

After several attempts, determined not to give up on my task, I finally managed to take my step forward and back. I then walked around the room like a robot would. The therapist walked me out to the car park where Naz was waiting for me. I was told that in a months' time I needed to come back for a follow up, just to make sure that my leg and foot were not getting sore from the new splint.

Initially it was a little bit difficult getting by with both legs in a splint, as people on the road were not always mindful that I may be taking my time to walk because I had a mobility problem. Hence, I decided to start exposing my splints so that it became visible to some of the people who I passed on my way to pick up and drop off the girls to school to see that I was not just being slow as I walked. But I had an issue with my legs.

I started to wear ankle length trousers and skirts, this helped show more of my splint. I found that this also made people more patient around me, they would not just brush past in a hurry, like how some used to, seeing my splints made them aware that something was wrong with my legs.

One of the issues that I still face, even now, is how some motorists park on the pavement, whilst getting to school and back, I find it a task and a half sometimes to walk comfortably. Especially in adverse weathers. People just park on the pavement, right in the middle, which leaves space neither on the left or the right to walk past, there are cars parked one after another on the pavement, some days I find walking on the actual road is safer, even with moving vehicles, as that way they slow down seeing me go down on the road.

However, walking in a style that is like weaving in and out of a congestion is much more difficult. I have had numerous falls on my way to, and back from school because people have just left their cars on the pavement. I have had my moments where I have cried about this, but now I am used to it, but to think that if I am finding it difficult to get past from standing position, someone in a wheelchair, or with a buggy and children gathered around must find it even more difficult to get past.

I am looking forward to the new year now, with my first ever written book on its way to being published. I really enjoyed the thought of the outcome.

It is nice to have a focus on something that means a lot to me. I enjoy the mindfulness exercises; they make me feel energetic and boost my morale levels even more. Now with the winter making its way out I am feeling more happier as the days are a little longer and there is more of daylight to enjoy.

I received the first draft of the cover on my book, it almost looks the way in which, how I had visualised it; I still cannot believe that the book is going to be out there for children to read. But it is still early days. I know that I cannot expect to see results straight away. I am going to be, a brand-new author, so I need to let people around me know that this is the step I have taken to prove myself. Then by word of mouth and social media, other people would be made aware of my work.

I have spoken to the school about my new venture, and they are incredibly supportive, the family workers have told me that when the book is ready then they would help me spread the word to the other parents of the school.

Finally, the day has come it is the 31ˢᵗ of May 2019 and I am officially a published author. My book is available to buy across the world via the online portal. I cannot believe that shops such as Waterstones, Amazon, WHSmith and Barnes and Nobles are selling my book. It is a long road from here to actually physically see a copy of the book in stores, but the online platform is a start, and I am happy with that.

The school has organised for me to attend a coffee morning to speak to other parents about my journey from living with a lifelong health condition to achieving my dream and becoming a children's author.

It was a pleasant experience as I got to speak about certain things included in my condition that could pull one down from living life as normally as possible, but I was able to talk about how I am living a very normal life as possible.

I explained that since September 2015, I have even been able to go on family day trips to the seaside, parks and sometimes even abroad, with my children, brother, and mum (to support me) for a couple of days. This experience has given my children the normality that they have seen within other families, whether it's their cousins or friends at school.

I am able to do things with my children that gives us quality family time. I make sure that I play a significant part in my children's education, making sure that they get all the help that they need and that they are achieving according to their age level or above.

All this has been possible because of being part of a strong family network. Throughout my journey my family members have always been there for me, waiting to jump in and support me when things seemed to be a struggle. They never let me feel alone. I have been able to make decisions with their support.

When I was able to share this with the other parents, I felt lighter and happier that I could talk about my experience without breaking down, like I used to at times, previously.

I feel as if I have now found Yasmin once again. I had lost myself in the expedition of life, but now I have finally managed to collect all the pieces of the puzzle and rediscover who I am. I can happily say that I am satisfied with what I have achieved, a few years back I would have never, in my wildest dream, thought that I would be an actual author. But now by moving on, I have faced my fears and achieved my childhood dream.

Since the launch of the book, I have completed drafting my second book, which I plan to type up soon and send to the publisher. While my health feels good, I want to continue with my work.

I had the opportunity to create some craft material at home with what I had and make some things that I was able to take along with me to the schools' summer fete, where I was given the opportunity to advertise my book to a broader range of audience. I had children come over to where I sat to design some puppets and props related to my book which I had created on my computer, with the help from my children who helped me cut everything out and colour code everything.

It was a lot of fun gathering colours, glue, and tape to sit at a stall of our own. My sister, Naz accompanied us to the fete with both her children which was a lot of fun.

In mid-July 2019, I went to the Junior school that my nephew attended to do a book read of my book. It was really nerve racking because I had only met the head of Year 3 once before the event to talk though my journey and then it was the actual thing, going into the school holding a copy of the book reading parts of the story to a group of approximately thirty children of five classes.

For this event I had designed some wordsearches and a quiz for the children to complete, after I had done the book read. It was really nerve racking at first, because they were a completely new group of children that I had just recently met on the day. I just had to sit as a confident adult introducing to them, who I was and then reading in front of the class, with the teachers also listening to me.

After facing the first two classes I had become a little more comfortable and managed the remaining three half hour sessions without showing the nerves on my face.

Following the events of that morning, of reading in front of complete strangers, I called a taxi to get home and rested myself for the rest of the duration of the day to calm the nerves down which caused a lot excitement inside me, which were good that they made me feel good about myself but at the same time, the energy inside me seemed to feel drained out.

I realised at this point that even when I was the most happiest, my body would disagree with me and feel very achy and sore. So, I had to take things very slowly, just like a little child, too much over excitement could lead to a little accident.

However, this is what I had to accept to stay happy. After all there is the saying "no pain no gain", which is what I always kept in mind.

I can only thank Allah, my lord for constantly supporting me through my challenges, had it not been for my faith in Allah, I would have been completely lost. The questions that I used to keep asking I now started getting their answers. I realised that going through with my physical condition, I had rediscovered my lost self. I had found my voice again, this was such a great feeling and it was only because I believed that Allah will show me the way.

I wanted to share my exciting news with my first family worker Clara, without whose support I would not have managed to take the first few steps towards thinking about what I wanted from my life after the breakup of my marriage.

It had been testing times, but luckily for me, I was able to move on, with the help and support from my family and kind people like Clara, who understood my fears and concerns and helped me to overcome these worries.

I wished to remind Clara, of the time, how five years ago

I had spoken to her for the first time saying that I had lost myself in my journey of life, from losing my self-confidence, the ability to make decisions on my own and the loss of having any financial control in my life.

I was even too scared to make any decisions when it came to the children and their future. With tears in my eyes and my voice trembling, I remember that one of the things that I had said to her was, "I want to find Yasmin, the Yasmin that I have lost in this difficult journey."

I felt my life would never be the same after becoming disabled, I felt that I would not be able to do anything the same as before. The road ahead seemed dull and full of doubts, it seemed impossible to rise above the dark clouds.

However, today I want to tell Clara that I have done it, "I have found Yasmin," it feels amazing to get my-self-worth back, to be proud of who I am. When I look into the mirror, I do not see a helpless weak person anymore, I see someone who is strong, who has hope in her heart and someone who has managed to embrace the changes in her life. Someone who is proud of her achievements and someone who is loved by her children, family, and friends.

That is what matters. Yes it would be nice to not have a chronic neurological disorder, however what I see now is, if I did not have this condition then I would have never been able to discover what I am capable of.

Clara was so pleased for me, and happy that she was a part of journey to help me through the difficulties I was going through. She could see the positive change in me and told me to remain happy and positive and wished me all the best for all my future ventures.

A few weeks after sharing my news with Clara, I was

invited by Flying Starts Children Centre to attend their volunteer's awards ceremony to talk about my story. I felt privileged to be invited. I was accompanied to the function, with one of my current family workers from school, Saher. Who along with her colleague Saba have supported me so much, especially in terms of being my standby transport people whenever I have felt really ill to do the school rounds.

After the release of my book, Saher had been very enthusiastic to share my story throughout the school, from arranging for me to be part of the school summer fete, to arranging a coffee morning in school, where I was given the opportunity to speak to other parents about myself and life with living with a disability. It is because of this I felt I had a strong support network within the school.

I had asked Saher to accompany me to the Flying Starts event, as I did not feel comfortable with going into a big crowd of people on my own especially as one of the guest speakers, because my nerves still get the better of me at times.

I start to feel claustrophobic and panicked but attending this function was an honour and a privilege that I felt, I had to come out of my way and face my fears, as I had wanted this love and respect from people for so long. Hence, I did not want to miss it and asked Saher to come with me to support me just in case I passed out with all the excitement.

Attending the awards function was lovely, I was able to not only share my story with the volunteers, but I was also able to show them my own certificate and trophy, from the time I had received my award for being a volunteer with Building Blocks Children Centre (the name previously used, before it became Flying Starts).

It was a really wonderful experience, the audience were

engaged and inspired by my story with how far I had come. My story did bring hope to many who were sitting there, it felt rewarding to be able to pass on some positivity.

I continued to promote my book throughout the summer. Saher had passed my details onto one of the charities she works with to help support families in different ways. I was invited by that charity to attend a festival of celebrating success in the local community. Again, this was a very lovely event to be part of, I was amongst many other people who had done something really exceptional in Luton to support families. Together we all explained who we were and how we made a difference in the community through our work.

I felt really good to be part of this event. This is because everyone who was there had an organisation or business of their own, through which they made a difference to the community in Luton. These were people who were physically having an impact on people's lives.

However, I did not have that, I was not a business neither an organisation. I only had my journey of experiences with me, to share faith, positivity and hope. I was able to quickly explain a little bit about myself and that I had become an author after facing a lot of struggles. But it was possible to achieve that dream through my faith, perseverance and self-belief.

Winter started to make its way and my health like usual started to feel a little rocky. During October I caught a cold, but it was a long lingering cold after which I developed a very horrible chesty cough. It was prolonged so much that it started draining all my energy.

My activities limited to only doing the school rounds and resting as much as possible. I started to feel uneasy and tired more often than usual. However, me being me I could not let my physical problems affect my mind. So, I decided to draft my third book. I was happy with the thought that I had sent the manuscript of the second book to the publishers, hence I wanted to make a start on the third book with some ideas for a storyline still fresh in my mind.

The year 2019 was a very hopeful and positive year for me. I had learnt so much and I had the opportunity to experience so many good things that really impacted on me as a person. I started believing in my abilities more and I knew that I had to always have a positive mindset as that is the healthiest option of living a productive and fulfilling life for me as a person.

We are all different and we all have different strengths and abilities as individuals, it is those strengths that help us through difficult in testing times. One should never give up on hope, even if it is a small amount of hope, with time things start to sort itself out.

To help us further there are organisations out there to support us, like our Doctors, Schools, Children Centres, Council, Certain Charities to name a few. There are many more services, and they are all doing an exceptional job to support people in need.

Nevertheless, I would have never imagined, that 2019 which had been such a fruitful year for me, would end on such a sad note for many of us. It was the first time the news of the corona virus had hit the news channels. None of us would have anticipated that the virus would make its way around the world as a global pandemic.

I do wish to write about my experiences of managing through the COVID-19 virus one day. However, that would have to be another account all on its own.

I want to finish my journey to self-discovery here, as I have achieved what I wanted. That was to prove to myself, more than to anyone else, that through faith, self believe, positive attitude, perseverance, and the attitude of learning from failures, we as individuals can achieve what we may have thought impossible at times.

I wanted to share a part of my journey with my audience. I hope this book will be a little bit inspiring and motivating for some of you out there. I know health problems can impact our life in a big way and sometimes we just feel like giving up. However, giving up only makes us more weak and we are the ones that feel most upset and miss some great opportunities that may come our way.

Sometimes if our minds are strong then through a strong mind, we are able to overcome many obstacles. My name is Yasmin, I am a single, disabled and an immensely proud mum. Author of the Zara Jannat adventure books.

As I finish this writing, I have been blessed to have my second book published. I hope that I never stop writing.

"I thought Transverse Myelitis was the end of the road for me, when I first found out what it had done to me. However, as I have started to live with its after affects, I have realised that it was key to my self-discovery. Had I not been diagnosed with a neurological disorder; I would have never discovered the strength and power I have in my own hands to make a difference to my life. I was scared, full of self-doubt, but my faith in Allah, my two wonderful girls and my family supporting me in every step showed me the way, guided me to what really matters. That is life, it's beautiful and I had to embrace the changes that came my way."